Cauca's Indigenous Movement in Southwestern Colombia

The Peoples of "Latin" America and the Caribbean

Series Editor
Martin Edwin Andersen,
author of *Peoples of the Earth: Ethnonationalism, Democracy, and the Indigenous Challenge in Latin America*

By means of monographs and edited collections, Lexington Books publishes new research on understudied aspects of both the history of and contemporary affairs affecting indigenous peoples and other, usually minority, populations in Central and South America and the Caribbean. Although a new specific effort, this initiative for thinking globally/historically builds upon Lexington works already published on the recent past and current affairs for the purpose of becoming a comprehensive resource and established publication series. Many important qualitative and quantitative determinants and aspects of the transformation affecting the peoples of the region have not yet been systematically analyzed, and Lexington's "The Peoples of 'Latin' America and the Caribbean" seeks to ensure that a space is made for this to occur.

An outlet for empirical research on a broad variety of themes, issues of specific interest that too often remain either under the radar of mainstream publishing on the region or effectively on the sideline include: ethnonationalism; colonialism and empire; concepts of identity; theories of race, nationalism, racism, and identity; political radicalization; mixed heritages and the study of ethnicity; religious identification; links of stress, poverty, and ethnicity among the indigenous and other ethnic/national populations; transnational organized crime and its threats to national/minority communities; comparative studies with indigenous peoples outside the region; local history; multicultural relations; cultural innovation; ethnic geography (including diaspora); minority protection; ethnic tensions and places of contested memory, etc.

Titles in the Series

Cauca's Indigenous Movement in Southwestern Colombia: Land, Violence, and Ethnic Identity, by Brett Troyan

Cauca's Indigenous Movement in Southwestern Colombia

Land, Violence, and Ethnic Identity

Brett Troyan

LEXINGTON BOOKS
Lanham • Boulder • New York • London

Published by Lexington Books
An imprint of The Rowman & Littlefield Publishing Group, Inc.
4501 Forbes Boulevard, Suite 200, Lanham, Maryland 20706
www.rowman.com

Unit A, Whitacre Mews, 26-34 Stannary Street, London SE11 4AB

British Library Cataloguing in Publication Information Available

Library of Congress Cataloging-in-Publication Data

Troyan, Brett, 1968-
Cauca's indigenous movement in southwestern Colombia : land, violence, and ethnic identity / Brett Troyan.
p. cm.
Includes bibliographical references and index.
ISBN 978-1-4985-0228-3 (cloth : alk. paper) – ISBN 978-1-4985-0230-6 (ebook)
1. Indians of South America–Colombia–Cauca (Department)–Politics and government–20th century. 2. Indians of South America–Colombia–Cauca (Department)–History–20th century. 3. Indians of South America–Colombia–Cauca (Department)–Government relations. 4. Cauca (Colombia : Department)–Politics and government–20th century. 5. Cauca (Colombia : Department)–Race relations. I. Title.
F2269.1.C375T76 2015
305.8009861'53–dc23
2015013244

∞™ The paper used in this publication meets the minimum requirements of American National Standard for Information Sciences Permanence of Paper for Printed Library Materials, ANSI/NISO Z39.48-1992.

Printed in the United States of America

This book is dedicated to my two children, Saskya and Julian.

Contents

Preface

In June 1997 I accompanied a human rights delegation to the indigenous communities of Cauca located in the southwest of Colombia. The purpose of this delegation was to foment solidarity between the United States and Colombian grassroots organizations. We visited the communities of Buenos Aires, Las Delicias, Pueblo Nuevo, Santa Leticia, and San Sebastián in the company of Avelina Pancho, the then-vice president of the CRIC—*Consejo Regional Indígena del Cauca*—Regional Indigenous Council of the Cauca.[1] These communities were located in the highlands of Cauca where most of the indigenous population of Cauca resides. The CRIC's objective in extending an invitation to the human rights delegation was to establish and cement transnational alliances with similar groups to raise awareness about the political and economic struggles that indigenous communities faced in Cauca.

Early one morning, we set off for San Sebastián to visit the Yanacona community, which Avelina Pancho identified as recently joining the CRIC. Our driver, a *mestizo* man from Cali, chain-smoked and drove recklessly terrifying the American passengers in the jeep. Our trip took us higher into the green mountains and onto unpaved roads. Along the way, we encountered a military roadblock. The driver declared that one never knows if the soldiers are guerrillas or members of the Colombian armed forces, but that in any event, he was prepared since he was armed; he then proceeded to take off his jacket and display his handgun. Needless to say, we became nervous and whispered amongst ourselves that our driver had a gun, and he seemed to relish the panic he had caused amongst the gringos. Eventually, the soldiers waved us on warning the indigenous leaders and drivers that guerrillas and perhaps common delinquents were still in the area. Avelina declared that there was nothing to fear since the CRIC had an agreement with the guerrillas, and that they would leave us alone.

After six hours of driving we arrived at the *cabildo* (council) of San Sebastián where a crowd of people greeted us. San Sebastián is a small isolated colonial town located in the southern part of Cauca. A small yellow sign on one of the whitewashed colonial houses read: *Cabildo Indígena de San Sebastián*/Indigenous Council of San Sebastián. Members of the cabildo told us that we, the *gringos,* needed to state who we were, why we were there, and reminded us that no videotaping or photographs were allowed since the photography of indigenous faces was a form of exploitation. We all duly presented ourselves and stated our intentions. The wary attitude of the inhabitants of San Sebastián toward the American delegation revealed their very recent affiliation to the CRIC. Shortly after lunch we were summoned back to the *cabildo* where we were told that the community had consented to talk to us. The indigenous members of the community were physically indistinguishable from their *mestizo* counterparts. The leader of the community stated that unfortunately they had forgotten their language (Quichua). A member of the community added that they had previously ignored that they were Yanacona Indians, but that the discovery of a colonial document had enabled them to recover their identity. The indigenous woman in charge of teaching folklore and crafts asked the Native American woman of our delegation if funds could be disbursed to the Yanaconas and if handcrafts techniques could be taught.

The conclusion of the meeting was that the Yanaconas of San Sebastián would appreciate any help from the Americans. Avelina pointed out somewhat apologetically that the Yanaconas were very much a part of the tradition of *clientelismo*[2] that existed in Colombian politics.

Our next visit was to Santa Leticia where the Nasa/Paez community of Juan Tama had resettled after the earthquake of 1994 in Tierradentro. When we arrived in Santa Leticia, the indigenous people of this community were celebrating a traditional feast, and many of the older people still spoke Nasa, their indigenous language. The older women were weaving wool. Bilingual indigenous teachers were teaching Nasa to the community's children. Inscriptions on the walls of school buildings stated: "*Conservemos los valores*/Let us preserve the values" and "*Vivamos nuestras tradiciones*/Let us live our traditions" in both Nasa and Spanish.

This first encounter in 1997 with the indigenous communities in Cauca led me to question whether all of Cauca's indigenous communities were automatically "Indian." The heterogeneity of indigenous communities in Cauca was palpable. On the one hand, there were communities that had maintained their traditional customs and still spoke their indigenous language; on the other hand, there were other communities whose only tie to their ethnic past was a colonial document that stated that the place where they resided was a communal land grant of the Spanish Crown to an indigenous group. I had witnessed as late as 1997 people claiming an indigenous ethnic identity and discovering colonial documents, which gave these indigenous rural folk a legitimate claim to collective landholding. What these communities did share was a relationship with the CRIC and an explicit agenda for ethnicization. So, both in Santa Leticia and in San Sebastián, the ethnicization of the community was promoted; in the case of Santa Leticia inscriptions on the wall instructed residents to preserve their culture, and in the case of San Sebastián, the leadership of the community sought to obtain funding and training for indigenous artisanal work, which would generate income as well as make members of the community more authentically indigenous.

I was also curious about the relationship between the guerrilla armies and the CRIC. In other meetings the indigenous leadership of the CRIC narrated how some members of the indigenous communities had formed a self-defense army, called *Movimiento Armado de Quintín Lame* (commonly known as Quintín Lame in the 1980s). By 1997 this armed group had demobilized, but according to the CRIC, the emergence of Quintín Lame had forced other guerrilla armies to respect the declared neutrality of indigenous communities in the armed conflict between guerrillas and the Colombian armed forces. In reality, while some guerrilla armies did indeed respect the neutrality of the indigenous communities, violent confrontations had occurred between the FARC/*Fuerzas Armadas Revolucionarias de Colombia*/Armed Revolutionary Forces of Colombia and Quintín Lame Armed Movement in the north of Cauca. In other words, the neutrality was a contested one.

My first visit to Cauca also made it clear that it would be impossible for me to live in an indigenous community in the rural area of the Cauca and do a "bottom-up" oral history of the indigenous movement. The ongoing violence in the rural areas of Cauca and my obviously foreign physical appearance (blond gringa) could have made me a target for kidnapping or worse. Consequently, my research centers on the leadership of the CRIC, the nonindigenous collaborators who helped advise indigenous interests, and the Colombian state.

Back in Ithaca, New York, I read Pedro Cortes's dissertation thesis on the indigenous movement in Cauca and realized that there were nonindigenous allies who played a crucial role in the indigenous movement's emergence.[3] When I returned to Cauca in February of 1998 for a third visit, I interviewed indigenous and nonindigenous people who had participated in the founding and formation of the CRIC in the 1970s. I began to gain a clearer picture of the role that nonindigenous collaborators had played in the formation of the CRIC and of the significance of Manuel Quíntin Lame self-defense movement (which I discuss in chapter 6).

My research in Bogotá in 1998 and 1999 led me to the archives of the Ministry of Interior where the files of the Division of Indigenous Affairs were located. These files were in the process of being transferred to the national archive. The study of this archive led to my discovery of petitions and letters from some indigenous communities dating from the 1930s and 1940s requesting the division of communal property. These documents suggested to me that there was no clear consensus in terms of what defined an indigenous ethnic identity in the 1930s amongst indigenous communities of Cauca. In addition, these sources shed light on the relationship between a central state that started a conversation with indigenous groups around the dissolution of communal land grants while intending to protect the rights of settlers and to redress some of the structural land inequalities of rural Colombia. More importantly the rural folk of Cauca—including some indigenous communities—were persuaded that an alliance with the Liberal central state would protect their rights to land and to their crops. They were sorely disappointed.

My research in the archive of the Indigenous Affairs also led me to ask how and why an indigenous ethnic identity was linked to the concept of a territory in Colombia. How was it that in the 1990s *resguardos* (communal property) and *cabildos* (councils) became code words for indigenous identity in Colombia? The next two archives that I looked at—the Ministry of Interior Archive and the Gregorio Hernández de Alba Archive—suggested that from 1958 on, the central state via the Division of Indigenous Affairs differentiated indigenous rural folk from other rural folk implementing laws and decrees that strenghtened communal landownership and government using laws that were created during the colonial period as well as Law 89 of 1890. The international trend of valorization of indigenous cultures and the placement of Gregorio Hernández de Alba, an *indigenista* since the 1930s, at the head of the Colombian Division of Indigenous Affairs agency led the Colombian state to promote an indigenous identity based on collective property.

The effectiveness of the state-agency was limited at first; however, it allowed indigenous communities to organize themselves and to come up with ethnic-based strategies to stop the loss of communal land. The nation state elaborated a political space for land tenure reform that allowed for communal landownership that was limited at first to the indigenous communities and was conditioned on a defined ethnic identity. Grassroots organizations and their allies have pushed the central state over the last twenty years to expand the definition of ethnic citizenship to include nonindigenous rural folk.

Thus, in 2014, seventeen years since my first trip to Cauca, the trend towards ethnicization to obtain state resources and to form collective land units is no longer limited to indigenous communities. Colombia's new constitution of 1991 recognized that Colombia was a multicultural nation and enshrined the rights of ethnic minorities privileging at first the indigenous ethnic communities. After a debate between the leaders of indigenous communities and that of Afro-Colombian communities as well as the participation of prominent Colombian intellectuals on whether Afro-Colombian communities deserved the same ethnic rights and state-sanctioned protections,

Afro-Colombian activism led to the passage of Transitory Article 55, which gave some communal landholding rights to black Pacific communities. Law 70 of 1993 solidified these landholding rights and recognized black culture as worthy of state protection (Wade 1995; Arocha 1998). Afro-Colombian communities on Cauca's Pacific coast gained recognition from the central state and obtained the collective titling of their land.

Mestizo rural communities in Cauca have also argued that they too deserve the same guarantees that "ethnic communities" have, and have demanded that the central state grant them collective land titles known as *Zona de Reserva Campesina*. This trend of the past twenty years makes it all the more important to document and analyze how and why the central state established a mode of rural citizenship based on an "ethnic identity."

Violence has continued to plague Cauca and in particular, indigenous and Afro-Colombian communities. The "truce" that Avelina Pancho discussed between the CRIC and the FARC that existed precariously in 1997 no longer exists. Massacres, displacement of entire communities, and targeted assassinations of political leaders carried out by paramilitaries and some guerrilla units are daily occurences in Cauca. While many rural regions of Colombia saw incidents of violence decrease during President Uribe's tenure (as controversial as his tactics were), Cauca remained a contested site. With President Santos's re-election, new initiatives for peace such as the state's plan to restitute land through an agency (*Unidad de Restitución*—Unit of Land Restitution) to victims of violence and the ongoing peace negotiations with the FARC in Havana, Cuba, have had a limited impact in Cauca. In municipalities of Cauca such as Miranda, Caloto, Toribio, and Corinto, the central state was unable to fully implement its peace initiatives due to the ongoing violence.[4]

While in Cauca in 1997, our human rights delegation peripherally and tangentially came into contact with armed factors; as mentioned earlier, we encountered military roadblocks, and our driver (unbeknownst to the CRIC organizers) was armed. The next day, our car ended up giving a ride to a member of the FARC whose only clues to his guerrilla identity were his plastic boots and his walkie-talkie. Fortunately, for us, the driver who had displayed his handgun was not hired that day and had been replaced by an unarmed indigenous driver. The member of the FARC, upon leaving our jeep, proudly announced his affiliation to the FARC and asked us if we would like to make a donation to the "cause." We declined, stunned by his announcement, with the exception of one woman who pulled out of her handbag a bar of soap, which she offered to the guerrilla. The member of the FARC, taken aback by the "gift," then stated, "cash/*dolares*." After he had made his request more explicit, the same woman donated five dollars. He thanked her, and we drove off. I mention this anecdote because of my belief that discourse, conversations, and dialogues matter. The exchange and conversation between the human rights delegation and the FARC guerrilla member was encrusted and entangled in the local, national, and international web of power and culture. The threat of violence hovered around us (although the man was not visibly armed, he was in communication with other members who presumably were), but the incongruous and somewhat comical offer of soap changed the dynamic between the FARC guerrilla member and us. This book maps out through an analysis of discourses moments of pivotal change where the conversation between different parties is forever altered.

NOTES

1. The CRIC was extremely generous and open with me. I was given full access to the archive and could photocopy any document. I wish to thank the CRIC, in particular the Avirama brothers and Avelina Pancho, for all the help and time they gave me.
2. By *clientelismo*, Avelina meant that they expected to be rewarded with gifts and other concrete favors for political allegiance to one or another party.
3. Cortes, Pedro. *Indian Social Movements: A Case Study in Cauca, Colombia, from a Marxist Perspective.* Ann Arbor, MI: University Microfilms International, 1991.
4. http://www.verdadabierta.com/lucha-por-la-tierra/5087-la-larga-y-cruel-lucha-por-la-tierra-en-el-cauca.

Acknowledgments

I hardly know where to begin with my acknowledgments since I am probably one of the most indebted authors in the field of Latin American history!

First, I must thank Barbara Weinstein who not only was a superb teacher and mentor when I completed my master's at Stonybrook University, but also the person who drove me home after our evening graduate class for an entire year! This act of generosity and solidarity was so meaningful to me because I had two small children under the age of three who were waiting for me to come home; taking the public bus (which was my only alternative) meant that the entire trip would have taken an extra hour. It also meant that Barbara would arrive later to her house and to her young children. This is just one example of how Barbara not only understood the predicament that I was in, but she stepped in to help. For the next twenty years, Barbara wrote numerous letters of recommendation (even though I was no longer her student after I left for Cornell University) and always made time to offer me sage and wise counsel.

I also wish to thank Brooke Larson who was my adviser at the time and who taught the most terrific and inspiring colonial Latin American history seminar that I still remember clearly (some twenty-plus years later). I must also thank Cecilia Mendez for her friendship and for the absolutely fascinating and stimulating intellectual exchanges that began twenty-two years ago.

I would never have made it to the next stage (after the master's) without Mary Roldán's providential help. Getting into Cornell University and obtaining six guaranteed years of funding were a game changer for my family. While at Stonybrook, I contemplated abandoning my ambitions of becoming a historian to pursue a career in social work. My acceptance to Cornell University came at just the right time.

Some of my best memories in the past twenty years are the wonderful directed readings on Colombia that Mary organized. I still remember being completely amazed and flabbergasted by her generosity with her time and knowledge; the weekly directed readings would last three to four hours. We would discuss the assigned readings for about two hours, and then the conversation would expand and veer into other delightful directions. I understood then that I was the recipient of a wonderful gift, but I am even more amazed now knowing firsthand now how busy and overwhelmed tenure-track faculty members are. Over my seven years at Cornell University, Mary rose above and beyond the call of duty listening and supporting me not only through academic challenges but personal ones. I am profoundly grateful for her support during what I can only describe as challenging years.

I also wish to thank Catherine Legrand who was generous enough to read my entire dissertation and provided me with some very useful comments and advice.

While raising two very lively children and then teenagers as a single mother, I was so blessed and fortunate to receive the help of so many wonderful women friends in Ithaca, New York. I quite literally would not be alive to tell the tale without their friendship. My close friends (Patricia Rivlin, Teresa Vasquez, Francoise Vermeylen, Quirine Ketterings, Gretchen Gilbert, Leigh Anne Eubanks, Felicia Kornegay, Hetty Krol, and Judy Podja) not only provided me with endless hours of emotional support, but also with logistical help. This logistical help consisted in lending me money, taking care of my children, taking me to the hospital for a 4:00 a.m. surgery an hour away and in the midst of a snowstorm, and covering for me at the principal's office to explain one of my lively children's behavior. This is not an inclusive list by any means; some events are not meant for publication! In addition, these wonderful close friends always encouraged me to pursue my work and celebrated every small milestone with me toward the completion of the book. Thank you!

I also owe a tremendous debt to two of my dear friends and colleagues at SUNY Cortland. Randi Storch was always there to remind me that I had a contribution to make and that it was possible for me to complete a book. She encouraged me gently but firmly to set deadlines for myself, which of course I did not always complete. After many years of not writing "the book," I began to doubt whether it would be possible or desirable for me to publish my manuscript. Randi's leadership of the history department at Cortland College (as chair) created a nurturing and supportive environment that allowed me to pursue my long-delayed objective of writing my book. She also was and is the very best friend one could have at work always ready to have lunch and to share her hot tub at a moment's notice. Luo Xu, my beloved office neighbor for the past decade, was and is also a crucial source of support at Cortland College. Our daily conversations about teaching, scholarship, and retirement gave me that very important daily dose of encouragement and laughter.

I also want to thank Paul Lovejoy and Rina Caceres for organizing a wonderful conference on the *Meaning of Blackness* in Costa Rica in February 2014. The supportive atmosphere at the conference where everyone was truly engaged and respectful of each other's contributions reminded me of why I had decided to become a history professor in the first place. This conference gave me the confidence and faith in academia that I needed in order to complete my book.

I also wish to thank my newfound friends that I made this past year in San José, Costa Rica; thank you Arlene, Manuel, Richard, Sharon, Macarena, Doña Gabriela, David, and Nela!

I must end my acknowledgments by thanking my mother and my stepfather; they took care of my children on many occasions when I attended conferences and did research abroad. Their generosity and enthusiasm for my academic career were truly astounding.

In terms of funding for this project I have been incredibly fortunate; I wish to thank the National Endowment for Humanities (for funding me twice—yearlong fellowship and summer stipend), the Woodrow Wilson Junior Democracy Grant, and the Fulbright Program.

I also wish to thank the many people in Colombia who shared their stories with me (this is not an inclusive list by any means due to privacy and confidentiality concerns): Marcos Avirama, Jesús Avirama, Graciela Bolaños, Víctor Daniel Bonilla, Jhon Jairo, Lorenzo Muelas, Avelina Pancho, Libia Tattay, Victor Daniel Bonilla, Edgar Avirama, Pedro Cortes, and Pablo Tattay.

Finally, thank you St. Jude.

Chapter One

Introduction

One of the most remarkable developments in recent Colombian history is the success of the indigenous political movement. The indigenous people, which represent only 3.43 percent of Colombia's population, have rights over almost 25 percent of the national territory. Scholars have attributed the success of the indigenous movement to the strength of the indigenous grassroots organizations (Hristov 2004; Findji 1992), to the weakness of the central state (Van Cott 2000), to the exceptional indigenous intellectual leadership of Colombian indigenous communities (Rappaport 1990), and, recently, to successful intercultural relationships established with nonindigenous sectors of society (Troyan 2002, 2008; Laurent 2005; Caviedes 2000; Rappaport 2005). While these factors played an important role in the success of the Colombian indigenous movement, this book argues that the success and development of the modern day indigenous movement in Colombia must be understood as resulting from the interaction between the national state, the Cauca department (birthplace of the Colombian indigenous movement), and grassroots organizations.

The central thesis of this book is that the Colombian central state at crucial junctures encouraged the formation of an ethnic-based movement amongst the indigenous rural folk of Cauca. My point of departure for an analysis of the Colombian state is that the state is not a monolithic institution that imposes its agenda unilaterally, but rather that the state comes into being in the process of its practices (Corrigan and Sayer 1985). These state practices are subject to negotiation and re-elaboration in the different local contexts where these are carried out. I argue that the Colombian central state's discourse and practices on ethnic identity prevailed not only because of key alliances with subaltern groups, but also due to the weakness of Cauca's elites and to their anachronistic regional discourse. The weakness of Cauca's elites stemmed from the national public discourse that portrayed them as antiquated (as standing in the way of modernity and progress)because of their declining economic position, and as a result of their failure to elaborate a regional project that included people of color.[1]

This book examines the triangular relationship between local elites, the national state, and the indigenous communities that mutually transformed the different parties involved from 1910 to 1991. I focused on pivotal moments when the central state, the local state, and indigenous communities came into contact, and I performed a textual and discursive analysis of these conversations. I zeroed into the discursive practices of the Colombian state in part because of the Colombian central state's limited clout and institutionalization outside of Bogotá for much of the twentieth century. I argue that grassroots organizations and political leaders like Ciro Trujillo (Liberal/Communist guerrilla in the 1950s) and Manuel Quintín Lame (indigenous leader of Cauca and Tolima) contributed to the formation of the Colombian central state upon imagining an ideal central government and making claims to a central state. This book also highlights how the Colombian central state relied on grassroots groups and their political leaders to carry out the institutionalization of the state's discourse. This process of state formation explains the intense democratic character of Colombian politics, but also its inherent weakness when faced with powerful local elites as well as with armed groups. While all central states are sometimes contradictory and not necessarily cohesive, the Colombian central state's sharply contradictory policies (colluding at times with the paramilitaries as well as protecting indigenous communities' legal rights) are better understood if one takes into consideration that the Colombian state's discourse was often implemented and altered by communities on the ground.[2] To clarify this point further, it is important to note that "communities on the ground" and their political leadership encountered resistance from local elites and faced a web of power and culture that was shaped by local discourse and practices.

The second chapter of this book examines the conversations that took place from 1913 to 1917 around Manuel Quintín Lame's political movement known as the *Quintinada*. Manuel Quintín Lame was a combative and tireless indigenous leader who led a political movement, which some scholars characterized as a series of indigenous "uprisings" against the landowners and the local state in Cauca from about 1910 to 1918.[3] The central demands of his movement were the defense of communal land grants (*resguardos*), strengthening of indigenous government (*cabildos*/councils), and the annulment of sharecroppers' labor obligations.[4] The analysis of the three-way conversation between the local state, the indigenous leader, and the central state around the so-called rebellion reveals that the local state used Manuel Quintín Lame's ethnic-based discourse to delegitimize the demands that his political movement made. The local state was able to revive old fears of race separation and rebellion, but this would be the last time that this discursive strategy would be effective. As we shall see, in tandem to the regional discourse about race and ethnicity, a subregional (from Tierradentro) identity and discourse formed in opposition to Manuel Quintín Lame's political movement.

In contrast to the local state, the central state adopted a contradictory approach legitimizing Manuel Quintín Lame's agenda by corresponding with him and promising to inquire about his legal matters while ultimately siding with the local state sending military troops. In spite of the central state's contradictory stance, the indigenous leader expressed steadfast belief that the central state was a just one and that it would intervene on behalf of Colombia's "poor and oppressed" indigenous peoples.[5] With a discourse based on his interpretation of Colombian *indigenista* laws Manuel Quintín Lame imagined a central state that was responsive to ethnic-based claims.

The third chapter focuses on the period from 1930 to 1947 when the national Liberal state (which had been out of power for thirty years) sought out new allies in the Colombian countryside. Vis-à-vis the indigenous communities of the Cauca, the national state adopted a two-pronged approach; on the one hand, it sought to push for an Agrarian Reform that promised individual land plots for all peasants, and on the other hand, it encouraged a discourse that valorized indigenous customs and identity through its cultural policies.[6] Chapter 3 examines the conversation between indigenous councils and the central state around collective landholding in the 1930s and 1940s in Cauca. Legislation (Law 89 of 1890) that protected indigenous communal landholding was due to expire. The central state contacted indigenous councils to start the process of division of *resguardos* (communal landholding grants); in many cases, it was the first time that the central state engaged in a direct conversation with these communities.

Indigenous communities responded in a myriad of ways: most opposed the breakup of their *resguardo*s, but some indigenous councils expressed their consent with this policy. As the chapter shows, the success of popular Liberalism in certain areas of Cauca led some indigenous individuals to argue that an indigenous identity was compatible with the celebrated settler identity.[7] In the aftermath of Manuel Quintín Lame's failed movement and his exile in Tolima, indigenous communities and individuals considered many different political avenues of participation including Liberalism. This chapter examines three specific cases of dissolution to shed light on the different motivations and contexts that led some indigenous communities to consider terminating collective landholding.

After the period of tremendous violence that engulfed Colombia from 1947 to 1953, the central state and its leaders sought to reestablish its presence and legitimacy in rural departments. The fourth chapter begins with a descriptive analysis of the impact of partisan violence in Cauca, in particular in Tierradentro. It then examines the case of the *resguardo* of Caldono in order to shed light on how land conflicts of the 1930s, the failure on the part of the central state to adjudicate land plots to former indigenous *resguardo* members, and the ongoing violence all contributed to the failure of a Liberal discourse, which upheld the settler's rights. The fourth chapter also discusses the so called "Independent Republic" of Riochiquito of the late 1950s, which was a multi-ethnic and armed community that formed itself in response to local state repression in Tierradentro as well as in response to partisan violence in Tolima. It examines the conversation/debates between the central state (in particular the Colombian armed forces), the Riochiquito Agrarian Self-Defense Movement, and the local state around land, citizenship, and ethnic identity.

The fifth chapter centers on the 1960s when the nation-state in the form of the *División de Asuntos Indígenas* (DAI, Division of Indigenous Affairs) took on a physical and institutional presence in Cauca. Previously the nation-state exercised its authority via correspondence, laws, and temporary visits made by national state employees. The DAI established a permanent albeit weak presence in the Cauca with its regional *promotores* or employees. The DAI hoped to strengthen the collective institutions of the indigenous communities. In 1959 the DAI put an end to all dissolution of *resguardos* until further notice. The employees of the DAI encouraged the formation of new indigenous councils/*cabildos*, strengthened existing councils, and protected collective landholding. This section of the book shows how the Division of Indigenous Affairs legitimized the claims of indigenous communities based on ethnic identity.

Chapter 6 examines the decade of the 1970s and the flowering of indigenous grassroots organizations. During this decade the central state was present in Cauca via the INCORA (*Instituto Colombiano de Reforma Agraria*/Colombian Institute of Agrarian Reform) and the ANUC (*Asociación Nacional de Usuarios Campesinos*/National Association of Peasants). By the 1970s, the economic and political clout of the local elite in the central part of Cauca was seriously weakened by an absence of economic development, which tipped the balance of power in favor of indigenous organizations and the central state. In addition, the central state continued to deploy a discourse that legitimized indigenous groups' ethnic-based claims. Utilizing the political space created by the central state's discourse, the indigenous groups with the creation of CRIC (*Consejo Regional Indígena del Cauca*) implemented the state's discourse and started recovering the land of lost *resguardos*, which was legally inalienable. Although the nation-state had legitimized the recovery of land, it was taken aback by the intensity of grassroots mobilization. The initial response of one branch of the nation-state was repression against members of the CRIC based on the argument that some members of the indigenous organization were "subversives." Ultimately, however, the emergence of leftist guerrillas and the formation of an indigenous self-defense movement eventually led to peace negotiations and to the formation of a clear alliance between the central state and indigenous people of Cauca.

THE SETTING

The Cauca department is located in the southwestern part of Colombia, totaling 29,308 square kilometers.[8] According to the *Historical Dictionary of Colombia*, the department of Cauca has 9,906 square kilometers of tropical climate, 10,203 square kilometers of temperate climate, and finally 6,184 square kilometers of cold climate.[9] The five neighboring departments are Nariño, Huila, Valle del Cauca, Tolima, Caquetá, and Putumayo. The Pacific Ocean borders the west coast of the Cauca Department. The central and western chains of the Andes mountains crisscross the department and produce widely diverging microclimates and ecologies. Consequently, the geography and the ecology of each subregion of Cauca not only determined the nature of the political demands that indigenous rural folk made, but also the external pressures that they faced. For instance, indigenous rural folk who lived in areas where coffee was widely cultivated encountered a different set of challenges than indigenous rural folk who resided in areas where only potatoes and maize were grown.

Cauca is also home to the highest mountain of the Colombian Andes, the Nevado Huila, which measures 5,365 meters.[10] Other mountains that have marked the geographical and cultural landscape of Cauca are *Puracé* and the *Pan de Azucar*.[11] The landscape next to the Puracé Mountain is moonlike with its craters and gray earth.[12] It is only at 4,500 meters, and under that vegetation appears; in the area known as high páramos only plants called "espeletias" and grasses appear at this altitude.[13] These plants carry water, and the whole area is saturated with water; lagoons are also present.[14] Although this ecological habitat is very fragile and not suitable for agricultural production, these ecological areas play a crucial role in maintaining the health of the other ecological areas of Cauca because of their key role in terms of water supply.

In the central valley of Cauca and at the lower levels of the Andes mountains, land is fertile, although erosion and deforestation present an ongoing challenge. At these altitudes the rural folk of Cauca in the first half of the twentieth century cultivated potatoes, ullucos, cubios, maize, arracacha, quinoa, sweet potato, maize, manioc, yucca, manioc, and beans.[15]

The other two geographical areas of Cauca are the lowlands located on the Pacific coast and the rain/"virgin" forest, which, as Arboleda Valencia points out, covers 60 percent of the Cauca Department.[16] Geographically and culturally speaking, this region is similar to the Choco department. Afro-

Colombians mainly populate the area, and indigenous people have a minimal presence. Today, in the municipality of Timbiqui, which is one of the two municipalities of the department of Cauca that is located on the Pacific, there are only three *resguardos*, which have a total population of 1,974 indigenous residents.[17]

The Pacific region is still not integrated with the rest of the department since there is no road from Popayán to Guapi; as of July 2011, an article in the regional newspaper, *El Liberal*, commented that Cauca was the only department in Colombia that had a coast on the Pacific Ocean and yet had no access to it.[18] Despite the nonintegration of the Pacific Coast with the Andean region some parts of this coast are densely populated, as José María Rojas and Sevilla Casas point out.[19] The ecological diversity of Cauca and paucity of internal infrastructure meant that Cauca was not a cohesive region, which would further hinder elites' attempt to fashion a regional identity.

The 1972 census divided Cauca's political economy into eight subregions: Tierradentro (located next to Huila and isolated until the mid-twentieth century because of mountains and absence of roads), the North (next to the Valle del Cauca), the northwest, the central valley (where Popayán is located), the Macizo subregion, the Bota Caucana, and finally the subregion of the Pacific.[20] This book centers principally on four of these sub-regions of Cauca: Tierradentro, the central Valley, northwest, and the north of Cauca. The majority of the indigenous population of Cauca resides in these areas. Since I refer throughout this study to specific municipalities, I will list which municipalities correspond to a particular geographic zone. The north of the Cauca encompasses the municipalities of Corinto, Miranda, Caloto, Padilla, Santander del Quilichao, and Puerto Tejada.[21] Tierradentro only has two municipalities: Páez (Belalcazar) and Inza.[22] The northwest area contains the municipalities of Toribio, Jambalo, Silvia, Totoro, and Caldono.[23] Finally, the center includes: Popayán, Sotara, Piendamo, Timbio, Purace, La Sierra, el Tambo, Cajibio, Morales, and Rosas.[24] The indigenous population in the north of the Cauca was quite minimal, but the inhabitants of this area played an important role in terms of the rise of Liberalism in the 1930s, and nonindigenous advisors of the CRIC also emerged from this area in the 1970s. One of the most publicized and conflictive land takeovers (Hacienda García Abajo) of the 1970s took place in the municipality of Santander del Quilichao. Four *resguardos* are currently located in the municipality of Santander del Quilichao.[25]

At the turn of the twentieth century most subregions of Cauca were poorly linked in terms of infrastructure and political economy; these sub-regions varied in terms of historical processes, ethnic composition, political economy, and ecology/geography. The formation of a unified indigenous political consciousness based on a "common" understanding of ethnicity had to overcome geographical isolation and divisions that existed between the many diverse indigenous groups that resided within the department of Cauca.

WHY CAUCA?[26]

Although approximately half of the eighty-one Colombian indigenous groups were from the Amazon and the rain forest areas located on the Pacific coast, the indigenous movement did not emerge from these geographical regions. It was only during the 1980s that the aforementioned ethnic groups began to play a crucial role in conjunction with the indigenous movement of Cauca. Maria Teresa Findji posed the crucial question of why the indigenous movement emerged in the Cauca department.[27] Following up on her pivotal question, the following discussion addresses the question of why Cauca was the perfect terrain for the emergence of an indigenous ethnic movement.

Overall, Cauca, along with the Guajira department, has the highest concentration of indigenous peoples in Colombia.[28] Major indigenous ethnic groups of Cauca are the Nasas (formerly referred to as the Páez), Misaks (referred to as Guambianos for most of the twentieth century), Coconucos, Totoros, Yanaconas, Guanaca, Totoró, Inga, and Embera.[29] According to the 1993 DANE census, the largest indigenous ethnic group was the Nasa, whose number was estimated at 100,000.[30] In 2005, 20.72 percent of Cauca's total population was considered indigenous.[31]

The significant indigenous population allowed for colonial and nineteenth-century central valley elites to rely on the labor of indigenous people who lived on communal land grants and who were organized by indigenous authorities. The utility of the maintenance of collective land grants and of the political organization (for the local elites) that accompanied this land structure signified that indigenous communities in Cauca were able to maintain collective landholding and cultural traditions to a far greater degree and for a longer period of time than in other regions of Colombia.

The presence of both a large Afro-Colombian (approximately 22 percent)[32] and indigenous population also differentiated Cauca from the rest of Colombia. Mestizos and "whites" were in the minority in many rural areas. In the north and northeast subregions of the department both indigenous people and Afro-Colombians were present. Additionally, in areas such as the north of the Cauca, the Patia Valley, and the Pacific Coast, the Afro-Colombian population represented approximately 80 percent of the population. As Nancy Appelbaum has pointed out, the large Afro-Colombian population in Cauca led to its external characterization as a region tainted with blackness and disorder.[33]

External representations of Cauca as backwards because of its large Afro-Colombian and indigenous population also impacted its internal racial hierarchy; the position that indigenous communities occupied in this regional racial hierarchy was not static and was elaborated in relation to other ethnic groups depending on specific historical contexts. Thus, the indigenous movement's trajectory and its success cannot be understood without taking into account the peculiarity and specificity of Cauca's historical experience.

Cauca presents a paradox, which also helps to answer the question of why Cauca was the setting for a successful grassroots indigenous movement. On the one hand, it was one of the most important regions for Colombia's economic and political life during the colonial period and for much of the nineteenth century. On the other hand, in 2005, as José R. Gamarra points out, its regional economy represented less than 2 percent of the gross domestic product of Colombia.[34] In a nutshell, the twin historical processes of a declining elite (due to its inability to modernize and loss of territory) and the maintenance of collective land and governmental structures of a significant indigenous population explain why the indigenous movement emerged first in Cauca.

HISTORICAL PROCESSES IN THE CENTRAL VALLEY, TIERRADENTRO, AND THE NORTH OF THE DEPARTMENT OF CAUCA

At the time of the Spanish Conquest, the principal indigenous groups of the department of Cauca were the Popayánenses, Nasas (Paeces), Guanaca, Coconucos, Pijaos, and the Moguexs.[35] Within each indigenous group there were subdivisions, and more names for each group. The dominant language of an area also had different close versions; the Nasa (Páez) language had a dialect called Paniquita.[36] In the early twentieth century, Castillo-Cárdenas stated that Paniquita, Guambiano, and Totoro were the three principal indigenous languages spoken.[37] According to Hernández de Alba, the different indigenous groups lived in separate ecological zones; the Coconuco and the Moquex lived in the highlands near the Cauca River, whereas the Nasas (Páez) and Guanacas resided in the paramos.[38]

It is somewhat misleading to speak of indigenous groups/tribes if trying to determine how indigenous rural folk identified themselves and interacted with nonindigenous peoples and authorities. From the 1910s to the 1960s indigenous rural folk petitioners identified themselves by the "parcialidad" that they belonged to. James Sanders states, "Parcialidades were divisions, more or less villages, within a resguardo, although some resguardos had only one parcialidad."[39] The close identification of an indigenous person or community with his or her parcialidad lessened the importance of an ethnic-based identity. It was only in the latter part of the twentieth century that ethnic affiliations acquired a greater relevance and were the basis for political action.[40]

The push to colonize the department of Cauca came from Ecuador.[41] In a myriad of ways the southern part of Colombia—Nariño and Cauca—was better linked to Quito than to Bogotá. In 1541 the Spanish Crown entrusted to the Spanish conquistador, Don Sebastián de Belalcázar (who had founded Popayán in 1537) with the province of Popayán, which measured 630,000 square kilometers.[42] The immensity of the province of Popayán's territory differentiated the settlement of this area from other regions in Colombia.

Popayán became one of Colombia's most important colonial centers. Gold mining was the basis for its economic importance. Gold was found in the mines of Almaguer, Guachicono, Purace, Caloto, Timbiqui, and Choco.[43] Initially, the *encomenderos* used indigenous labor to work the mines.[44] At the beginning of the seventeenth century, Spanish landowners imported African slaves to work in the mines due to the rapid decline in population of indigenous population and ongoing resistance. By the eighteenth century, Africans had replaced many of the indigenous groups as workers on the haciendas and in the mines.[45] The region achieved a pre-eminence during this time period that it would never regain in later historical times. Ironically, its privileged status during the colonial era of Colombia would later bolster its detractors' claims that Popayán and consequently the Cauca and its elite were backwards and were in need of "modernization."

The other distinguishing factor about the area that later corresponded to the department of Cauca was the vigorous and prolonged resistance that some indigenous groups (Nasas and the Yalcones) mounted against the establishment of Spanish authority. For instance, the Yalcones and Nasas carried out the assassination of two Spanish leaders: Juan de Ampudia and Anaco.[46] These indigenous groups enjoyed a momentary triumph when they defeated the Spaniards at the Penon of Talaga in 1541.[47] They continued to fight the settlement of Spaniards throughout the sixteenth century. Although the Spaniards were only momentarily defeated, the reputation of the Nasas as brave and ferocious fighters endures to this day. In the 1990s Nasa indigenous communities and nonindigenous activists often referred to this past of resistance to the Spanish conquest to explain the depth and strength of indigenous activism in Cauca. While the depth of indigenous resistance should not be underestimated, as in other places in Latin America, some groups such as the Pijaos fought until they were exterminated, whereas others such as Guanaca chose to make an alliance with the Spaniards.[48]

In response to the rapid decline of the indigenous population and its horrific treatment in Cauca, the Spanish Crown created the first *resguardos*.[49] These resguardos were land grants given to a specific group of indigenous people. The land was inalienable and could not be sold or rented to nonindigenous people. An indigenous council elected on a yearly basis was in charge of allocating land to individual families. Hernández de Alba described the council thus: "The native Indian government consisted generally of a governor, a first mayor (alcalde mayor), a second mayor (alcalde menor), a trustee (sindico o fiscal), and constables (alguaciles), the last a kind of police who transmitted to the people the orders which the Whites gave through the governors or mayors, and who carried out penalties of imprisonment of placing in stocks, and whipping, which the first Spaniards introduced into the punishment of the natives."[50] Although the stated purpose of the creation of *resguardos* was to protect indigenous people, indigenous authorities (as seen in Hernández de Alba's description) were given political and legal authority to facilitate the governing of indigenous communities and their compliance with the demands of local elites.

The different responses of indigenous groups in the Cauca department and the difficult topography of some of its subregions signified that the region was not colonized in one fell swoop. For instance, Spaniards established a significant presence in the central valley area at a much earlier date than in the subregion of Tierradentro, which continued to be isolated from the center of the department well into the mid-twentieth century.

CENTRAL VALLEY INDIGENOUS GROUPS: THE CASE OF THE COCONUCO COMMUNITY AND THE MOSQUERA FAMILY

Indigenous groups of the Central Valley provided subsistence products to local markets and were integrated into the colonial regional economy from the sixteenth century. The experience of the Coconuco community not only illustrates the relationship between indigenous people residing in the Central Valley and its local elite, but it also became an emblematic example for Liberal public intellectuals who sought to show that Cauca's elites were trapped in the past.

For all intents and purposes the fate of an indigenous community in the central valley was closely linked to the elite family that acquired the land that originally belonged to the indigenous community. For instance, the Coconuco community's destiny was intertwined with the Mosquera family's fortune. The Mosquera family was one of the most prominent clans in the Cauca department; in the nineteenth century one of the members of this family became President of Colombia. Members of the Coconuco indigenous group worked on the hacienda of the Mosqueras for hundreds of years.

The Mosquera family acquired the Coconuco hacienda after the Jesuits were expelled in 1767.[51] Leon Helguera characterized the relationship between the Coconucos and the Mosqueras as semi-feudal.[52] This semi-feudal relationship was manifest in that the Mosqueras forced the Coconucos to give tribute; this tribute was only officially abolished in 1834.[53] In 1842, a new arrangement was put into place when the Coconuco indigenous people became sharecroppers (known in Cauca as *terrazgueros*).[54] The practice of sharecropping/known as *terraje* endured until the second half of the twentieth century; the abolition of this labor arrangement was not only one of Manuel Quintín Lame's central demands, but also of the CRIC in 1971. The feudal character of the labor arrangement gave greater legitimacy to the indigenous communities and their allies to argue for the dismantling of this labor practice in the second half of the twentieth century; Liberal intellectuals speaking to a national audience could argue that Cauca's elites stood in the way of modernity.[55]

Continued participation in partisan politics and wars throughout the nineteenth century also weakened the central valley elite. Colonel Hamilton's travel account of 1827 narrates how elite families of Cauca suffered on account of their participation during the War of Independence.[56] Subsequently, the nineteenth-century civil wars such as the War of the Supremes and the democratizing politics of Obando hit the Mosqueras hard.[57] The abolition of slavery and the forced contributions exacted by Obando's army weakened the Mosquera family economically.[58] The Mosquera family's prosperity depended on gold mining and cattle ranching; during the nineteenth century the Mosquera gold mines were abandoned and their cattle confiscated.[59] Helguera points out that the hacienda of Coconuco was part of a larger family economy/fortune that rested upon diversified production (cattle, gold mines, and slaves). Once access to the economic activities such as slavery, gold mining, and cattle ranching were removed, the hacienda turned on itself and became a site of subsistence production.[60] The Mosquera family's economic decline led in part to its representation as an elite lacking practical know-how and therefore undeserving of its preeminent status.

TIERRADENTRO AND THE NASAS

The historical experience of the Nasas who resided in the mountain ranges of Tierradentro differed considerably from that of indigenous groups of the center of Cauca. Because Tierradentro was isolated geographically and topographically (the high Andes mountains and the absence of paved roads until the mid-twentieth century), its linkage to the local economy of Cauca did not occur until the 1960s. Indigenous groups of Tierradentro did not bring their subsistence products such as potatoes and corn to the central valley because they lived too far away. Moreover, while indigenous communities of the center of the department coexisted with other ethnic groups and were integrated into the economic and political life of the department, the indigenous communities in Tierradentro were placed under the "protection" of missionaries in the early 1900s, which further isolated them. The presence of missionaries who had control over large swaths of territory was also to provide further fodder for Liberals who argued that the political control that religious orders exerted over indigenous communities was an obstacle to the modernization of Colombia.

In reality, although missionaries controlled much of the political life of the subregion, they were also ardent proponents of economic modernization based on roads and the cultivation of coffee. Many missionaries published newspaper editorials advocating for Progress and for the building of roads. In other words, in the 1930s and 1940s Liberals did not have an exclusive monopoly around a discourse that advocated the need for Colombia to modernize. In the 1930s coffee's emergence as a commercial and lucrative crop in the southwestern part of Tierradentro altered the political economy of this subregion and led to its economic integration with neighboring Huila.[61] The growing importance of coffee and establishment of transportation networks within Cauca in the twentieth century also brought an influx of colonists from other regions to this area, and an increase in tensions around land.[62]

Other national economic and political changes of the twentieth century signified that certain subregions of the Cauca department became more important economically and politically. The growth of coffee exports and an indemnity of twenty-five million dollars that the United States paid Colombia for the loss of Panama financed the building of certain roads that altered the route by which goods transitioned through. During the colonial era, the building of the road, Guanaca, which linked Popayán to the Magdalena River, ensured that Popayán was an obligatory stop for goods whose final destination was Valle del Cauca, Choco, and Pasto.[63] Until the early twentieth century, the Magdalena River played a crucial role in terms of enabling the transportation of products and peoples given Colombia's difficult topography. Once the railroad between Cali and Buenaventura (a major port on the Pacific Coast) was completed in 1914, goods could bypass Popayán entirely.[64] Since development closely followed the routes of transportation, the economic opportunities for the department of Cauca were severely limited after this change in transportation networks. This development dealt a serious blow to Popayán's elites.

NORTH OF CAUCA

In contrast, the department of Valle del Cauca benefited from the above change since investment began to pour into this area at the turn of the twentieth century.[65] As a consequence of the development of the Valle del Cauca, the northern area of the department of Cauca was integrated into the economic orbit of the Valle del Cauca.[66] Prior to the modernization of the department of Valle del Cauca, the northern part of the department of Cauca bordering Valle del Cauca was populated by groups of ex-slaves who had run away and who established communities in isolated areas. Once slavery was abolished in 1851, ex-slaves refused to work on the sugar plantations and devoted themselves instead to working on their own plots.[67] As Michael Taussig has shown so well in his work, the economic development of this area in the twentieth century brought about a painful disruption to Afro-Colombian communities' way of life. From the turn of the twentieth century rural folk of this geographical area began losing their land and were gradually transformed into a rural proletariat.[68] The development of capitalism based on sugar production (Colombia became an important exporter of sugar to the United States in the 1960s when it replaced Cuba due to the United States imposed economic blockade against that country) signified that a powerful bourgeoisie emerged in the department of El Valle del Cauca alongside a rural proletariat.[69] This bourgeoisie eclipsed the power of the elite of Cauca.

CAUCA AND LAND

The reduced importance of Cauca's elite was evident when in 1905 Gran Cauca was broken up into several departments leaving the current department of Cauca with a small territory and temporarily cut off from transportation networks.[70] The current departments of Nariño, Valle del Cauca, Huila, Putumayo, Amazonas, Chocó, and Caquetá had all formed part of the extinct Gran Cauca.[71] The subsequent building of two roads, one which linked Popayán to the south of the country, and the other which connected Cauca to Huila, only partially ended Cauca's isolation and led to limited economic growth in the subregions of Valle del Patia and in the southwest.

Overall, Cauca never achieved any significant level of modernization and development compared to other regions in Colombia. While the rest of Colombia became a mostly urban country after the 1950s, the department of Cauca remains mainly rural. According to the DANE (Departamento Administrativo Nacional de Estadistica/National Administrative Department of Statistics) census of 2005, Cauca's total population in 2005 was 1,268,937 people. In 1993, the majority of its inhabitants (at that date 979,231) were rural residents.[72] In the 1970s 80 percent of the population residing in the Cauca worked in the agricultural sector.[73] Thus, one of the central themes of this book is land; the desire to acquire more land and/or to maintain collective landholding patterns fueled most of the violence and conflict in twentieth century Cauca. The central demand of indigenous communities and its leaders was territory; non-indigenous settlers and local elites' interactions with indigenous communities revolved around land and agricultural labor. This interaction around land was shaped by the previously described economic trends, but also by the national legislation that protected indigenous communal land grants/*resguardos*.

LAW 89 OF 1890

Any discussion of land in Cauca rests on a basic knowledge of Law 89 of 1890, which I explain in the following paragraphs. As mentioned earlier, Manuel Quintín Lame's political movement's main objective was to recover land that indigenous communities of Cauca were entitled to through colonial grants; the Republican legislation that upheld these land grants was Law 89 of 1890.[74] Although the proper application of Law 89 of 1890 was a central demand of Manuel Quintín Lame's movement, the general tone of this law was paternalistic and racist. It stated that Colombian general law would not apply to *salvajes/[savages]* who were on their way to becoming civilized. The protection that Law 89 of 1890 gave was based on the notion that indigenous rural folk who lived on *resguardos* were not "civilized." The measure was conceived as temporary since the belief was that eventually indigenous people would achieve "civilization" and would no longer need the protection of their *resguardos*.

The law also established, however, that the land belonging to indigenous *resguardos* could not be sold or alienated. The indigenous people living on the existing land *resguardos* were considered minors in matters of land transactions and had to obtain permission from both the indigenous council and the municipality to settle land matters. Law 89 of 1890 also clearly placed the indigenous council under the municipality's power: the mayor of the municipality where the *resguardo* was located had to approve the election of officials of indigenous councils; otherwise, the election was invalidated.

Law 89 of 1890 also permitted the creation of areas from 10 to 70 hectares in size within the resguardo that could be occupied by nonindigenous people.[75] Even though Law 89 of 1890 was a national law that was in force for the entire national territory, each department decreed laws that determined how Law 89 of 1890 was to be carried out.

In the case of Cauca, while the municipality was in charge of designating areas of nonindigenous settlement, the local government of Cauca through decree 74 of 1898 gave indigenous councils the power to veto or to approve the settlement of nonindigenous people within the resguardo.[76] In 1926, the governor of Cauca, Carlos Vernaza, used decree number 435 of 1926 to eliminate the veto power that indigenous councils had in the department of Cauca.[77] Such a change in legislation eroded the power of the indigenous councils considerably.

Law 89 of 1890 also meant that vast amounts of the Colombian territory were turned over to religious missions who essentially governed the indigenous tribes and the area they occupied or were assigned to. The nation-state effectively handed over its authority to the Catholic Church and gave legal, political, and judicial power to the missions through a series of agreements between the Vatican and the Colombian government. The areas where missionaries took over were generally designated as "territorios nacionales"/ national territories because these geographic entities were not yet part of the national administrative structure. These agreements or "convenios" could bypass the Congress since they did not require its approval.[78] Law 72 of 1892, for instance, essentially gave the missionaries the power to decide how indigenous societies should be governed.[79] The first "convenio" was signed in 1903, and the idea behind this agreement was that the missionaries would evangelize and "civilize" the various indigenous groups that were dispersed in Chocó, Caquetá, Darien, the Llanos, Antioquia, Tierradentro, and Pamplona.[80] A second agreement was signed in 1928 when border conflicts with neighboring nations emerged and a push for occupying the frontier zones with missionaries was made. The rationale for sending missionaries to these border areas was that these missionaries would be the pioneers in these inhospitable zones, and in turn, would encourage Colombian hispanicized settlers to come to these areas. Peruvians and other possible invaders would also thereby be discouraged from making land claims in the Colombian territory. This legislation established a state claim on border areas and/or strategic sites.

This legislation meant that a French order (the Pere Lazaristes) along with the Vicentinos came to Tierradentro, Cauca in 1905.[81] The irony of the case of Tierradentro and indeed of other national territory areas (such as Sierra Nevada) was that many of the missionaries were not Colombian, but foreign so that they were not exactly effective agents of Colombian nationalism.[82] The agreements of 1903 and 1928 mentioned above gave the Catholic missionaries the direction over public schools for boys. Forced attendance at these Catholic schools, often boarding schools, was one of the preferred methods for the Catholic missionaries to "civilize." In contrast to jungle areas of Caquetá where missionaries sometimes played a protective role, in Tierradentro, the missionaries were not dealing with an indigenous population that was isolated from any contact with Western society. The indigenous inhabitants of Tierradentro had a long history of involvement with the larger Colombian society. The arrival of these missionaries who were openly racist and condescending created a number of conflicts with some indigenous councils.

Law 89 of 1890 and the legislation that governed national territories had special importance and impact not only for Tierradentro, but also for Cauca in general since it was one of the departments with the largest numbers of *resguardos*. In many ways the stage was set for Manuel Quintín Lame's political movement, which emerged in 1910. The arrival of missionaries to a fully politically integrated subregion (Tierradentro), an elite faced with a loss of economic and political prestige (reduced to a tiny fraction of its former territory and its economic power diminished and eclipsed by the nascent bourgeoisie of Valle del Cauca), and finally indigenous communities, which had a long history of political activism, all contributed to make Cauca fertile ground for Manuel Quintín Lame's political mobilization based on ethnic identity.

NOTES

1. See Nancy Appelbaum, *Muddied Waters Race, Region, and Local History in Colombia, 1846–1948* (Durham: Duke University Press, 2003) for a compelling analysis of Cauca's representation in contrast to Antioquia (in particular chapter 1), and James Sanders' *Contentious Republicans: Popular Politics, Race, and Class in Nineteenth-Century Colombia* (Durham: Duke University Press, 2004). Both Sanders and Appelbaum have argued that nineteenth-century Cauca elites failed to establish elite hegemony.

2. Alan Knight's arguments about the Mexican postrevolutionary state negotiating with subaltern groups to implement its state policies have also shaped my understanding of the Colombian state.

3. Joanne Rappaport points out the heterogeneity of scholarly views on Manuel Quintín Lame's political movement in *The Politics of Memory, Native Historical Interpretation in Colombian Andes* (Durham: Duke University Press, 1998), 115–16. See Gonzalo Castillo Cárdenas, *Liberation Theology from Below: The Life and Thought of Manuel Quintín Lame* (Maryknoll, NY: Orbis Books, 1987) for a chronology of the "rebellion."

4. Joanne Rappaport, *The Politics of Memory, Native Historical Interpretation in Colombian Andes* (Durham: Duke University Press, 1998), 114.

5. I have put in quotation marks "poor and oppressed" not to cast doubt on the real exploitation and misery that many indigenous communities faced in Cauca at the turn of the twentieth century but to refer to the language that Manuel Quintín Lame used in his petitions.

6. See Brett Troyan, "Re-Imagining the 'Indian' and the State: *Indigenismo* in Colombia, 1926–1947," *Canadian Journal of Latin American and Caribbean Studies* 33, no. 65 (2008): 81–106.

7. See James Sanders, "Belonging to the Great Granadan Family: Partisan Struggle and the Construction of Indigenous Identity and Politics in Southwestern Colombia, 1849–1890," in *Race and Nation in Modern Latin America*, ed. by Appelbaum et al. (Chapel Hill: North Carolina Press, 2003), for an analysis of how southwestern indigenous communities of the nineteenth century adopted a Republican discourse while maintaining an indigenous ethnic identity.

8. Robert H. Davis, *Historical Dictionary of Colombia*, 2nd Ed (Metuchen, NJ: Scarecrow Press, 1993), 125.

9. Davis, 125.

10. Gustavo Wilches-Chaux, "Breve historia natural del Cauca" in *Homenaje al Cauca* (Bogotá, Colombia: Villegas Editores, 1991), 21. For a magnificent description of the natural habitat of Cauca one should read Gustavo Wilches-Chaux's chapter.

11. Ibid.

12. Ibid, 21.

13. Gustavo Wilches-Chaux, "Breve Historia Natural del Cauca" in *Homenaje al Cauca* (Bogotá, Colombia: Villegas Editores, 1991), 29. Gregorio Hernandez de Alba, "The Highland Tribes of Southern Colombia," in the *Handbook of South American Indians Vol. 2. Andean Civilizations* ed. By Julian Steward (Washington, D.C.: United States Government Printing Office, 1946), 918. Hernández de Alba explains that *frailejón* is known in Latin as *Espeletia harwegiana*.

14. Wilches-Chaux, 29–32.

15. Gregorio Hernández de Alba, "The Highland Tribes of Southern Colombia," in the *Handbook of South American Indians Vol. 2. Andean Civilizations*, ed. by Julian Steward (Washington, DC: United States Government Printing Office, 1946), 918.
16. Julio Arboleda Valencia, "Perfil cultural del Cauca," in *Homenaje al Cauca* (Bogotá, Colombia: Villegas Editores, 1991), 113.
17. Raúl Arango and Enrique Sánchez, *Los pueblos indígenas de Colombia 1997: Desarollo y territorio* (Colombia: TM editors, 1998), no page number.
18. "Los diez proyectos que permitirán reconstruir el Cauca," *El Liberal*. Com 17 Jul. 2011. Accessed on June 27, 2012.
19. José María Rojas and Elías Sevilla-Casas, "El campesinado en la formación territorial del Suroccidente Colombiano," in *Territorios, regiones, sociedades*. Ed. Renán Silva (Bogotá, Colombia: Cerec, 1994), 178.
20. María Teresa Findji, *Elementos para el estudio de los resguardos indígenas del Cauca, censo indígena del Cauca 1972* (Bogotá, Colombia: Departamento Administrativo Nacional de Estadística, 1978), 7.
21. Jacques Aprile Gniset, *Los pueblos negros caucanos y la fundación de Puerto Tejada* (Cali, Colombia: Imprenta del departamento del Valle del Cauca, 1994), 11.
22. María Teresa Findji, Mapa 2 "Cauca: época de la constitución de los municipios." No page number.
23. Ibid.
24. Ibid.
25. Raúl Arango and Enrique Sánchez, *Los pueblos indígenas del Colombia 1997: Desarollo y territorio* (Colombia: TM editors, 1998), no page number. The list of resguardos is located in an appendix titled *Listado Base Guía Etnográfica de Colombia-GEC-Los Pueblos Indígenas 1997*.
26. Maria Teresa Findji asked this question first; I am using the same question here.
27. Maria Teresa Findji, "From Resistance to Social Movement: The Indigenous Authorities Movement in Colombia," pp. 112–35 in Arturo Escobar and Sonia Alvarez (eds.), *The Making of Social Movements in Latin America: Identity, Strategy, and Democracy* (Boulder: Westview Press, 1992).
28. Raúl Arango and Enrique Sánchez, *Los pueblos indígenas del Colombia 1997: Desarollo y territorio* (Colombia: TM editors, 1998), 26. The total population of Cauca according to the DANE census of 2005 was 1,268,937.
29. Roberto Pineda Camacho, *Tierra profanada: Grandes proyectos en territorios indígenas de Colombia* (Bogotá: Disloque Editores, 1995), 29.
30. Pineda Camacho, 13.
31. Gildardo Vanegas Muñoz and José Nicolás López, "El Departamento del Cauca en cifras: Situación social y política." Observatorio Político no. 5 (February 2008), no page number. Accessed October 2014, www.cauca.gov.co/nuestro-departamento/ . . . /item/ . . . /4. The 1995 estimate was that 22.9 percent of Cauca's population was indigenous according to Roberto Pineda Camacho. See *Tierra profanada: Grandes proyectos en territorios indígenas de Colombia* (Bogotá: Disloque Editores, 1995), 13.
32. DANE Census of 2005 estimated that the number of Afro-Colombians represented 22.9 percent of the total population of Cauca.
33. See Nancy Appelbaum, *Muddied Waters Race, Region, and Local History in Colombia, 1846–1948* (Durham: Duke University Press, 2003), 38.
34. Jose R. Gamarra Vergara, "La economía del departamento del Cauca: Concentración de tierras y pobreza" (Banco de La Republica. Centro de Estudios Economicos Regionales, CEER, Cartagena, 2007).
35. Gregorio Hernández de Alba, "The Highland Tribes," 919–23.
36. Gregorio Hernández de Alba, "The Highland Tribes," 923.
37. Gonzalo Castillo-Cardenas, *Liberation Theology from Below: The Life and Thought of Manuel Quintín Lame* (Maryknoll, NY: Orbis Books, 1987), 15.
38. Gregorio Hernández de Alba, "The Highland Tribes," 917.

39. James E. Sanders, *Contentious Republicans: Popular Politics, Race, and Class in Nineteenth-Century Colombia* (Durham: Duke University Press, 2004), 13. For an excellent description and overview of Cauca during the nineteenth century see Sanders, chapter 1.

40. Sanders sees the emergence of a pan-Indian identity emerging in the nineteenth century in Cauca, whereas I coincide with Nancy Appelbaum in seeing indigenous identity as a local one in the nineteenth century. See James Sanders, "Belonging to the Great Granadan Family: Partisan Struggle and the Construction of Indigenous Identity and Politics in Southwestern Colombia, 1849–1890," in *Race and Nation in Modern Latin America*, ed. by Appelbaum et al. (Chapel Hill: North Carolina Press, 2003), 56–87.

41. Diego Castrillón Arboleda, "Trazo etnohistórico," in *Homenaje al Cauca* (Bogotá, Colombia: Villegas Editores, 1991), 63.

42. Diego Castrillón Arboleda, "Trazo," 69.

43. Diego Castrillón Arboleda, "Trazo," 75.

44. Diego Castrillón Arboleda, "Trazo," 75.

45. Hernández de Alba, "Highland Tribes," 927.

46. Nina S. de Friedemann and Jaime Arocha, *Herederos del jaguar y la anaconda* (Bogotá: C. Valencia, 1985). Accessed at http://www.banrepcultural.org/node/19047.

47. Ibid.

48. Hernández de Alba, "Highland Tribes," 915 and 925.

49. Hernández de Alba, "Highland Tribes," 926.

50. Ibid.

51. J. Leon Helguera, "Coconuco: datos y documentos para la historia de una gran hacienda caucana: 1823, 1842, y 1876." in *Anuario Colombiano de historia social y de la cultura* 5 (1970), 189–203.

52. J. Leon Helguera, "Coconuco," 190.

53. J. Leon Helguera, "Coconuco," 192.

54. Ibid.

55. This discourse about Cauca's elites was not new to the twentieth century; Nancy Appelbaum shows compellingly how nineteenth-century Colombian public intellectuals (notably geographers) and foreign authors of travel narratives characterized Cauca as a place where elites were non-entrepreneurial in contrast to Antioquia's "modern elite." See *Muddied Waters Race, Region, and Local History in Colombia, 1846–1948* (Durham: Duke University Press, 2003).

56. Colonel John Hamilton Potter, *Travels through the Interior Provinces of Colombia*. 2 vols (London: J. Murray, 1827). Col. Hamilton was a commissioner traveling in Colombia on behalf of the British government.

57. J. Leon Helguera, "Coconuco," 192.

58. J. Leon Helguera, "Coconuco," 193.

59. Ibid.

60. Helguera, "Coconuco," 194.

61. Joanne Rappaport citing Earle discusses how coffee was planted in Tierradentro in the 1920s. See the earlier version of *Politics of Memory* (Cambridge: Cambridge University Press, 1990), 130. Also field diaries (in particular *Notas de Viaje sobre Region de Tierradentro*) produced by ethnologists for the Ethnological Institute of the University of Cauca discussed the growth of the importance of coffee from the 1930s to 1940s.

62. Joanne Rappaport, *The Politics of Memory, Native Historical Interpretation in the Colombian Andes* (Durham and London: Duke University Press, 1998), 143–44.

63. Diego Castrillón Arboleda, "Trazo," 75.

64. Mateo Mina, *Esclavitud y libertad en el valle del Rio Cauca* (Bogotá: Publicaciones de la Rosca, 1975), 84. Taussig also points out that the completion of the Panama Canal meant that the Pacific route became a viable one for the exportation of Colombia's products.

65. Mateo Mina, *Esclavitud y libertad en el valle del Rio Cauca* (Bogotá: Publicaciones de la Rosca, 1975), 85.

66. See Michael Taussig, *The Devil and Commodity Fetishism in South America* (North Carolina: University of North Carolina Press, 1980).

67. See Taussig.

68. Michael Taussig, *The Devil and Commodity Fetishism in South America* (North Carolina: University of North Carolina Press, 1980).

69. José María Rojas and Elías Sevilla Casas, "El campesinado en la formacion territorial del Surroccidente Colombiano," in *Territorios, regiones, sociedades*. ed. Renan Silva (Bogotá, Colombia: Cerec, 1994), 171. See also Taussig, *The Devil and Commodity Fetishism in South America* (North Carolina: University of North Carolina Press, 1980), 84.

70. María Teresa Findji points out that the reduction of Cauca's territory had a great impact on Cauca's elite. See Findji *Elementos para el estudio de los resguardos indígenas del Cauca, censo indígena del Cauca 1972* (Bogotá, Colombia: Departamento Administrativo Nacional de Estadística, 1978), 3.

71. Ibid, 3.

72. Raúl Arango and Enrique Sánchez, *Los pueblos indígenas de Colombia, 1997: Desarrollo y territorio* (Colombia: TM Editores, 1998), 3.

73. Christian Gros, *Colombia indígena, identidad cultural y Cambio social* (Bogotá, Colombia: Editorial Cerec, 1991), 177.

74. Joanne Rappaport, gives an overview of Law 89 of 1890 in her book, *Cumbe Reborn* (Chicago and London: University of Chicago Press, 1994), 26. Another author who discusses extensively Law 89 of 1890 is Gonzalo Castillo-Cardenas. See *Liberation Theology from Below: The Life and Thought of Manuel Quintín Lame* (Maryknoll: Orbis Books, 1987), 20–21.

75. Elias Sevilla Casas, *La pobreza de los excluidos, economía y sobrevivencia en un resguardo indígena del Cauca-Colombia,* (Cali: Ethnos, 1986), 43.

76. Ibid.

77. Ibid.

78. Alberto Pinzon Sánchez, *Monopolios, misioneros y destruccion de indígenas* (Bogotá: Ediciones Armadillo, 1979), 95.

79. Pinzon Sánchez, 96.

80. Ibid.

81. Sevilla Casas, *La probeza*,42.

82. See Juan Friede's *La explotación indígena en Colombia bajo el Gobiemo de las Misiones: El Caso de los arhuacos de la Sierra Nevada de Santa Marta* (Bogotá: Punta de Lanza, 1973) on the Aruacos and his funny yet sad description of indigenous people being taught to sing a German hymn in the midst of the Colombian jungle.

Chapter Two

Manuel Quintín Lame and His Political Movement

Manuel Quintín Lame's life, activism, and physical representation have tremendous symbolic power for the indigenous community and for the larger Colombian and international public. Scholars have characterized him as an organic intellectual, as a bicultural leader, and as a founding "father" of the Colombian indigenous movement.[1] The very image of Manuel Quintín Lame is central to the Colombian indigenous movement. One of his most iconic representations is his photograph taken at his 1916 arrest at San Isidro, Cauca; he is center stage and has long hair.[2] The long hair sets him apart from other men in the photograph; his long hair is usually interpreted as an outward manifestation of his political mobilization based on his indigenous ethnic identity. The historical moment of this photograph is also charged with meaning; here he was arrested and in an open confrontation with the Colombian authorities. Thus, this photograph suggests what many scholars and political activists have argued, which is that Manuel Quintín Lame's life and activism placed him in constant opposition with the state in Colombia.

My aim in this chapter is not to give an overview of his life, which is well documented in various compelling and well-documented works from various angles.[3] Instead, I examine the voluminous correspondence from approximately 1913 to 1918 to advance the overall argument that while Manuel Quintín Lame was a tireless and combative leader of indigenous communities who fought the local states of Cauca and Huila, he also was constantly appealing to the central state as a possible ally. The following quote encapsulates Manuel Quintin Lame's approach toward the national state; he expressed this profound belief in the good will of the national government toward indigenous communities throughout his political life. He stated,

> You are just, you are an upstanding man. I must clarify with a message of truth and not of error, in this chapter about the good will of non-indigenous men, those that make up the National Government of Colombia. That since 1910 until today all my claims have been heard in favor of all the resguardos of indigenous people in the departments of Nariño, Cauca, Valle del Cauca, Huila and Tolima.[4]

Thus, Manuel Quintín Lame established a certain type of ethnic political mobilization based on an alliance with the central state that would later be taken up by the modern day indigenous movement of Colombia with success.

This chapter focuses specifically on the historical moment known as the *Quintinada* Rebellion, which is traditionally given the dates of 1910 to 1920, and which took place in various departments of Southwestern Colombia, but was centered in Tierradentro, Cauca. I argue that this "rebellion" named after Manuel Quintín Lame was not really a rebellion if understood as an attempt to take over an area in a military fashion, but rather a political movement that was essentially nonviolent. The indigenous leader did hint at violence, adopt intimidating postures, and engage in inflammatory rhetoric (for the times), but Manuel Quintín Lame was a man who believed in the might of the pen and the force of the law.[5] He sincerely believed that the central state would ultimately side with him and his cause and would intervene in an effective manner in favor of the indigenous people. The explosion of violence that finally came was clearly from the nonindigenous sector of the population who can be viewed as the precursors of paramilitary forces that would plague this subregion of Cauca for years to come.

This chapter outlines the various false alarms when the local government and local subregional elites claimed that Manuel Quintín Lame and his cohort had attacked a town or various areas. It is important to consider these false alarms or exaggerations of the actual events because they provide a lens into the dynamic of the interaction between the local elite, the regional state, and the central state.[6]

Here I show how the central state (even at this early stage) was more sympathetic to the indigenous cause and cautioned the regional state in terms of its response. The national state had its own reasons for suggesting restraint (at first), which did not necessarily stem from a benevolent position vis-à-vis Manuel Quintín Lame, but rather on a desire to maintain its monopoly on violence and to assert its newfound status as the center of political power.[7] My focus on the state's actions and agenda from 1913 to 1918 is an integral part to my larger argument, which is that the central state would ultimately create and legitimize a political space for indigenous communities to push forward their claims based on ethnic identity. Nonetheless, the national state did (in dating language) give mixed signals to Manuel Quintín Lame in terms of what he could expect. Ultimately, the central state sided with the local state, but during a substantial period it allowed for Manuel Quintín Lame to imagine a central Colombian state that would side with the indigenous cause. The absence of effectiveness and mixed messages would have fatal consequences (although limited ones compared to today's number of dead in Colombia during the most recent outbreak of violence) when the local subregional elites took matters into their own hands.

After the dismemberment of the state of Gran Cauca (as seen in the previous chapter) the regional elite of Cauca (even in 1910) was a fractured one. Partisan disputes between Liberals, Conservatives, and "Republicans" divided local elites; the central state controlled by the Conservative Party during the 1910s was more inclined to listen to Conservative merchants and members of the new bourgeoisie.[8] There were, of course, ties between the old Central Valley elite and the new bourgeoisie; for instance, Guillermo Valencia (a member of the old elite and future president of Colombia) was the son-in-law of one of the richest men of Cauca (Ignacio Muñoz). However, elite partisan differences, which were greater in Cauca than in other regions, heightened electoral competition for the distinct political parties; Manuel Quintín Lame was keenly aware of indigenous communities' political clout.[9] While other scholars have pointed out the weakness of Cauca's central valley elites and the importance of partisan differences, I make the novel argument in this chapter that divisions amongst local elites will create new opportunities for alliances between the indigenous communities and the central state.[10] Overall, Manuel Quintín Lame sought to position himself as the key intermediary between the central state and southwestern indigenous communities seeking to bypass the local structures of power. While the local Cauca elite successfully repressed Manuel Quintin Lame's political movement, the indigenous leader had begun to undermine the political legitimacy of Cauca's elite and the local state's hegemony.[11]

The organization of this chapter is chronological. I focus on pivotal moments when Manuel Quintín Lame's actions or perceived actions bring the central state, the local state, the local elites, and the indigenous communities into contact.

BRIEF SUMMARY OF HIS LIFE UNTIL THE OUTBREAK OF THE *QUINTÍNADA*

In many regards, Manuel Quintín Lame was predestined to become Cauca's most famous indigenous leader. Manuel Quintín Lame's life was an intersection of Colombian national politics and of the economic and social trends in Cauca. In 1880, he was born on a hacienda, *La Polindara*,[12] located near Popayán that belonged to one of Cauca's most elite families, the Arboledas.[13] His parents, both indigenous, were sharecroppers/*terrajeros* like many indigenous people of central Cauca. The fact that they did not initially own land was a reflection of earlier historical periods of conquest and colonization of indigenous people in Cauca. In the central valley of Cauca many indigenous people experienced land dispossession; they went from collectively owning the land they farmed to becoming tenants of the same land.

However, his father, Mariano Lame, was an astute businessman who managed to buy a land plot and set up a small cattle ranching business while performing his sharecropping duties. The ability to buy a land plot and to set up a business in ranching came about in part because the new owner of *La Polindara* decreased the number of days that his sharecroppers had to serve.[14] While Mariano Lame was fortunate, he was not atypical. Other indigenous families blessed with a large number of sons and a "benevolent" hacienda boss could and did purchase private property. I point this out because the later discourse about indigenous people, which erased class differences, painted them as uniformly poor and oppressed. While the larger narrative of land dispossession of indigenous community is absolutely correct, some indigenous families managed to achieve a certain degree of economic prosperity with cattle ranching and agricultural work. Manuel Quintín Lame was a product of Cauca's central valley's environment that simultaneously exploited indigenous people and also offered some opportunities for economic mobility.

Economic mobility for indigenous rural folk was limited to commercial and agricultural ventures; access to formal schooling and to professional careers was seriously limited. Manuel Quintín Lame's life and political agenda reflected these two trends. After visiting with his uncle (who could read) and hearing him read bits and pieces from newspapers, Manuel Quintín Lame (who was obviously extraordinarily bright) asked his father if he could go to school. According to Diego Castrillón Arboleda, his father pointed to some agricultural tools informing his son that was all the education he needed as an "Indian."[15] His father's reaction makes perfect sense if we consider that economic advancement for most indigenous rural folk was achieved through agricultural work. The indigenous leader was a self-taught reader and writer by necessity. Manuel Quintín Lame's political agenda repeatedly emphasized the importance of access to education for indigenous rural folk.[16]

National and partisan politics forever changed Manuel Quintín Lame's family. In 1886, during one of Colombia's many civil wars, his sister, who was mute, was raped and then died five years later. During the *War of a Thousand Days* (1899–1902), Liberal guerrilla soldiers attacked Manuel Quintín Lame and his family known for their support for Conservatives and for the Conservative government.[17] Manuel Quintín Lame and one of his brothers (Gregorio) managed to escape from the soldiers, but his brother Feliciano was killed. In 1901, Manuel Quintín Lame joined the Conservative army and served as an orderly for General Carlos Albán in Panama where he improved his literacy skills. Manuel Quintín Lame's military service in Panama lent him an air of prestige amongst indigenous communities and gave him an understanding of national politics.[18]

Upon his return to Cauca, Manuel Quintín Lame's first wife's death upended the economic and psychological stability he had achieved; he was also frustrated with the hacienda's owner's refusal to sell him a land plot. Faced with personal tragedy and the impossibility of economic mobility, he began drinking heavily and acquired the reputation as a womanizer. A second marriage in 1911 and his introduction to the book *El abogado en casa* (a legal manual) not only provided him with emotional stability, but set him on the path of advocating for indigenous communities as an amateur lawyer, *tinterillo*.[19]

1913–1914: "FIRST SKIRMISHES"

One of the early conflicts between Manuel Quintín Lame and local authorities took place in Tacueyó, which is the head of the municipality of Toribío, located in the northwest of Cauca. The municipality of Toribío was the site of terrible violence in the 1980s when a rogue/dissident unit of the FARC (called Ricardo Franco) carried out a large-scale massacre of women, men, and children.[20] As recently as 2012, the conflict between the FARC and the Colombian armed forces caused the displacement of the civilian population, including many indigenous peoples in the area of Toribío.[21] One of the unfortunate trends that this book confirms is that the sites of conflict in Cauca during the second decade of the twentieth century are often the same in the twenty-first century.[22]

From the very beginning of what would become an incredibly voluminous correspondence, Manuel Quintín Lame portrayed the municipal authorities (whether it be in Cauca, Tolima, or Huila) as unjust, arbitrary, and illegitimate. While he also complained about the regional state representatives, his greatest outrage was reserved for the low-level municipal authorities. The indigenous leader's response to the abuses committed by the local state at the municipal level was to write extensive missives to the national government. In the process of writing to the national government, Manuel Quintín Lame imagined a national state that was benevolent and all-powerful.

In October of 1914 Manuel Quintín Lame was arrested and sent to Popayán's jail because the prefect, the judge, and the municipal mayor of Tacueyó had requested it.[23] The indigenous leader narrated how on October 3, 1914, a captain of the police force arrested him while he was at the Popayán produce market selling onions and wheat. To make matters worse, he was not allowed to entrust his produce to someone else. Thus, he suffered a monetary loss due to this arbitrary and unjust arrest. The second violation of his rights was when he was transported with a tight rope around his neck and with his hands tied behind. The instigator of this violation of human rights was the local municipal authority, which had requested that he be treated in such a manner.[24]

Subsequently, the municipal mayor of Caloto placed him in isolation and did not allow him to communicate with anyone. After six days of isolation and of being incommunicado, he was allowed to start writing letters/memorials. He was only able to obtain his freedom after sixty-six days of jail and was not given any money for his rations while he was in jail. The local authorities were thus portrayed as behaving in an unjust and illegitimate manner. Equally important to note here is that Manuel Quintín Lame assumed that the central state shared his notions of how justice should be carried out and how a legitimate political authority should behave.

The source of conflict between Manuel Quintín Lame and the local authorities of the district of Tacueyó was over a limestone quarry, which the local authorities stated was a mine of gold. Local authorities misrepresented the true nature of this mine because if the mine was a gold mine then municipal rights trumped the rights of the indigenous people on whose land the mine was located. In addition, to this misrepresentation, local authorities forced the indigenous people to work on a road, and in the process of building this road, their crops and sections of wooded land were destroyed. Initially, Manuel Quintín Lame appealed to the Prefect of Caloto (the local authority), who responded by telling him that he had no jurisdiction over this matter. Facing the absence of an official response to his complaint about the misappropriation of labor and land, Manuel Quintín Lame "ordered" (term he used) that the indigenous council of Tacueyó destroy the machinery that was used to extract the desired materials; he also informed the minister of government that hay was burnt. In response to this confrontation, local authorities charged Manuel Quintín Lame with arson.

Two petitions directed to the Ministerio de Gobierno/Minister of Government during the time and shortly after the incident of the quarry mine shed light on Manuel Quintín Lame's discourse and on the symbolic power he gave to the central state. He characterized the President of Colombia as the "father of humanity" and indigenous people of the department of Cauca as inept.[25] Manuel Quintín Lame's discourse about indigenous people in Cauca was empowering in the sense that he stressed the rights that indigenous peoples had over the land, but it was also condescending because he represented indigenous people as needing rescuing from the national state and in a terrible condition.

In order to remedy this unfortunate state of affairs, the indigenous leader petitioned the national government to grant him legal power to represent the councils of indigenous *resguardos*. The stated concern of this missive was that indigenous *parcialidades* needed a new *reglamento*/regulation and that they should follow Law 89 of 1890.[26] Manuel Quintín Lame alleged that the Camilo Torres municipality's prefect ordered the council of the *parcialidad* Tacueyó to take away his right to represent the council of Tacueyó (that had been given to him so he could defend their rights). Here, we can see how the local state in response to Manuel Quintín Lame's "orders" that led to the destruction of the mine quarry's machinery had pressured the indigenous council to officially revoke the power of attorney it had previously granted to the indigenous leader. The petition also asked the national government to order the governor of Cauca to recognize Manuel Quintín Lame's right to represent all of Cauca's *parcialidades* (which numbered around sixty).

The underlying issue was who decided on the political representation of indigenous communities. As the reader will remember, Law 89 of 1890 allowed for indigenous *resguardo* members to elect their council representatives, but the municipality's mayor could veto the election. Manuel Quintín Lame in this petition sought to bypass the municipality's veto power with his petition that the national government grant him the political authority to represent all sixty *parcialidades.*

Manuel Quintín Lame had a view of Colombian political authority as extremely hierarchical. He believed the national government could simply order the governor to comply with an order and thought all orders were carried from the top down within the department. Unfortunately for him, reality did not match his vision or the pretensions of the Colombian national government. In all fairness, the 1886 Regeneration Constitution outlined a national government that was the ultimate arbiter; and the new model of political organization in Colombia was one where centralization prevailed. The new bureaucratic post of prefect (created after the period of the 1886 constitution) was modeled after the French system renowned for its centralization and for the iron control that Paris exerted over its provinces. The central state's willingness to correspond with Manuel Quintín Lame and to consider his claims in 1914 stemmed in part from its desire to show regional states and elites that the central state (in Bogotá) could intervene in local affairs and that it was the ultimate arbiter of political claims.[27]

To obtain protection from the national state, Manuel Quintín Lame decided to travel to Bogotá, which he called the capital of Colombia thus giving it a larger and more powerful symbolic importance.[28] For a central state that had recently acquired its status as the center of political power, Manuel Quintín Lame's representation of the state was politically expedient. His last request to the national government embedded in musings about the lack of education for indigenous people was that he should be given the title of Leader or "Mariscal." Thus, Manuel Quintín Lame's aim was not to topple or question the central state, but rather was to establish himself as the go-to person in terms of the relationship between the central state and the indigenous communities. After all, Law 89 of 1890 that he kept referring to and lauding was one that the central Colombian state had enacted. Although this was not necessarily Manuel Quintín Lame's goal, his correspondence with the central state legitimized the Colombian state.

FIRST FALSE ALARM: FEBRUARY OF 1915

The local state's response to Manuel Quintín Lame's political activities was one of complete alarm and almost panic.[29] From 1915 on, the local state and municipal authorities seized on the slightest information to claim either that an indigenous rebellion was underway or that Manuel Quintín Lame was conspiring to carry out one. On February 6, 1915, Leandro Medina, the Cauca secretary of government, portrayed Manuel Quintín Lame as conspiring to foment an indigenous rebellion while taking advantage of the ignorance of indigenous people. Interestingly, both Leandro Medina and Manuel Quintín Lame agreed on the need for education for the indigenous people of the area but obviously had entirely different objectives. Leandro Medina thought that the departmental schools should be nationalized thereby providing financing for the local schools (which otherwise would not be funded in poor areas) so that indigenous people would not be so easily swayed and susceptible to the messages preached by "characters" such as Manuel Quintín Lame.

Medina claimed that Manuel Quintín Lame's message was one of separation from "whites" and of seizing land that had previously belonged to the indigenous population. In contrast to later periods of the twentieth century when an ethnic agenda was seen as less dangerous than a class-based one, at the turn of the twentieth century an ethnic-based message was seen as profoundly subversive by local authorities.

The alleged plot before it was carried out was to gather in Calibío on February 14, elect Manuel Quintín Lame as a representative, and to proclaim separation from whites. The Cauca state authorities alerted the governors of Valle del Cauca, Tolima, and Huila of the complot; thirty commissioned men from the battalion of Junín were sent to Tierradentro. Manuel Quintín Lame and his brother along with five other indigenous "helpers" were imprisoned.

The theme that the Cauca state would assert throughout all of its correspondence to the national government was that Manuel Quintín Lame was the primary cause for the indigenous uprising. Later on, Cauca government representatives such as Governor Paredes would even go as far as to assert that the indigenous people of Cauca held no significant political, economic, and social grievances vis-à-vis the landowners and the local political authorities, but rather that Manuel Quintín Lame preached a message that was so seductive (the return of the land to the indigenous people) that they could not resist it. However, Leandro Medina while emphasizing Manuel Quintín Lame's role in this supposed plot, also laid the blame on the legislation that governed indigenous people (Law 89 of 1890), which he stated prevented the indigenous people from progressing yet left them vulnerable to the *gamonales*/local political bosses.[30] It is not clear from other correspondence what real "danger" existed other than Manuel Quintín Lame summoning a group of indigenous people in Calibio to deliver a speech.

This allegation of a plot, which led to Manuel Quintín Lame's imprisonment, spurred a response from the indigenous people of Tacueyó and Toribío. In a memorial to the Ministry of Government the letter writers complained about how local authorities and various judicial authorities had not respected Law 89 of 1890.[31] This lack of respect for Law 89 of 1890 led them to give Manuel Quintín Lame the power of attorney. The other cited motivation to the conferral of power of attorney was that Manuel Quintín Lame offered to travel to Bogotá to obtain the titles of the properties that the indigenous petitioners alleged were taken away by "racionales" (meaning white people). The indigenous letter writers stated that the indigenous race was a wretched one and that not a single historian, orator, journalist, or philosopher had spoken in favor of the indigenous people. Here, we have an example of how indigenous people internalized the discourse that Manuel Quintín Lame held on indigenous people of Cauca as a wretched race in need of education and salvation. For these letter writers, Manuel Quintín Lame had promised a way for indigenous people to be empowered by education and by morality. This was in opposition to the teachers of the area who were described as opposed to the education of the children of indigenous people because it would be detrimental to the white race.

According to the letter writers, the reason that the local authorities had charged Manuel Quintín Lame with sedition was because he wore a uniform given to him by the Ministry of War; their leader and his brother were shifted around from jail to jail to a total of five jails. In a manner similar to Manuel Quintín Lame, the indigenous petitioners portrayed the local authorities as illegitimate; they specifically accused the governor of Cauca of being on the side of the rich usurpers of their land. The evidence of the governor of Cauca's illegitimate conduct was that he opposed the release of Lame on bail even when the Superior Tribunal had decreed it.[32] The tone of the missive turned confrontational when they threatened to sue the governorship of Cauca and other authorities with the Supreme Court of Justice because the imprisonment of Manuel Quintín Lame had caused great losses in terms of their properties. In addition, the petitioners alleged that the prefect of Silvia obliged the indigenous council of Totoró to revoke the legal power conferred to Manuel Quintín Lame, and that the prefect of Caloto had ordered them to give a beating to their leader.[33] The response to this petition from the national government was that it could not decree Manuel Quintín Lame's freedom and that this petition should be sent to the authority that incarcerated him.

In July of 1915 a missive addressed to Manuel Quintín Lame gives us insight into the national government's response to the "indigenous problem." The first claim was that the district attorney was the stated protector of indigenous people; the ministry of government maintained that Manuel Quintín Lame was in jail because of the crime of arson and other charges brought against him before the court of Caloto and not because of the charge of rebellion or sedition that was being investigated in the court of Silvia. However, the Ministry of Government promised to investigate the theft of five thousand pesos and the wound inflicted on Ignacio Lame. As far as the theft of his uniform, the national government advised him to follow a certain procedure; Manuel Quintín Lame had accused the mayor of Belalcázar of stealing his uniform. While it cannot be said that the national government supported Manuel Quintín Lame's agenda, the willingness that the national government showed to correspond with the indigenous leader and its follow-through with the local state gave him a certain legitimacy.

In August of 1915 Manuel Quintín Lame wrote again to the Ministry of Government to protest his continued detention; he was still imprisoned after eight months accused of the crime of rebellion.[34] In this missive, he continued his attempt to undermine the legitimacy of the local state by portraying it as irrational and as biased in favor of the rich; he stated that the Secretario of Gobierno of Cauca was colluding with the rich usurpers of the land of many *resguardos* whose members Manuel Quintín Lame represented. Manuel Quintín Lame singled out the secretary of the governorship of Cauca and advanced that he was irrational and swayed by passion rather than by the logic of law and rationality.[35] Manuel Quintín Lame also portrayed the local authorities as contradicting themselves; according to him the attorney general said he was in jail because of the charge of arson and property damage while the Secretary of Gobierno of Cauca told him that he was in jail for the charge/crime of rebellion or sedition.

SECOND FALSE ALARM: FEBRUARY 1916

In February of 1916 Miguel Arroyo Díez (the governor of Cauca at this time) sent a telegram to the Minister of Gobierno to alert him that the Superior Tribunal had cleared Manuel Quintín Lame of the charges of sedition and freed him.[36] To the governor's dismay Manuel Quintín Lame was now active in the *parcialidades* where he was proclaiming that he was a cacique and a restorer of indigenous land. He also assembled indigenous people everywhere, requested money for his expenses, and prepared to challenge local authorities starting with the expulsion of the departmental revenue agents.

The governor of Cauca requested that fifty soldiers from the Junín Regiment be sent to Cauca so that Manuel Quintín Lame could be arrested. Since the governor of Cauca thought that it was likely that Manuel Quintín Lame would be freed again (by the Tribunal) if he was imprisoned, he suggested that Manuel Quintín Lame be sent to Puerto Asis or to another penal colony where he could be constantly watched. Manuel Quintín Lame's exile was to prevent any further rebellion attempts and was intended to tranquilize the people of the *cordillera* who were supposedly profoundly alarmed.[37]

Miguel Arroyo Díez went from warning that an incipient rebellion was about to occur to claiming that the indigenous people had risen up organized by Manuel Quintín Lame.[38] The local population in the central *cordillera* terrified by the imminent indigenous uprising was apparently asking for weapons and munitions, but the department of Cauca had none to give. Julio Borrero, the governor of Huila, echoed the same warning and even went a step further characterizing Manuel Quintín Lame's movement as revolutionary. [39] The prefect of the area was given orders to watch events closely.

On February 12, according to the mayors of Belalcázar and Inzá, Manuel Quintín Lame was in Mosoco with three hundred armed men; the mayors of these towns asked for help.[40] The governor of Cauca stated that even though an armed detachment of the Junín regiment was marching to the region of Tierradentro, he needed two hundred rifles to arm the citizens (called *vecinos*) of Silvia, Inzá, Belalcázar, and Caloto to stop the indigenous uprising. The indigenous rebels were thought to be plotting to burn the towns of Silvia, Inzá, Belalcázar, and Caloto. The governor of Cauca did state that the indigenous insurrection was restricted to the region of Tierradentro and Cordillera; in the other parts of the department total calm reigned and not even the news of Manuel Quintín Lame's movement had spread. The governor of Cauca thought that fifteen days would be sufficient to terminate the movement. Although the governor of Cauca stressed the alarming nature of Manuel Quintín Lame's movement, he clearly did not want to convey the impression that he had lost control of the department. On the same day, Julio Borrerro, the governor of Huila requested that one hundred men be "organized" in what can only be described as a paramilitary force so that they could work in conjunction with the armed forces of Popayán and Cali to respond to the indigenous rebellion led by Manuel Quintín Lame. [41]

The response from the national government came swiftly on February 12, 1916.[42] Abadía Mendez, the Minister of Interior, narrated that he met with the President of the Republic and with the Minister of War to discuss the Manuel Quintín Lame issue. The high-level talks indicated that this indigenous uprising was taken very seriously by the national government. Order was to be restored through General Velasco's (the military leader of the area) actions. Although the national government was clearly concerned with maintaining order and security in the region of Tierradentro, it also conveyed its deep reservations about arming ordinary citizens. Abadía Mendez stated,

> The President and the Minister also believe that in military operations, regular forces of the army and of the Police should intervene with absolute discipline and prudence, since untrained forces could carry out premature, unjustified, and hostile acts that would prevent any friendly intelligence and would leave the seed for terrible reprisals by indigenous people. This is without taking into account the danger of taking out arms and munitions from national parks to put them in the hands of individuals, since experience has shown that they are almost never returned and they (the arms) become a threat for public order. It would be convenient before implementing harsh measures to send a commission that enjoys prestige amongst indigenous people to convince them of the irrationality of their hostile attitude, of how Lame has them deceived, and to offer them what can legitimely be offered to eliminate the causes for their complaints. Hopefully, General Castellanos will be contacted and an efficient plan will be put together, but most of all a prudent plan, to avert conflict. Will be grateful for frequent information.[43]

This passage is worth quoting in its entirety since it shows how the national government was open to negotiations with the indigenous population and sought to try more conciliatory methods to deal with the indigenous uprising before moving on to military repression. This was in sharp contrast with the local authorities' desire to respond to the indigenous uprising with force first and foremost. The governor of Cauca and the governor of Huila made no reference to any sort of legitimacy to the demands made by the indigenous rebels. This is not to say that the national government was sympathetic to Manuel Quintín Lame, but that the overall tone and approach to the indigenous population was distinct to that of the local government. Of course, the central state had its own agenda separate from the indigenous issue, which was to maintain control over its national territory and to secure a monopoly on violence. However, this agenda of state formation led to a different approach and vision of indigenous peoples, which would be reasserted at different historical junctures throughout the twentieth century. Another long-term historical trend that was established at this moment was that local authorities of Tierradentro had no qualms in arming private citizens and on relying on the use of force to deal with the indigenous population.

The governor of Cauca (Miguel Arroyo Díez) sought to reassure the national government that he had no intention of using force to repress the indigenous movement, but rather that he sought to guarantee the "life and rights" of the citizens in the affected towns and municipalities.[44] The governor's assertion seems disingenuous since once military troops arrived in the area, the line between defending the "citizens" and repressing the indigenous people's movement was a tenuous one. In his very discourse he made it clear that for him indigenous people were not citizens to be protected unlike the nonindigenous people of the area. The governor of Cauca also asserted that in all likelihood the indigenous rebels would simply disband once they saw that the military troops had arrived. The local authorities sought to delegitimize the indigenous movement by claiming that there was no political content to their agenda, but rather that they were embarked on a race war. Again, here for the local state, the mere mention of race and ethnicity somehow invalidated and delegitimized the political message of indigenous communities. The governor then engaged in a bold-faced lie stating that there were no complaints made by indigenous people against local authorities. The complaints were directed (according to the governor) exclusively toward the white merchants who were seen as exploiters. In addition, the governor of Cauca sought to delegitimize Manuel Quintín Lame further by stating that several *resguardos* had expressed their disapproval of Manuel Quintín Lame's plans via telegrams sent to the Gobernación. Julio Borrero, the governor of Huila, stated that he was adopting the prudent attitude suggested by the national government and also informed the executive branch of government that thirty gendarmes were leaving for La Plata.[45]

The next round of correspondence between the local government and the national state revealed that rumors had run wild and that the so-called indigenous uprising existed only in the fears and imagination of certain inhabitants of Tierradentro. The governor of Cauca explained that the mayor of Paez received a telegram that alleged that Manuel Quintín Lame had presented himself with three hundred armed men to Mosoco; this telegram proved to be a falsehood.[46] Under pressure (presumably of the inhabitants of Mosoco), the telegrapher of Mosoco had sent a telegram that stated the fears of the Mosoco inhabitants. The mayor of Paez had relayed the telegram (believing it to be true) to the governor of Cauca. The governor of Cauca had received other alarming telegrams that notified him of Manuel Quintín Lame inciting indigenous people to disregard local authorities.[47]

What had really occurred was that Manuel Quintín Lame after his release from jail had returned to the central *cordillera* and had continued spreading his message that the land belonged to the indigenous peoples and that many of the titles of the land that the "whites" possessed were invalid.[48] Manuel Quintín Lame's very appearance in Tierradentro free to wander must have lent enormous credibility to his message of indigenous rights and caused what can only be described as hysteria amongst the local authorities. After all, he had triumphed over the local authorities (mayors and governor of Cauca) through his legal maneuvers and apparent (even if it proved to be illusory) support of the national state. We know that Manuel Quintín Lame showed the correspondence that he received from the national state to the indigenous people of the area as evidence of his good standing with the central state much to the local elite's annoyance.[49]

The local elite, here Ignacio Muñoz and Alcibiades Valencia, stated in a letter to the President of the Republic, "*Acogida inconsiderada que ha prestado Bogotá a esa clase vagos ha sido funestísima*/Thoughtless welcome that Bogota has given to these shiftless individuals has been fatal." The local landowners clearly viewed Bogotá's/the central state's willingness to receive and to listen to Manuel Quintín Lame as deeply problematic and as giving the impression that he was a powerful agent in the eyes of the indigenous population. The governor of Cauca claimed that as a result of Manuel Quintín Lame's release and his return to Tierradentro, the indigenous leader was able to persuade the indigenous *terrajeros* that they did not have to comply with their labor obligations.[50] Thus, indigenous peoples of the area were challenging the established social order alarming the local elites and authorities.

JUNE 1916: ANOTHER FALSE ALARM AND EVIDENCE OF THE LARGER IMPACT OF THE INDIGENOUS POLITICAL MOVEMENT LED BY MANUEL QUINTÍN LAME

The flurry of correspondence started up again with another allegation that Manuel Quintín Lame was preparing a general uprising of indigenous peoples against whites in June of 1916.[51] Manuel Quintín Lame's plan consisted of recovering all the land taken from them, of founding a separate indigenous government, and of establishing capitals for the new indigenous nation. According to Governor Paredes, the "white" population was deeply alarmed, especially the *hacendados*. Paredes requested that the commander of the Brigade be ordered to send men from the military regiment to Cauca because the department only had a few policemen at its disposal to maintain order. The fear was that if they captured Manuel Quintín Lame without military support, the indigenous people would rise up and rescue him.

The specter of an all-race war was also raised to the national state; both governor Paredes and the local elites suggested to the central state that the unrest was not limited to the indigenous people of Cauca, but had spread to include people of color in general (blacks were mentioned specifically).[52] Don Guillermo Valencia (we can safely assume that this is the same Guillermo Valencia who was Manuel Quintín Lame's archenemy) would have told Paredes that people of color in Nariño, Cauca, Valle, Tolima, and Huila were all conspiring together. It was not made clear what the conspiracy was about, but clearly the author of the telegram thought it was to end "white power." The final warning shot to the national government from the local elites (who introduced themselves as members of the same party as President Concha/Conservatives) was the allegation that Caucano blacks were beginning to protest and to adopt the attitude of the indigenous people. Given that Afro-

Colombians of Cauca had participated valiantly and effectively in a number of civil wars, this rumor was meant to alarm the central state. In addition, in the north of Cauca, Afro-Colombians had organized self-defense committees in 1915 that challenged landowners' rights to demand labor from sharecroppers.[53]

The national state again in June of 1916 (as it had in February of 1916) responded to the local authorities with a message of caution.[54] While the national state agreed to send military support, it insisted that only regular armed forces be used, and it warned that arming private citizens was a bad idea. It reminded the current governor of Cauca that the national state had given the same advice to its predecessor, Miguel Arroyo Díez. Also, the advice to find a nonviolent and conciliatory way to defuse the situation was repeated such as organizing a commission to visit with the indigenous people to convince them that their grievances were without any basis.

On June 8, 1916, Manuel Quintín Lame was arrested; Governor Paredes claimed that indigenous people reacted violently to the news of Manuel Quintín Lame's arrest and that on one occasion indigenous people clashed with soldiers from the Junín Regiment in Las Piedras located on the road toward Puracé.[55] The local state used the example of this confrontation to advance that indigenous people were preparing an uprising and were resorting to violence. However, it is important to note that the indigenous people who clashed with the soldiers of the Junín did so only after Manuel Quintín Lame was arrested, and that the confrontation resulted in the death of an indigenous person not of a soldier. In addition, undermining the local state's theory that vast number of indigenous people were prepared to respond with violence at the news of Manuel Quintín Lame's arrest and were preparing an all-out race war, was the Governor of Cauca's own report on June 10 that the situation of Cauca had improved and that there was no need for a declaration that the public order of Cauca was disturbed.[56]

By June of 1916 Manuel Quintín Lame's movement intersected with partisan disputes and played into the larger racial dynamics of Cauca. One of Manuel Quintín Lame's key allies in his legal and public defense was Teófilo Sarria who wrote frequently for the Liberal newspaper, *El Liberal*.[57] Governor Paredes suggested that certain people of Popayán (enemies of the Conservative Presidency of Colombia) were helping Manuel Quintín Lame with the objective of furthering their own political aims. Teófilo Sarria had not only published Manuel Quintín Lame's speeches in his newspaper, but had also stormed into the police barracks after Manuel Quintín Lame's arrest and capture to protest his arrest that he characterized as an arbitrary procedure and to declare that he was Manuel Quintín Lame's defender. Much to Governor Paredes's annoyance, Teofilo Sarria protested Manuel Quintín Lame's arrest not only at the police station but also publicly.[58]

A series of articles in local newspapers revealed partisan tensions amongst the local elites and poked fun at those who saw Manuel Quintín Lame as a threat. One such article, "Manuel Quintín Lame," stated that the indigenous leader was still in jail in July of 1916 for the alleged insurrection and that the so-called sedition of Manuel Quintín Lame would be judged by history as a ridiculous notion.[59] A quote from the article, "Ni Gonzalo de Oyón"[60] gives a sense of the ridicule heaped upon the authorities; "Manuel Quintín Lame y diez individuos más se hallan detenidos por estar sindicados por delitos contra la paz interior, contra el Gobierno existente y contra la Constitución. Según se ve, a estos revolucionarios no les va a a alcanzar la vida para purgar esa rebeldía! Estuvo en peligro el Gobierno del doctor Concha!!/ Manuel Quintín Lame and ten more individuals are imprisoned charged with the crime of disturbing the peace against the existing Government and against the Constitution. As one can see, the revolutionaries' lifetime will not be long enough to serve their sentences for their rebellion. Dr. Concha's government was in danger!!"[61]

Another lengthier article, "No mas ridiculeces por Dios! No more absurdities for the Love of God" from the same newspaper dated August 5, 1916, narrated how a rumor circulated that five hundred indigenous people were coming toward Popayán to rescue their leader.[62] Fortunately, the prefect of Popayán marched alone to the "battlefield" (meant ironically and not specified where he was) and met with indigenous communities. Once he talked to indigenous people, he realized that only a group of them intended to travel to Popayán with the sole and peaceful objective of talking with the governor of Cauca. The anonymous author of the article stated his full confidence that once the governor of Popayán met with indigenous people, he would realize that no threat of violence existed.[63]

A subsequent article, "Ya es tiempo. . . . It is time" pressured the judicial system to come to a decision about Manuel Quintín Lame's case.[64] The author stated that either Manuel Quintín Lame was a socialist revolutionary and a criminal and therefore should be tried or he was the victim of legends made up by nervous imaginations. The author of the article stressed his full confidence in the judicial branch and in its impartiality; since the judicial branch had already compiled a file three hundred pages long on Manuel Quintín Lame, there was no reason to delay a prompt resolution of the case. The local press campaign probably played a role in the Superior Court's decision to release Manuel Quintín Lame and his followers on September 23, 1916.[65]

NOVEMBER 1916: VIOLENCE ON NOVEMBER 12TH/VIEW FROM INZÁ'S INHABITANTS AND THE LOCAL STATE

On November 12, 1916, in Inzá, Tierradentro, at least five indigenous people were killed, and twelve were wounded.[66] During and shortly after these events, the local state and the municipality of Inzá presented the five deaths as a clear indication of Manuel Quintin Lame's rogue intentions and of his propensity to violence. Manuel Quintín Lame had a completely different version of the events that took place that I will discuss later. I focus first on the versions produced by the local state and the inhabitants of Inzá because they essentially monopolized the conversation around the November events of 1916 and successfully unleashed a campaign of repression. The narrative that the local state and the inhabitants of Inzá produced was similar to many frontier narratives where an "ethnic fiction" of whiteness was produced.[67] While other scholars have summarized the events that I discuss below, the textual analysis of the communications between the local state and the national state allows me to shed light on how the local state of Cauca and Tierradentro's nonindigenous inhabitants defined Colombian citizenship in a manner that clearly excluded Manuel Quintín Lame and his indigenous followers. This exclusion did not stay in the realm of ideas and ended with a massacre.

The earliest versions of this confrontation (available in the national archive) came from telegrams sent by the inhabitants of Inzá. Throughout the different reports from the local authorities, Manuel Quintín Lame was portrayed as a bandit, his followers as "savages," and the nonindigenous inhabitants of Inzá as responsible citizens of the town (*vecinos*). According to the nonindigenous inhabitants of Inzá, on November 6, 1916,[68] Manuel Quintín Lame entered the main plaza of Inzá with his two thousand armed (with revolvers, machetes, and rifles) indigenous men from *parcialidades*.[69] According to these eyewitnesses, once in the main square of the town, the indigenous leader ridiculed the Colombian national hymn, alleged that whites had stolen the land of the indigenous people, and promised swift revenge for past abuses. Manuel Quintín Lame also warned the citizens of Inzá that they had ten days to vacate the area of *población* (the area that was established within the *resguardo*) or force would be used. The telegram writers were careful to portray the local authorities in a positive light stating that the mayor and the parish priest advised the *vecinos* to be prudent so as to avoid catastrophe because the attitude of indigenous people was thirsty for revenge. According to the authors of the telegram, Manuel Quintín Lame was stirring up hatred amongst indigenous people toward white people in the region. There was also a reference to Manuel Quintín Lame's release by the judicial authorities that had annulled the force of the actions taken by political authorities to repress Lame's "seditious" attempts. Here, a certain frustration with the legal system was apparent.

On November 11, 1916, Antonio Paredes, the governor of Cauca, sent a telegram to the Minister of War stating that the situation created by Manuel Quintín Lame was extremely serious.[70] Evidently, Manuel Quintín Lame's entry into Inzá was the "final straw" for local authorities because attacks on rural properties preceded his bold declarations in that main square of Inzá. Additionally, Paredes, who was an inveterate racist, saw Manuel Quintín Lame as supported and led on by political opponents to the regime. This legal and moral support was partially to blame for the release of Manuel Quintín Lame by Primitivo Fernandez, Magistrate of the Superior Tribunal, which emboldened the indigenous leader even further.[71] While Governor Paredes' version of events must be read skeptically, there is no doubt that Manuel Quintín Lame must have felt empowered by his release once again by the judicial system.

The indigenous leader's political agenda (as described by Paredes) was basically unchanged; he instructed indigenous people to disregard local authorities, to challenge the property rights of whites, to distill *aguardiente* (which was a monopoly of the state), to end unpaid labor, and to slaughter cattle without paying any tax. The relationship between Manuel Quintín Lame and that of his followers was depicted as one of total control; Lame would imprison indigenous people who did not follow his orders. Attributing to Manuel Quintín Lame total control over his indigenous followers allowed the regional state to blame the entire conflict on the indigenous leader and to dismiss the possibility that indigenous communities had legitimate grievances.

Despite the governor's request, the judicial branch refused to order the capture of those up in arms/"*revoltosos*" (rebels). The local authority despite their portrayal of Manuel Quintín Lame as an armed rebel never produced any evidence of actual violence carried out by indigenous people; the term, rebels, revealed more about the local state's attempt to delegitimize Manuel Quintin Lame and his followers. Governor Paredes informed the national government that the local population had started arming itself and asked for the army to be sent. He also declared that the time had come for national political authorities to proceed with great energy. The local state's discourse presented the "whites" as under siege stating that the white race was threatened. It is worth pausing here to consider that "whiteness" in this context did not necessarily correlate with pigmentation of skin but rather was associated with a cultural mind-set that despised indigenous people and customs.

On November 12, 1916, Governor Paredes announced to the central government that as result of Manuel Quintín Lame's attack on the town of Inzá five people had died and fifteen people were wounded. The governor repeated his request (that he had made the day before the deaths had occurred) that armed forces be dispatched to give military support to the police force.[72]

The governor of Huila (Julio Borrero who always confirmed Paredes' statements) informed in a telegram to the Minister of Government that he had just received a telegram from the prefect of La Plata who was relaying information he had received from Inzá that stated that Manuel Quintín Lame with many "indians" had attacked the population taking advantage of the fact that its inhabitants were attending mass at the Church.[73] Despite this unfair advantage, the whites of Inzá had "valiantly" resisted. Here language matters because the term *indios* was generally considered an insult in Colombian Spanish whereas *indígena* was not.[74] The Prefect of La Plata expressed his contempt of indigenous people by using the term, *indios*. Manuel Quintín Lame and his followers were accused here of being completely "uncivilized" and "un-Christian" in that they had supposedly used the religiosity of Inzá's inhabitants for nefarious ends. It is interesting to note that this accusation of taking advantage of the fact that Inzá's inhabitants were attending mass was not found in other versions. This was yet another attempt on the part of the municipal authorities to delegitimize Manuel Quintín Lame by depicting him as un-Christian.

The local authorities of Inzá, specifically the mayor of Inzá, requested that the director of police be given the order to give one hundred rifles and 2,400 cartridges to the civil guard of Inzá so that they could organize a brigade.[75] Clearly, the local authorities insisted on arming themselves and the population in what can only be described as a paramilitary force rather than relying on the national police and/or army. Here the justification for this request came from a portrayal of Manuel Quintín Lame entering the town with an indigenous mob. The mayor told him not to enter the town of Inzá, and this refusal would have resulted in a fight where four people died and nine people were wounded. We can see how different versions existed of why and how Manuel Quintin Lame's so-called attack resulted in violence.

Meanwhile in Bogotá, the Minister of Government notified General Velasco that two thousand indigenous people had risen up and that they were attacking Inzá's inhabitants. He took it upon himself to notify General Velasco because the minister of War was out of town.[76] The government minister, alarmed by the report given by the prefect of Garzón that two thousand Indians were armed and attacking the inhabitants of Inzá, gave the advice that the "executive and political" branches of Cauca should react "energetically" (in other words with force) to this rebellion given the attitude of the judicial branch (the fact that they had authorized Manuel Quintín Lame's release).[77] Specifically, the Minister of Government told the governor of Cauca to utilize the armed forces that were available to respond to the attacks. Once the Minister of War and the President returned to the capital, further orders would be given to restore order and to repress the rebellion.

The full force of repression was to come down on the indigenous revolt since the tolerance shown to them had proven to be prejudicial.[78]

Otero, the inspector in Garzón, explained that indigenous people (again called *indios*) had retreated to the nearby mountains and were preparing a second attack that they thought was irresistible. They asked for the military to come and help. The number of dead reported by this telegram was five people, and the number of reported wounded was twenty.[79] On November 13, the telegram from Julio Borrerro to the Ministro de Gobierno indicated that the *Indios* had made no movement during the night. The prefect of La Plata had sixty armed men at his disposal; these men were policemen.[80]

Antonio Paredes provided yet another summary of events to the Minister of Gobierno that had transpired on November 12, 1916.[81] This summary suggested that five people had died and that fifteen people were wounded as a result of Manuel Quintín Lame's entrance in Inzá, depicted by the governor of Cauca as a clash between indigenous people and the white people of this town. The governor of Cauca requested reinforcements from the Brigade given the small number of armed men he had at his disposal so that they could support the police force that was present in Cauca. Nothing new had been reported from Inzá on November 13, but he was confident that a new attack would not take place (by the "adventurer Lame" and his followers) given that the indigenous people had suffered a lesson and that help had arrived from Belalcázar.[82] The regional state's favorite accusation toward Manuel Quintín Lame was that he was an "adventurer" and that he did not possess the virtues of a productive citizen. No doubt to ward off any accusation of rash actions, Paredes also maintained that he was recommending the greatest prudence and discretion to avoid any bloodshed when capturing Lame and his followers.

On November 14, the situation had improved for the local government given that it had managed to imprison some of the rebels and was pursuing others with some agents and auxiliary forces at the town's disposal.[83] The military commission was slowly making its way to Inzá and was due to arrive the next day demonstrating that the national government had a very slow response to rebellions/insurrections. Despite Antonio Paredes' claim that relative calm had returned to the area of Tierradentro, a telegram dated the same day informed Bogotá that the indigenous people of Turmina had sent a written statement and that they were challenging the inhabitants of this town to a new fight.[84] The town of Turmina was depicted as completely surrounded by indigenous people and that all its inhabitants were afraid of a new attack. The military support had still not yet arrived from Popayán.

On November 15, 1916, the rebellion was still not over; according to the prefect of La Plata, Lame's indigenous followers who were armed with rifles, machetes, and garrotes, were in the town of Turmina; Pio Collo, the indigenous leader (accompanied by people of Belalcázar, Segovia, and Pedregal) was pursuing them.[85] Given that the regular armed forces were due to arrive, and that sixty policemen from Inzá were also coming, the governor of Huila did not think it necessary to receive the one hundred rifles and other elements that the national police had but it was good to have them on hand in case they decided to organize armed forces in La Plata and Nataga. On the very same day, Bogotá received the news that Manuel Quintín Lame was seriously wounded and that he was being pursued.[86] Manuel Quintín Lame's brother was captured as well as Cenón Ramírez who was characterized as one of the leaders of the alleged rebellion.

FALLOUT AND REACTIONS FROM THE LOCAL PRESS AND LOCAL AUTHORITIES IN THE AFTERMATH OF THE "REBELLION" OF NOVEMBER 1916

Conservative Interpretation of the Events of November 1916

The local press, *Union Conservadora*, depicted Manuel Quintín Lame in a negative manner.[87] The article, titled *El Mariscal Lame*, advanced that Lame was a lazy individual who had no real profession and who exploited his people echoing the local state's discourse. This newspaper also repeated the local state's version of events in Inzá, which was that Manuel Quintín Lame arrived to the town of Inzá and ordered the mayor of Inzá to summon the local council; Lame delivered a threatening lecture and insulted the inhabitants of the town. The local authorities with the support of Silvia's prefect voiced their concerns to the governor of Cauca who responded with great prudence given the accusations of overreaction in prior instances. The *Union Conservadora* newspaper went on to attack other newspapers of different political persuasions (in particular *Opiniones)* for their view on the clash between Manuel Quintín Lame and the citizens of Inzá.[88]

The very next day, November 12, the news came from Inzá that Lame had attacked and from the brawl that ensued, six people died and fourteen people were wounded. To counterattack the notion that this was somehow orchestrated by the local state authorities and conservative politicians, the author of the article in *Union Conservadora* asserted that it should be known that there was not a single policeman or soldier in the town and that it was the civilian population that armed itself to defend itself from the aggression of the "audacious Indian" and of his *compañeros*. While the author of the article argued that this was proof that the governorship could not be accused of attacking indigenous people, it was also evidence of vigilante justice.

Immediately, after the news spread, Pio Collo came out with one hundred volunteers from Belalcázar (called the prestigious *caudillo*) to defend the defenseless and unfortunate population, victimized by the brutality of an idle man who had been portrayed by the press as a martyr, liberator, and an advocate. It was the attitude of Collo and of his companions that deserved the gratitude of the entire Caucano society according to this author. In other words, the Caucano society should be grateful that Pio Collo had restored "calm and order" according to *Union Conservadora*. The author of this article stated that the recent events showed that the actions taken by the governor in June of 1916 were justified (even though these actions had been ridiculed). The following rhetorical question was posed: Will the newspaper *El Cauca Liberal* continue to publish speeches and lectures with socialist leanings made by the poor indigenous man who was a victim of his own rashness. A patronizing and racist view of Manuel Quintín Lame emerged in this article; the belief that Lame was used as an instrument by other political forces (probably Liberals) was also present.

In the aftermath of the "rebellion," a letter from Antonio Paredes, which was sent to the President of the Republic, gave an overview of Manuel Quintín Lame's political trajectory and agenda.[89] He portrayed yet again Lame as a free agent who was lazy and idle; Manuel Quintín Lame was not a *terrajero*/did not have to pay tribute to a landowner and did not belong to a *parcialidad*.[90] The larger point that Paredes made was that Manuel Quintín Lame was involved in a cause that did not directly concern him and was thus an outside agitator. Therefore, his agenda was even more suspect. Lame's political agenda was to regain indigenous land that was now cultivated and occupied by whites, and if necessary to eliminate the white race. Paredes described this message of recovery of land as the "good news" (which was probably a reference to the gospels) to the indigenous people of the area. Manuel Quintín Lame imparted his political agenda in numerous lectures that indigenous people came to attend from a great distance. Paredes contradicted himself because on the one hand he depicted indigenous people as enthusiastically attending the conferences, while on the other hand he advanced that these indigenous followers only came because they were obliged to do so under the orders of the councils of the *parcialidades*.

Paredes suggested that Manuel Quintín Lame was no better than a charlatan who was seducing the indigenous population with his discourse that fanned the fantasies and hopes of the indigenous inhabitants of Cauca. The governor of Cauca feminized the indigenous population of Cauca depicting indigenous people as vulnerable and easily led, and portrayed Manuel Quintin Lame as the unscrupulous seducer.

The governor sought to take advantage of the political opportunity that Manuel Quintín Lame's supposed attack on Inzá presented to him; he wished to destroy what he saw as the key political linchpin in the organization of Manuel Quintín Lame's political organization. The key to understand the power that Manuel Quintín Lame had over his indigenous followers was in the control that indigenous councils had over the *parcialidades*; indigenous individuals (Paredes argued) followed their *cabildos*'s orders blindly, and these orders carried greater weight than the authority of the mayor, prefect, and even the governor of the department. Therein lay the problem. Once a person (in this case Manuel Quintín Lame) had achieved power or influence over the indigenous councils, it was very easy then to manipulate the entire indigenous population. Interestingly, Paredes advanced that part of the power that Manuel Quintín Lame had acquired over the indigenous councils stemmed from the papers that he had obtained in Bogotá; here he was indicting the national government for receiving Manuel Quintín Lame. The indigenous leader's trips to Bogotá gave him an aura that led indigenous people of the area to consider him as a Messiah and a restorer.[91] All of these elements meant that the indigenous people of Southwestern Colombia followed him blindly and supported him with their financial contributions.

The other complication (according to Paredes) was that Lame had allies that he calls *parciales civilizados* (nonindigenous people). These people encouraged Manuel Quintín Lame and portrayed him as a victim of intolerance. The real motivation behind this support for Manuel Quintín Lame was the desire to cause trouble for the Conservative government in power and also, to take away the votes that would normally be cast in favor of the Conservative government by members of the *parcialidades*. Here, the governor of Cauca was no doubt trying to appeal to the national state on a partisan basis warning that votes for the Conservative Party could be lost should Manuel Quintín Lame's movement continue unchecked. Paredes suggested that most indigenous people voted for Conservatives: he stated that they were faithful to la "buena causa/good cause" until recently. This intrusion of politics was very preoccupying not only because everyone should be worried about the possibility of a war of races, but also because of how it had affected the course of events. Paredes suggested that the Magistrate of Superior Tribunal's decision on September 19 to release Manuel Quintín Lame was politically motivated; the proof was that other members of the judiciary branch had previously denied him his freedom. Paredes was all the more irate because Lame had asked for a conditional release/release on bail, but the magistrate decreed his unconditional freedom thus giving him even more than he had asked for.

According to Paredes, this decision was not based on Lame's entire file and also gave the governor's political opponents a great political triumph. Paredes enclosed some of the correspondence between the magistrate and the governorship; this correspondence showed how the "delitos" of sedition or of *conatos* against the peace and tranquility that did not exist in the judicial code. In any event, once Lame was freed, he returned to Inzá, which led to bloody results.

According to Paredes, Manuel Quintín Lame arrived in Inzá in the early days of November, and the indigenous people and his followers, notified of his arrival to the town of Inzá, met him a few hundred yards away from the town. They were three hundred of them, and they were armed mostly with rifles and peinillas; Lame stayed in town for three days and delivered his menacing conferences/lectures against the while citizens of the town (called *vecinos* again). Apparently, Lame and his followers retreated to a camp that was right outside of Inzá and were proposing to increase the number of (protesters) and announced that on November 12 they would be coming back to Inzá.

Prior to November 12, the *vecinos* had also announced that they were preparing to defend themselves; on the 12th, they resisted the indigenous people's attack and a fight ensued, which resulted in the death of seven of Lame's followers and about seventeen wounded from both sides. Paredes described Manuel Quintín Lame's forces as defeated and chastened. Immediately after this clash, a group of "voluntary auxiliary forces" of the nearby town, *Belalcázar*, led by the caudillo José Pio Collo and fifty armed men sent by the prefect of La Plata "liberated" the town of Inzá. Shortly after the military commission of Junín made up of one hundred men arrived along with a detachment of the police contributed to restore the "tranquility" and obliged the *parcialidades* on the outskirts to present themselves to show submission and respect to the authorities. The description of this event (even through Governor Paredes' eyes) makes it clear that local "volunteers" with the complicity of the army and the police waged a campaign of terror and intimidation on indigenous communities.

Although on November 17 Lame was still at large, final steps were taken to ensure the end to Manuel Quintín's Lame political movement. "Ringleaders" were imprisoned (amongst them Lame's brother who was the general secretary); the prefect of Silvia was transferred to Inzá (under orders of the governorship) where he completed a report, interrogated prisoners, and reestablished "normality" with the presence of the garrison of Junín while awaiting for a police presence that the central state had offered to provide.

Evidently not satisfied with the repression carried out in Inzá, Paredes declared that the inhabitants of *parcialidades* of the same *cordillera central* Tacueyó, Toribío, etc. had banded together creating alarm amongst the neighboring towns. The governor of Cauca stated that he was not sure whether this was because they were unaware that Lame was wounded or if it was because indigenous people wanted revenge, which the governor stated was not unlikely. Insisting that Manuel Quintín Lame and his followers still presented a danger allowed for the governor to push forward his agenda of diminishing the power of indigenous councils.

The governor argued that an abnormal situation existed in the department that required immediate attention. Evidently, confident that his version of the events in Inzá would prevail, the governor returned to his real objective in contacting the national state, which was to convince the central state to weaken the political organization of indigenous communities. The governor of Cauca objected to the recognition that the laws/justice system gave to indigenous authorities; he argued that these laws should be changed so that the danger of a race war could be avoided. He also requested the creation of a national police force unit since the department was unable to maintain a large enough unit. To bolster his argument, Paredes suggested that the army could only act in very specific conditions and was not really a police force.

He also requested severe punishment for Manuel Quintín Lame and suggested that he should be imprisoned in a manner that would incapacitate him permanently so that he could not continue fanning the flames of rebellion amongst the indigenous people of Cauca. According to the governor, the ordinary system of justice was not powerful or efficient enough for people like Manuel Quintín Lame, and the governor thought that extraordinary measures were required for the "health of the people."

Alternative View of the Events

Shortly after the events of November 12, some local voices of opposition to the local state's narrative emerged.[92] The anonymous author of "Si los muertos hablaran"/"If the dead could talk," published in *Opiniones*, suggested that not all parties had been listened to; in other words there was a rush to judgment. He objected to the narrative that characterized the inhabitants of Inzá as heroes; he stated that the acts of one party were celebrated without considering whether their conduct was justified let alone worthy of applause. He pointed out that only the point of view and report from the authorities of Inzá was available, and since they were participants in this conflict, they could hardly be called objective. The Inzá reports should be read carefully (he argued), and it should be taken into consideration that undoubtedly these authorities would not admit that their imprudence had led to the events that unfolded.

He stated that the most elementary responsibility of the national government was to send a representative who would be impartial and ethical to establish what actually had happened. He also suggested that it was necessary to look at prior events to assess the situation; previously Lame was giving conferences in many towns in a peaceful and respectful manner. He gave the example of the town of Totoró where the inhabitants were at first nervous about Lame making speeches, but then they changed their minds and instead offered protection to the indigenous leaders so he could give his conferences. Manuel Quintín Lame lectured mostly about the importance of sending indigenous children to school. The author of the article was also racist in that he characterized Manuel Quintín Lame as giving lectures in a rustic and simple language.

He stated that one could not reproach Lame for trying to "improve" the race through education. The other point he made was that Lame was in Inzá for many hours with many of his companions and that nothing had occurred.

They did not attack anyone and were instead threatened by the opposing band. Lame left the town without harming anyone and intended to return the next day to meet with the municipal town council.

The article posed the question of whether the eruption of conflict was the result of an idle man or if it was the manifestation of a larger social problem. The author suggested that if it was the suffering of the indigenous race, then the solution was not to punish or to persecute. The article presented Manuel Quintín Lame as an Indian who was pursuing noble objectives, which were the improvement of his race, the end of abuses against indigenous people, and the same rights for indigenous people that other Colombians possessed.

A letter dated May of 1918 from Manuel Quintín Lame's followers addressed to the Minister of Gobierno clearly refuted all the charges made and presented a very different view of the so-called rebellion.[93] The authors of this memorial pointed out that after an exhaustive judicial investigation that resulted in 1,600 pages not a single serious charge (of sedition, of rebellion, or any charge deserving of imprisonment) was proven. Instead, they argued compellingly that the various meetings (which were all entirely legal and protected by various laws and the Colombian Constitution) held by indigenous councils had caused a state of panic and fear amongst nonindigenous inhabitants.

In 1924, Manuel Quintín Lame himself offered a very different version of events that took place in Inzá; he stated that he was indeed present in Inzá on November 12, 1916, but it was for the baptism of several indigenous children.[94] He was in church when militia units came in and attacked him and his followers killing seven indigenous people and wounding eighteen people including indigenous women and children.[95] The indigenous leader also claimed that a certain parish priest instructed members of the militia units to kill the Indians because they were not Christians.[96]

My own interpretation of the events is that Manuel Quintín Lame did not come to attack the town of Inzá on November 12; he came with only sixty men to Inzá on that particular day even according to his enemies' testimony. If he really had the intention of starting a general insurrection, he would have brought the two thousand that allegedly came with him the previous day/week. The most compelling evidence that demonstrates that this was not a planned attack carried out by Manuel Quintín Lame was that those killed were all members of his political movement. Although the numbers vary, the most conservative estimate is that five indigenous people/Manuel Quintín Lame's followers died and that fourteen indigenous people were wounded.

The obvious question that emerges is why and how the massacre of indigenous people came to be portrayed as the moment when Manuel Quintín Lame's movement veered into what the local state and the nonindigenous inhabitants of Inzá called an uprising/a rebellion. The many times that the local elite and the inhabitants of Inzá had falsely accused Manuel Quintín

Lame of violence should have destroyed any credibility to their version of events. The other connected question is why was the local state and non-indigenous inhabitants of Tierradentro so fearful of Manuel Quintín Lame's movement. Espinosa Arango argues that Manuel Quintín Lame provoked fear because he was an indigenous person who was both "civilized" and a "rebel."[97] While I agree with Espinosa Arango that Manuel Quintín Lame was a disquieting figure because of his "rebellious" attitude despite his "Westernization," the fear and panic that Manuel Quintín Lame caused came from his direct challenge to land ownership.

Two factors contributed to making his challenge a serious one. The first factor was that the higher level of the judicial system released him on several occasions and defied the governors of Cauca's orders and political pressures to keep in him in prison. The second factor was the central state's indirect legitimization of Manuel Quintin Lame's political agenda. One might argue that this legitimization was a superficial one; after all, the central state ultimately sided with the local state by eventually providing military support to the campaign of repression that ensued after the massacre of Inzá. However, in Cauca, the news that Manuel Quintín Lame was received in an audience by the Minister of Foreign Relations and that the Minister of Gobierno corresponded with him and/or asked the local state for an accounting of their actions toward the indigenous leader was profoundly alarming to the local state at both the municipal and state levels. In numerous instances, the local elite (as demonstrated in my analysis of the correspondence) asserted that engaging in a conversation through correspondence with the indigenous leader was at the very least regrettable. Members of the local elite and state authorities were most concerned about the central state's correspondence with Manuel Quintín Lame because of its effect on the indigenous population. We know that Manuel Quintín Lame showed his correspondence to his indigenous followers; many of his followers were not literate (which was typical for many rural Colombians) and thus could not actually read the correspondence received from the national government that could be quite noncommittal. It is quite possible that the indigenous leader who was given to hyperbole stressed the positive elements of his correspondence with the central government to his indigenous audience. The initial quote where Manuel Quintín Lame states that his claims were always well received by the central state demonstrates his inclination to portray his relationship with the central state in the most positive light.

The local authorities of Tierradentro were especially concerned with the indigenous leader's objects that gave him an aura of legitimacy; it is quite likely that the mayor of Belalcázar did indeed steal Manuel Quintín Lame's uniform that the Minister of War had given him because of its highly symbolic value. Manuel Quintín Lame's followers thought that the uniform was the cause for why the local state had charged him with sedition. My interpretation is that the local authorities of Tierradentro knew perfectly well that a seditious act had not been committed but were concerned with the legitimacy that this uniform gave to Manuel Quintin Lame.

The local state and in particular the municipal authorities of Tierradentro were losing an ideological battle over the meaning of Colombian citizenship. Manuel Quintín Lame offered a new way to define citizenship and inclusion in the nation for indigenous people and in this process upset the cultural and moral order of this subregion. Manuel Quintín Lame's vision of indigenous citizenship was one that relied on the central state as a guarantor of indigenous rights; Law 89 of 1890 was in essence a founding document for indigenous rights as the indigenous leader envisioned it. He sought to transform the passages of the law that placed indigenous communities under the power of the municipality; he also envisioned himself as the key intermediary between the central state and indigenous communities. The conservative press and local government officials mockingly and repeatedly called him *El Mariscal*, which has led some scholars to characterize him as a *caudillo*. In particular, the reader will remember how the local state representative stressed (and no doubt exaggerated) the total control that the indigenous leader had on his indigenous followers. At stake here in this exchange of words was the designation of cultural and political brokers for Tierradentro's indigenous population and more importantly the decision of who the gatekeepers of Colombian citizenship were. Manuel Quintín Lame enthusiastically sought the education and the betterment of the "indigenous race" that he also saw as in a wretched state and in need of salvation. However, he did not see members of the local government and the Catholic Church as ideal brokers for indigenous people's transformation, but rather argued that an education based on indigenous traditions along with his leadership would bring about full inclusion into the Colombian nation.

Manuel Quintín Lame's discourse and path to citizenship were especially threatening to the political and cultural brokers of Tierradentro. In contrast to Cauca's central valley political and cultural authorities that were well established, the municipalities of Belalcázar and Inzá were only constituted in 1907; Catholic missionaries had only just arrived in 1905 with the stated purpose of "civilizing" the indigenous population. Thus, the political power that the municipal authorities exercised in Tierradentro was only recently created; the entire legitimacy of the presence of the missionaries rested on their designation as the preferred cultural brokers for the task of transforming indigenous people into Colombian citizens. The gulf between Manuel Quintín Lame's view of citizenship in Colombia and Tierradentro's cultural and political brokers' conception of citizenship was immense. For the Catholic missionary the only way to achieve full inclusion into the Colombian nation was to abandon indigenous traditions and for indigenous peoples of Cauca to be subservient to the Catholic authorities. The most chilling example of psychological warfare is present when the governor of Cauca states in his report after the so-called rebellion's repression that the inhabitants of the neighboring *parcialidades* were forced to come and show subservience to the local authorities. The message delivered through violence was that indigenous councils had to acknowledge the authority of the local state and of the Catholic missionaries.

However, the act of violence also showed the fragility of the local state's hegemony and its inability to persuade Cauca's indigenous communities and peoples that the power resided only in the local state. The initial support that Manuel Quintín Lame received in local Liberal newspapers, and from the judicial system allowed indigenous communities and their councils in particular to envision a different type of inclusion into the Colombian nation.

Furthermore, Manuel Quintín Lame brought the central state into Cauca into this dialogue of who was the legitimate citizen and who enjoyed the support of the Colombian nation. The local state had to respond to numerous questions from the central state that came from Manuel Quintin Lame's petitions; in addition, it faced accusations of unfair treatment from local intellectuals that it then accused of partisanship. Even in its final triumphant hour in November of 1916 in Inzá, it had to appeal to the central state for help to carry out its campaign of repression. The governor of Cauca, while he was one of Manuel Quintín Lame's most ferocious enemies, did not want to abdicate control of the subregion of Tierradentro to the hands of the civilian force. Hence, the local state asked for a more substantial police force to ensure its hegemony over the non-indigenous inhabitants of Tierradentro.

The question remains of how the Inza authorities and the local state were able to spin a narrative where the Inzá citizens were the victims of an indigenous uprising when in fact they were responsible for the deaths of seven indigenous people. The first crucial element was that they controlled the information that came out of Inzá; they told the same story that the brave citizens of Inzá defended themselves from a horde of indigenous people led by Manuel Quintín Lame who came to attack them. The governor of Cauca transferred a prefect (that he must have known was sympathetic to his cause) and had him verify that all the information that the local state had provided was correct. Indigenous people sympathetic to Manuel Quintín Lame's message were rounded up and placed in detention. In addition, as seen earlier, local councils were summoned to pay homage to the local authorities. In other words, all opposing views from Tierradentro were silenced very effectively; the lone voice of the Liberal newspaper in Popayán spoke out, but he was clearly isolated. By the time Manuel Quintín Lame and his followers spoke out, it was years later and too late to change the events that came after the rebellion.

Another important reason contributes to Manuel Quintín Lame's political movement's continued portrayal as an armed uprising.[98] The recent armed self-defense movement of Quintín Lame that emerged in the 1980s rested part of its legitimacy on maintaining that indigenous resistance and self-defense originated with Manuel Quintín Lame rather than on an alliance with leftist guerrilla movements. It was politically powerful for the indigenous movement sector that supported the armed self-defense movement that the man who wrote the seven points of the Consejo Regional Indígena del Cauca's political and ethnic agenda was also the originator of armed resistance. In my view, in 1916, indigenous communities' armed response consisted of a few isolated incidents and only emerged after the events in Inzá. Indeed, the close analysis of the extensive correspondence of this time period known as the *Quintinada* demonstrates that Manuel Quintín Lame was not organizing indigenous communities to resist militarily nor was he relying on a guerrilla strategy; he had full confidence in the laws of the Colombian nation and in the central state.

Manuel Quintín Lame's entire approach, which is evident in his correspondence to the national state was to present himself as a legitimate political actor who sought an alliance with the central state. He asked repeatedly for the central state's intervention based on his understanding of Law 89 of 1890. His objective throughout his correspondence was to portray local authorities (especially municipal ones) as illegitimate and unjust. To organize an armed insurrection would have placed him outside of the parameters of legitimate political activity. Manuel Quintín Lame was a political leader who engaged in provocative and theatrical gestures, but his entire correspondence was aimed at inclusion into the world of Colombian politics.

Manuel Quintín Lame thought that with this inclusion he could achieve his most important objective, which was to recover the land that legally belonged to indigenous communities. Amidst the accusations of violence it is easy to forget that the indigenous leader's primordial aim was to recover land that belonged to indigenous communities of Cauca through the proper application of Law 89 of 1890 and through an alliance with the central state; this recovery of land would also end the practice of indigenous labor servitude. Manuel Quintín Lame's political agenda and tactics failed momentarily when the local state and the armed volunteers of Tierradentro delegitimized his political movement by accusing him of violence and by emphasizing the ethnic character of his claims. Within Cauca, certain Liberal voices and the justice system also lent legitimacy to Manuel Quintín Lame's movement and allowed the indigenous leader to regain his freedom after numerous and arbitrary arrests and detentions. The central state adopted a contradictory attitude, legitimizing Manuel Quintín Lame's message by corresponding with him, by inquiring about his legal affairs with the local state, and by cautioning the local state to be prudent. Ultimately, the central state sided with the local state, but its wavering had given Manuel Quintín Lame's movement its initial elan.

On the May 9, 1917, Manuel Quintín Lame was captured and sent to Popayán's jail where he was beaten and tortured.[99] He was sentenced to four years and some months of imprisonment, and was only released in 1921.[100] Manuel Quintín Lame took refuge in the department of Tolima where he wrote thousands of pages of petitions to the national government (with little or no success) and continued to argue for his vision of indigeneity and of Colombia.

NOTES

1. Joanne Rappaport, in particular, has written extensively on Manuel Quintín Lame as an organic intellectual. Also see Fernando Romero Loaiza, *Manuel Quintín Lame Chantre: El indígena ilustrado, el pensador indigenista* (Pereira, Colombia: F. Romero Loaiza, 2005) and Luis Guillermo Vasco, "Quintin Lame: Resistencia y Liberación." See http://www.luguiva.net/percent5C/articulos/detalle.aspx?id=68.

2. See Joanne Rappaport's description in *Politics of Memory* (Durham: Duke University Press, 1998) of Manuel Quintín Lame in that photograph, 134.

3. See Diego Castrillón Arboleda, *El indio Quintín Lame* (Bogotá: Tercer Mundo, 1973) and Gonzalo Castillo-Cárdenas, *Liberation Theology from Below: The Life and Thought of Manuel Quintín Lame* (Maryknoll, NY: Orbis Books, 1987). See also Monica Espinosa Arango, *La civilización montés: la visión india y el trasegar de Manuel Quintín Lame en Colombia* (Bogotá: Ediciones Uniandes, 2009).

4. Manuel Quintín Lame and Gonzalo Castillo-Cárdenas, in *En defensa de mi raza* (Bogotá: Rosca de Investigación y Acción Social), 1971, 61. This quote comes from Manuel Quintín Lame's memoir, which was published posthumously in 1971. I have translated the quote from Spanish.

> Eres justo, eres hombre de bien. Debo aclarar, con una antorcha mensajera de verdad y no de error, en este Capítulo sobre la buena voluntad de los hombres no indígenas, los que forman el Gobierno Nacional de Colombia. Que desde el año 1910 hasta hoy he sido atendido en todos mis reclamos en favor de todos los resguardos de Indígenas de los departamentos de Nariño, Cauca, Valle del Cauca, Huila, y Tolima.

5. Manuel Quintín Lame's most radical and bold speeches against "white" authority were when he was speaking to an audience of indigenous people. In addition, his rhetoric was considered inflammatory in the decade of the 1910s because he stressed how the "indigenous race" had special rights and had a valid and prior claim to land that "whites" held. In the 1920s his discourse grew more radical in that he rejected partisan electoral politics. See *El derecho de la mujer indígena en Colombia: Manifiesto de catorce mil mujeres lamistas* (1927).

6. The most recently published and comprehensive discussion of many of the sources around the Quintinada can also be found in Monica Espinosa Arango's *La civilización montés*, chapter 4. See also David D. Gow, *Countering Development-Indigenous Modernity and the Moral Imagination* (Durham and London: Duke University Press, 2008), chapter 6.

7. Colombia's constitution of 1886 reversed previous trends of federalism and political decentralization when it made Bogotá the center of political power.

8. Ignacio Muñoz was the perfect example of the new economic elite that emerged at the turn of twentieth century. See Gonzalo Castillo Cárdenas, *Liberation Theology from Below: The Life and Thought of Manuel Quintín Lame,* 20. Castillo Cárdenas describes him as one of the richest men in Cauca.

9. In his memoir, Manuel Quintín Lame lauded Dr. Marcos Fidel Suárez, and in a footnote, Gonzalo Castillo Cárdenas states that Quintín Lame supported Suárez in his campaign against Guillermo Valencia in 1918. Quintín Lame, 61–62.

10. Monica Espinosa Arango argues that the local elite of Cauca was divided. See Espinosa Arango, 122. See also María Teresa Findji (1978) and José María Rojas and Elías Sevilla Casas, "El campesinado en la formacion territorial del Surroccidente Colombiano" in *Territorios, regiones, sociedades*. Ed. Renan Silva (Bogotá, Colombia: Cerec, 1994).

11. Manuel Quintín Lame in his memoir referred to the elite of Popayán as poets mocking them for their lack of courage; he also stated that he did not hire a lawyer or anyone to help him with his legal defense from Popayán despite Popayán's fame as the capital of sages. This was also a way for him to insult Guillermo Valencia who was his archenemy and who was known for his poetry. Manuel Quintin Lame, *En defensa de mi raza*, 16 and 48.

12. As Espinosa Arango points out, the hacienda *La Polindara* was annexed in 1894 to the Hacienda San Isidro. Espinosa Arango, 22.

13. Information about Manuel Quintín Lame's life that follows in this section of the chapter comes mainly from Diego Castrillón Arboleda's *El indio Quintín Lame* (Bogotá: Ediciones Tercer Mundo, 1973). Monica Espinosa Arango has an excellent discussion of Manuel Quintín Lame's life, which is based not only on Diego Castrillón's book, but also on an interview with the same author. There is some controversy about Manuel Quintín Lame's birth date. Diego Castrillón suggested 1880, but Espinosa Arango suggests that it is 1883 based on Manuel Quintín Lame's memoir. Vasco has reproached historians for ignoring this discrepancy and reminds readers that his name on the baptism certificate was not Manuel but Juan.

14. http://www.banrepcultural.org/blaavirtual/biografias/lamemanu.htm. The bibliographic entry of the Banco Cultural mentions this reduction of days by a "new owner," but it is not stated that the new owner is Ignacio Muñoz. Castrillón Arboleda in his biography does not specify who the new owner is. However, in other texts such as the prologue to Manuel Quintín Lame's memoir, Gonzalo Castillo Cardenas states that the owner of San Isidro was Ignacio Muñoz.

15. Diego Castrillón Arboleda, *El indio Quintín Lame*, 30.

16. See Fernando Romero Loaiza, *Manuel Quintín Lame Chantre: El indígena ilustrado, el pensador indigenista*, 1 ed. Pereira, Colombia: F. Romero Loaiza, 2005, for an extensive discussion on Manuel Quintín Lame's positions vis-à-vis education.

17. http://www.banrepcultural.org/blaavirtual/biografias/lamemanu.htm.

18. See Ary R. Campo Chicangana, *Montoneras, deserciones e insubordinaciones: Yanaconas y Paeces en la Guerra de los Mil Días*. (Cali: Secretaría de Cultura y Turismo, Municipio de Santiago de Cali, 2003) for a wonderful overview of the *War of a Thousand Days* and its impact on the Yanaconas and Paeces (Nasas). Campo Chicangana states in his book that he did not find any archival records of Manuel Quintín Lame's military service.

19. Castrillón Arboleda states that on one of his trips to Popayán Manuel Quintín Lame met with Dr. Perez who gave him a copy of the manual, *El abogado en casa*, 72.

20. http://www.semana.com/portada/articulo/yo-sobrevivi-masacre-Tacueyó/76546-3.

21. http://www.coha.org/leave-us-in-peace-security-in-colombias-cauca-department/.

22. Mary Roldán's research on *La Violencia* in Antioquia demonstrates the continuity of conflict and violence in certain municipalities from the pre-*Violencia* period to the 1980s.

23. Universidad del Cauca. Archivo Instituto de Investigaciones Historicas. José María Arboleda. Archivo Republica. Grupo 3. No.1 Manuscrito. Memorial from Manuel Quintín Lame to the Magistrates of the Supreme Court of Justice. Dated: October 16, 1914.

24. Universidad del Cauca. Archivo Instituto de Investigaciones Historicas. José María Arboleda. Archivo Republica. Grupo 3. No.1 Manuscrito. Memorial from Manuel Quintín Lame to the Magistrates of the Supreme Court of Justice. Dated: October 16, 1914.

25. Letter from Manuel Quintín Lame to Minister of Gobierno dated May 25, 1914. Archivo General de La Nación, Republica, Fondo Ministerio de Gobierno, Sección 4 varios, TOMO 107, folio 0002-00026.

26. Letter from Manuel Quintín Lame to Minister of Gobierno dated May 25, 1914. Archivo General de La Nación, Republica, Fondo Ministerio de Gobierno, Sección 4 varios, TOMO 107, folio 0002-00026.

27. In 1908 the number of "departamentos"/states multiplied. As seen earlier, Gran Cauca was broken up into several states. In 1910, the department of El Valle del Cauca was created.

28. Letter from Manuel Quintín Lame to Minister of Gobierno dated May 25, 1914. Archivo General de La Nación, Republica, Fondo Ministerio de Gobierno, Sección 4 varios, TOMO 107, folio 0002-00026.

29. Telegram from Leandro Medina/Secretario Gobierno Encargado Leandro Medina to the President of the Republic. February 6, 1915. Archivo General de la Nación, Republica, Fondo Ministerio de Gobierno, Sección 4 varios, Tomo 107. 1915 "Comunicaciones y Telegramas Cauca" ff. 00016-00030.

30. Telegram from Leandro Medina/Secretario Gobierno Encargado Leandro Medina to the President of the Republic. February 6, 1915. Archivo General de la Nación, Republica, Fondo Ministerio de Gobierno, Sección 4 varios, Tomo 107. 1915 " Comunicaciones y Telegramas Cauca" ff. 00016-00030.

31. Memorial from the indigenous people of Tacueyó and Toribío to the Ministry of Gobierno on June 1, 1915. Archivo General de la Nación, Republica, Fondo Ministerio de Gobierno, Sección 4 varios. 1915.

32. Memorial from the indigenous people of Tacueyó and Toribío to the Ministry of Gobierno on June 1, 1915. Archivo General de la Nación, Republica, Fondo Ministerio de Gobierno, Sección 4 varios. 1915.

33. Memorial from the indigenous people of Tacueyó and Toribío to the Ministry of Gobierno on June 1, 1915. Archivo General de la Nación, Republica, Fondo Ministerio de Gobierno, Sección 4 varios. 1915.

34. Memorial from Manuel Quintín Lame to Minister of Government, August 18, 1915. Archivo General de la Nación, Republica, Fondo Ministerio de Gobierno, Sección 4 varios. 1915. He was transferred from one prison to the next: from Popayán to Santander and from Santander to Caloto.

35. Archivo General de la Nación, Republica, Fondo Ministerio del Gobierno, Sección 4 varios. Tomo 107. 1915. "Comunicaciones y Telegramas sobre orden público relacionados con Lame." Ff. 42–96 (ff. 00048-0049). Letter from Lame to Ministro de Gobierno, August 18, 1915.

36. Archivo General de la Nación, Republica, Fondo Ministerio de Gobierno, Sección 4 varios. Tomo 107. 1915. "Comunicaciones y Telegramas sobre orden público relacionados con Lame." Ff. 42–96. Telegram from Miguel Arroyo Díez to Minister of Gobierno, February 9, 1916.

37. According to Manuel Quintín Lame, Guillermo Valencia as a congressman requested Manuel Quintin Lame's exile, but Abadía Méndez then Minister of Government opposed it.

38. Archivo General de la Nación, Republica, Fondo Ministerio de Gobierno, Sección 4 varios. Tomo 107. 1915. "Comunicaciones y Telegramas sobre orden público relacionados con Lame." Ff. 42–96. Telegram from Miguel Arroyo Diez to Minister of Gobierno, February 11, 1916.

39. Archivo General de la Nación, Republica, Fondo Ministerio de Gobierno, Sección 4 varios. Tomo 107. 1915. "Comunicaciones y Telegramas sobre orden público relacionados con Lame." Ff. 42-96. Telegram from Julio Borrero to Ministro of Gobierno, February 11, 1916.

40. Archivo General de la Nación, Republica, Fondo Ministerio de Gobierno, Sección 4 varios. Tomo 107. 1915. "Comunicaciones y Telegramas sobre orden público relacionados con Lame." Ff. 42–96. Telegram from Miguel Arroyo Diez to Minister of Gobierno, February 12, 1916.

41. Archivo General de la Nación, Republica, Fondo Ministerio de Gobierno, Sección 4 varios. Tomo 107. 1915. "Comunicaciones y Telegramas sobre orden público relacionados con Lame." Ff. 42–96. Telegram from Julio Borrerro to Ministro de Gobierno, February 12, 1916.

42. Archivo General de la Nación, Republica, Fondo Ministerio de Gobierno, Sección 4 varios. Tomo 107. 1915. "Comunicaciones y Telegramas sobre orden público relacionados con Lame." Ff. 42–96. Telegram from Abadía Mendez to Governor of Cauca, February 12, 1916.

43. Presidente y Ministro creen también que en operaciones deben intervener de preferencia fuerzas regulares del Ejercito y la Policía, a fin de poder proceder con absoluta disciplina y prudencia, pues fuerzas colecticias podrían ejecutar actos de hostilidad prematuros e injustifica-

dos que impidiera cualquier inteligencia amistosa y dejarian un germen de represalias espantosas para mas tarde por parte de indigenas. Esto sin contar el peligro de sacar armas y municiones de los parques nacionales para ponerlas en manos de particulares, pues la experiencia a demostrado que casi nunca vuelven a ellos, y se convierten en una amenaza para la paz pública. Convendría tentar antes de las medidas de rigor, proposiciones conciliatorias, enviando comisonados de prestigio entre los indios que les demuestren la sinrazón de su actitud hostil, el engaño en que los tiene Lame y les ofrezcan lo que legítimamente pueda ofrecérseles para remover causas de queja. Ojala se ponga al habla con el General Castellanos y combinen un plan eficaz, pero mas que todo prudente, para conjurar conflicto. Agradecerle informacion frecuente.

44. Archivo General de la Nación, Republica, Fondo Ministerio de Gobierno, Sección 4 varios. Tomo 107. 1915. "Comunicaciones y Telegramas sobre orden público relacionados con Lame." Ff. 42–96. Telegram from Governor of Cauca to Ministro de Gobierno, February 13, 1916.

45. Archivo General de la Nación, Republica, Fondo Ministerio de Gobierno, Sección 4 varios. Tomo 107. 1915. "Comunicaciones y Telegramas sobre orden público relacionados con Lame." Ff. 42–96. Telegram from Governor of Huila to Ministro de Gobierno, February 13, 1916.

46. Archivo General de la Nación, Republica, Fondo Ministerio de Gobierno, Sección 4 varios. Tomo 107. 1915. "Comunicaciones y Telegramas sobre orden público relacionados con Lame." Ff. 42–96. Letter sent to President from the Governor of Cauca, February 17, 1916.

47. The Governor of Cauca received news from the district of Caldoso that Lame was preparing a race war in that district and that indigenous people were preparing to attack the authorities specifically the tax agents. See Archivo General de la Nación, Republica, Fondo Ministerio de Gobierno, Sección 4 varios. Tomo 107. 1915. "Comunicaciones y Telegramas sobre orden público relacionados con Lame." Ff. 42–96. Letter sent to President of Colombia from the Governor of Cauca, February 17, 1916.

48. Archivo General de la Nación, Republica, Fondo Ministerio de Gobierno, Sección 4 varios. Tomo 107. 1915. "Comunicaciones y Telegramas sobre orden público relacionados con Lame." Ff. 42–96. Letter sent to President from the Governor of Cauca, February 17, 1916.

49. Archivo General de la Nación, Republica, Fondo Ministerio de Gobierno, Sección 4 varios. Tomo 107. 1915. " Comunicaciones y Telegramas sobre orden público relacionados con Lame." Ff. 42–96. Letter to José Vicente Concha, dated June 5,1916.

50. Archivo General de la Nación, Republica, Fondo Ministerio de Gobierno, Sección 4 varios. Tomo 107. 1915. "Comunicaciones y Telegramas sobre orden público relacionados con Lame." Ff. 42–96. Letter sent to President from the Governor of Cauca, February 17, 1916.

51. Archivo General de la Nación, Republica, Fondo Ministerio de Gobierno, Sección 4 Varios. Tomo 107. 1915. "Comunicaciones y Telegramas sobre orden público relacionados con Lame." Ff. 42–96. Telegram dated June 7, 1916, from Antonio Paredes to President and Ministers of Government and War.

52. Archivo General de la Nación, Republica, Fondo Ministerio de Gobierno, Sección 4 varios. Tomo 107. 1915. "Comunicaciones y Telegramas sobre orden público relacionados con Lame." Ff. 42–96. Letter to José Vicente Concha from Alcibíades Valencia Zambrano and Ignacio Muñoz, dated June 5, 1916. The authors of the letter suggested capturing Manuel Quintín Lame along with his closest associates immediately to avoid the danger of a "giant" revolution.

53. Miguel Angel, "Los Negros Caucanos en el Siglo XX." Semana. http://www.semana.com/opinion/expertos/articulo/los-negors-caucanos-en-el-siglo-xx/323107.

54. Archivo General de la Nación, Republica, Fondo Ministerio de Gobierno, Sección 4 varios. Tomo 107. 1915. "Comunicaciones y Telegramas sobre orden público relacionados con Lame." Ff. 42–96. Telegram to the Governor of Cauca from Minister of Government, June 7, 1916.

55. Archivo General de la Nación, Republica, Fondo Ministerio de Gobierno, Sección 4 varios. Tomo 107. 1915. "Comunicaciones y Telegramas sobre orden público relacionados con Lame." Ff. 42–96. Telegram dated June 9, 1916, from Antonio Paredes to President and Ministers of Government and War.

56. Archivo General de la Nación, Republica, Fondo Ministerio de Gobierno, Sección 4 varios. Tomo 107. 1915. "Comunicaciones y Telegramas sobre orden público relacionados con Lame." Ff. 42–96. Telegram to the Governor of Cauca from Minister of Government, June 10, 1916

57. Archivo General de la Nación, Republica, Fondo Ministerio de Gobierno, Sección 4 varios. Tomo 107. 1915. "Comunicaciones y Telegramas sobre orden público relacionados con Lame." Ff. 42–96. Telegram to the Governor of Cauca from Minister of Government, June 9, 1916.

58. Archivo General de la Nación, Republica, Fondo Ministerio de Gobierno, Sección 4 varios. Tomo 107. 1915. "Comunicaciones y Telegramas sobre orden público relacionados con Lame." Ff. 42–96. Telegram dated June 9, 1916, from Antonio Paredes to President and Ministers of Government and War.

59. *Opiniones*. "Manuel Quintín Lame." Archivo José María Arboleda. Universidad del Cauca. Popayán, July 10, 1916.

60. Julio Arboleda was a well-known conservative of Cauca who wrote a famous epic poem that depicted love between a Spaniard (Gonzalo de Oyón) and an indigenous woman in the Valley of Popayán. Gonzalo de Oyón was driven to suicide by the Belalcazar family (original conquistadors). See http://eldiario.com.co/seccion/OPINION/pubenza110904.html.

61. *Opiniones*. "Ni Gonzalo de Oyón". Archivo José María Arboleda. Universidad del Cauca. Popayán, July 29, 1916.

62. *Opiniones*. "No mas ridiculeces por Dios!!" Archivo José María Arboleda. Universidad del Cauca. Popayán, August 5, 1916.

63. Since the director of the newspaper was Laurentino Quintana, it is reasonable to assume that he was also the author of the article.

64. *Opiniones*. "Ya es tiempo . . ."Archivo José María Arboleda. Universidad del Cauca. Popayán, August 24, 1916.

65. *Opiniones*. "La revolución de Lame." Archivo José María Arboleda. Universidad del Cauca. Popayán, September 8, 1916. Also, *Opiniones*. "La sedición de Lame." Archivo José María Arboleda. Universidad del Cauca. Popayán, September 23, 1916.

66. Gonzalo Castillo-Cárdenas, *Liberation Theology from Below: The Life and Thought of Manuel Quintín Lame* (Maryknoll, NY: Orbis Books, 1987), 34. See also Gow, 213.

67. Here I am borrowing Ana María Alonso's discussion of ethnic fiction. See *Thread of Blood: Colonialism, Revolution, and Gender on Mexico's Northern Frontier* (Tucson: University of Arizona Press, 1995), 51. See Espinosa for a discussion of whiteness and Colombian racial discourses, 130–36. Also Mary Roldán for how certain subregions of Antioquia were othered.

68. Archivo General de la Nación, República, Fondo Ministerio de Gobierno, Sección 4 varios. Tomo 104. 1916. "Comunicaciones y Telegramas sobre orden público relacionados con Lame." Ff. 263–88. Telegram from Inzá to Presidentes of the Camara, November 6, 1916.

69. Archivo General de la Nación, República, Fondo Ministerio de Gobierno, Sección 4 varios. Tomo 104. 1916. "Comunicaciones y Telegramas sobre orden público relacionados con Lame." Ff. 263–88. Telegram from *vecinos* of Inzá to Minister of War and Gobierno, November 6, 1916.

70. Archivo General de la Nación, República, Fondo Ministerio de Gobierno, Sección 4 varios. Tomo 104. 1916. "Comunicaciones y Telegramas sobre orden público relacionados con Lame." Ff. 263–88. Telegram from Antonio Paredes to Ministro de Gobierno. November 11, 1916.

71. Governor Paredes' anger toward Primitivo Fernandez was manifest in much of the correspondence about Manuel Quintín Lame. One particular exchange between Paredes and Primitivo Fernandez after the events in Inzá shows how Paredes gloated over what he saw as a justification for his previous insistence that Manuel Quintín Lame was dangerous. Primitivo Fernandez tried to obtain some sort of protection from the governor of Cauca when he faced considerable opprobrium regarding his decision to release the indigenous leader; the governor took great pleasure in rejecting this request. See, in particular, Archivo General de la Nación, República, Fondo Ministerio de Gobierno, Sección 4 varios. Tomo 104. 1916. "Comunicaciones y Telegramas sobre orden público relacionados con Lame." Ff. 263–88. Letter from the

Governor of the Department /Antonio Paredes to Primitivo Fernandez, Popayán, November 15, 1916.

72. Archivo General de la Nación, República, Fondo Ministerio de Gobierno, Sección 4 varios. Tomo 104. 1916. "Comunicaciones y Telegramas sobre orden público relacionados con Lame." Ff. 263–88. Telegram from Antonio Paredes to Ministerio Gobernación and Guerra, November 12, 1916.

73. Archivo General de la Nación, República, Fondo Ministerio de Gobierno, Sección 4 varios. Tomo 104. 1916. "Comunicaciones y Telegramas sobre orden público relacionados con Lame." Ff. 263–88. Telegram from Julio Borrero to Ministro de Gobierno, November 12, 1916.

74. The racist connotation of *indio* endured in Colombia until the late 1980s. For example, it was common to hear Bogotanos say, "No seas Indio"/"Don't be an Indian." The meaning was generally understood that an *indio* was an uneducated and ill-mannered fool.

75. Archivo General de la Nación, República, Fondo Ministerio de Gobierno, Sección 4 varios. Tomo 104. 1916. "Comunicaciones y Telegramas sobre orden público relacionados con Lame." Ff. 263–88. Telegram from Julio Borrero to Ministro de Gobierno, November 12, 1916 (second telegram of the day that included excerpts or quotes from the Inzá telegrapher).

76. Archivo General de la Nación, República, Fondo Ministerio de Gobierno, Sección 4 varios. Tomo 104. 1916. "Comunicaciones y Telegramas sobre orden público relacionados con Lame." Ff. 263–88. Telegram from Ministro de Gobierno to General Velazco, November 12, 1916.

77. Archivo General de la Nación, República, Fondo Ministerio de Gobierno, Sección 4 varios. Tomo 104. 1916. "Comunicaciones y Telegramas sobre orden público relacionados con Lame." Ff. 263–88. Telegram from Ministro de Gobierno to Governor of Cauca, November 12, 1916.

78. Archivo General de la Nación, República, Fondo Ministerio de Gobierno, Sección 4 varios. Tomo 104. 1916. "Comunicaciones y Telegramas sobre orden público relacionados con Lame." Ff. 263–88. Telegram from General Velasco to Ministro of Gobierno, Cali, November 12, 1916.

79. Archivo General de la Nación, República, Fondo Ministerio de Gobierno, Sección 4 varios. Tomo 104. 1916. "Comunicaciones y Telegramas sobre orden público relacionados con Lame." Ff. 263–88. Telegram from Inspector Otero to Bogotá, November 12, 1916.

80. Archivo General de la Nación, República, Fondo Ministerio de Gobierno, Sección 4 varios. Tomo 104. 1916. "Comunicaciones y Telegramas sobre orden público relacionados con Lame." Ff. 263–88. Telegram from Julio Borrero to Ministro de Gobierno, dated November 13, 1916.

81. Archivo General de la Nación, República, Fondo Ministerio de Gobierno, Sección 4 varios. Tomo 104. 1916. "Comunicaciones y Telegramas sobre orden público relacionados con Lame." Ff. 263–88. Telegram from Antonio Paredes to Ministro de Gobierno, November 13, 1916.

82. He ended the telegram requesting funds to pay for the expenses that he had incurred so far (in the sending of armed forces).

83. Archivo General de la Nación, República, Fondo Ministerio de Gobierno, Sección 4 varios. Tomo 104. 1916. "Comunicaciones y Telegramas sobre orden público relacionados con Lame." Ff. 263–88. Telegram from Antonio Paredes to Ministro de Gobierno, November 14, 1917.

84. Archivo General de la Nación, República, Fondo Ministerio de Gobierno, Sección 4 varios. Tomo 104. 1916. "Comunicaciones y Telegramas sobre orden público relacionados con Lame." Ff. 263–88. Telegram from Inspector Otero to Bogotá, November 14, 1916.

85. Archivo General de la Nación, República, Fondo Ministerio de Gobierno, Sección 4 varios. Tomo 104. 1916. "Comunicaciones y Telegramas sobre orden público relacionados con Lame." Ff. 263–88. Telegram from Julio Borrero to Minister of Gobierno, November 15, 1916. Pio Collo was also a *Nasa* and was a former Liberal guerrilla leader. See Ary R. Campo Chicangana, *Montoneras, deserciones e insubordinaciones: Yanaconas y Paeces en la Guerra de los Mil Días*.

86. Archivo General de la Nación, República, Fondo Ministerio de Gobierno, Sección 4 varios. Tomo 104. 1916. "Comunicaciones y Telegramas sobre orden público relacionados con

Lame." Ff. 263–88. Telegram from Julio Borrero to Minister of Gobierno (second of the day), November 15, 1916.

87. *La Union Conservadora*, "El Mariscal Lame," November 17, 1916. www.proyectoQuintínlame.org.

88. The writers of *Opiniones* stated that one should not forget that this clash occurred on the eve of elections (article or statement published on November 11).

89. Popayán, November 22, 1916. Letter from Antonio Paredes to President of Republic. Archivo General de la Nación. Fondo Ministerio de Gobierno. Sección 4 varios. Tomo 108. 1916.

90. He also pointed out that Manuel Quintín Lame's father owned property. I am not the first to notice Manuel Quintin Lame's representation as a lazy and free agent whose father owned property. See Monica Espinosa Arango, 135.

91. Popayán, November 22, 1916. Letter from Antonio Paredes to President of Republic. Archivo General de la Nación. Fondo Ministerio de Gobierno. Sección 4 varios. Tomo 108. 1916.

92. *Opiniones*. "Si los muertos hablaran." Archivo José María Arboleda. Universidad del Cauca. Popayán. www.proyectoQuintínlame.org.

93. Archivo General de la Nación, República, Fondo Ministerio de Gobierno, Sección 4 varios. Tomo 131. 1918. Memoriales indígenas Cauca, ff. 219–21. Memorial dated May 1918 from Manuel Quintín Lame's followers (including Cenón Ramirez who was mentioned in local state documents as an important member of Manuel Quintín Lame's organization and Ignacio Lame).

94. Gonzalo Castillo-Cárdenas, 34. See also David Gow, 213.

95. Manuel Quintín Lame, *En defensa de mi raza*, xxii. An excerpt of an interview that he gave in July of 1924 to a journalist of *El Espectador* is cited.

96. Ibid.

97. Monica Espinosa Arango, 135. I have placed quotations marks around civilized and rebel because Espinosa Arango uses those exact terms: "civilizado" y "rebelde."

98. See Luis Guillermo Vasco's "Quintin Lame: Resistencia y Liberación" for an interpretation that emphasizes the armed/guerrilla nature of Manuel Quintín Lame's movement.

99. http://www.banrepcultural.org/blaavirtual/biografias/lamemanu.htm.

100. Castillo-Cárdenas, 21.

Chapter Three

Conversations between Indigenous Communities and the Central State in the 1930s and 1940s

This chapter examines how the central state interacted with indigenous people in Cauca from the 1930s to 1940s; it focuses primarily on its attempt to dissolve communal landownership. The central state, local state, indigenous communities, and municipal authorities were all engaged in a dialogue about the dissolution of indigenous *resguardos*. This dialogue evolved into a conversation about land, "progress," and ethnic identity as the different parties tried to justify their position against or for the dissolution of a specific *resguardo*. The broader argument that this chapter makes is that the ideology of the Liberal Party in the 1930s was attractive to some indigenous communities especially to those located in the northern and western subregions of Cauca. Scholars have traditionally argued that Liberalism was an ideology in direct opposition to indigenous communities' agenda because of its emphasis on individual rights. However, in Cauca in the 1930s indigenous groups as well as Afro-Colombians voted for the Liberal party. In 1939 the Liberal party had received a majority of the votes cast in twenty-seven out of thirty-three municipalities.[1] Even municipalities with a majority indigenous population voted for the Liberal platform. Popayán's Liberal newspaper captured the mood of triumphant liberalism with the headline of this article: "Triunfo arrollador del Liberalismo en Corinto en el debate pasado"/"Overwhelming victory of Liberalism in Corinto in the last debate."[2] Liberals had received 997 votes versus only 57 for the Conservatives.[3] The Liberal candidate, López Pumarejo, received 30,572 votes in Cauca, which was significant, if we consider that the population of the Cauca was estimated in 1905 at 206,113.[4]

Tierradentro, in particular, had long-standing ties to the Liberal Party and voted en masse for the Liberal party in the 1930s. An example of the historical ties that existed between Liberals and indigenous people in Tierradentro was that in the nineteenth century the indigenous communities of Pitayo and Jambalo obtained the land of Julio Arboleda, a Conservative, as a reward for their military allegiance to Tomás Mosquera de Cipriano who represented the Liberal Party in the War of 1859–1862.[5] During the *War of a Thousand Days* (1899–1902) Liberal and Conservative Nasas fought on opposing sides.[6]

Intrinsic to the attraction of Liberalism was a more fluid notion of ethnic identity. In the 1930s indigenous rural folk did not necessarily see a contradiction between being a settler/*colono* and being an indigenous person. Many indigenous families held land both inside the *resguardo* and had settled/cultivated land outside of the *resguardos* (see Lorenzo Muelas's memoir). For all his insistence on the importance of the *resguardo*/communal landholding Manuel Quintín Lame was not a member of a *resguardo* and owned land outside of the communal landholding framework. In part the rigidity and essentializing of what it means to be an indigenous person in Colombia will come from outsiders such as Gregorio Hernández de Alba and his team of ethnologists who arrived to Cauca under the aegis of the cultural policy of the Liberal State in the 1940s.

In addition, indigenous activists of the North of Cauca were quick to exploit the contradictions that existed within the Liberal Party, which on the one hand preached an ideology of progress and modernization, which often benefited landowners, but at the same time encouraged grassroots mobilization through the formation of unions and peasant leagues thus empowering the lower classes. Indigenous people joined peasant leagues and unions in an effort to shape the Liberal Party's policy and made alliances with *indigenista* intellectuals. A perfect example of this trend was José Gonzalo Sánchez's (a former Manuel Quintín Lame associate) participation in the *Federación Departamental Indígena y Campesina del Cauca*.[7] This federation at its fourth conference (via José Gonzalo Sánchez who was part of the executive committee) voiced its strong opposition to the policy of dissolution of *resguardos* while stating its strong support for the Liberal government, which in the 1940s faced an attempted coup d'état. It also reminded the Liberal state in this statement that many intellectuals and "democratic personalities" rejected this policy.

The Liberal central state viewed indigenous peoples of Cauca as possible political allies, and general rural based initiatives such as Law 200 of 1936 brought the indigenous rural folk into contact with the central government. The other aspect of the state's gaze and interaction with indigenous people of Cauca stemmed from the Liberal government's cultural policies. These cultural policies were important not only because they emphasized the importance of indigenous culture to Colombian nationalism, but also because they created an alternative discourse that stressed the state's need to protect indigenous communities. Institutions such as the *Instituto Etnologico de Cauca* were loosely affiliated with the central government;[8] while the director of the institute (Gregorio Hernández de Alba) published extensively on the need to maintain the collective landholding structure, he was not in charge of land policy vis-à-vis indigenous rural folk. Thus, in the 1930s and 1940s the *indigenista* discourse and its stance against the dissolution of *resguardos* were still on the margins of the state's land policy.

Instead, the Liberal discourse and policy that the Ministry of Agriculture adopted emphasized the commonality of indigenous rural folk with their *mestizo*, white, and Afro-Colombian counterparts. According to this view, the central state's role was to help bring indigenous rural folk to an era of progress and modernity. The division in charge of land and colonization (which changed its name several times) presented the indigenous rural folk as oppressed by Law 89 of 1890 and at the mercy of colonial institutions such as the indigenous councils.

Indigenous people of Cauca responded to these various state initiatives in a myriad of ways. The diversity of reactions was due in part to the very different situations that indigenous communities residing on *resguardo* land faced. As we shall see, indigenous communities that resided on a territory that had access to urban markets and whose land was coveted and taken over at times by nonindigenous settlers and merchants appealed to the central state for protection even if it meant the breakup of the *resguardo*. The other development that weakened certain indigenous communities was that their indigenous councils came under increased pressure from the municipal authorities who could veto land adjudication and the election of indigenous council members. As the reader will remember, in 1926, the governor of Cauca, Carlos Vernaza, used decree number 435 of 1926 to eliminate the veto power regarding the settlement of nonindigenous people in the *resguardo* that indigenous councils previously had in Cauca.[9] Such a change in legislation eroded the power of the indigenous councils considerably. Overall, only ten out of fifty-four resguardos legally recognized in 1937 sought their dissolution through official channels.

RESGUARDOS IN THE CAUCA[10]

National Context

In 1930, after decades of political exclusion, the Liberal party gained control of the central government and of the presidency. Of particular relevance here are the broader political and economic trends of the Colombian countryside to understand the development of the indigenous political movement and its interaction with the central state. In 1930 most of Colombia was rural; 76

Table 3.1.

Municipalities	*1937/56 resguardos*	*1935/61 resguardos*
Popayán	1 Poblazón	1
Almaguer	1	1
San Sebastian	1	1
Bolívar	1	1
Jambaló	1	1
Cajibío	1	1
Sotará	1	1
El Tambo	2	5
La Vega	2	2
Puracé	2	2
Totoro	3	3
Toribío	3	3
Caldono	4	4
Morales	4	4
Silvia	4	4
Inzá	8	9
Páez	15	15
Timbío	0	1

percent of the Colombian population lived in the countryside (Vega Cantor 2002, 11). Furthermore, as seen in the introduction, the indigenous communities of Cauca resided overwhelmingly in the countryside; Cauca was and is still a predominantly rural department in contrast to the rest of modern Colombia.

The broad economic trends from 1910 to 1940 in the Colombian countryside were the growing importance of the coffee export, the development of roads and transportation networks that linked Bogotá to the other regions more effectively (which was financed in part by the U.S. payment for Panama), and finally the changing land tenure patterns. Although the division within the Conservative Party facilitated in particular the election of Alfonso López Pumarejo in 1934, the 1929 Stock Market Crash with the subsequent fallout in terms of coffee prices and rising rural unemployment deepened the discontent of many middle-class and rural Colombians toward the Conservative government. In addition, the broadly publicized massacre of banana workers of the United Fruit Company carried out by the Colombian Conservative government in Cienaga in response to the workers' protest and growing radicalization also discredited and delegitimized the Conservative Party.

The growing unrest in the Colombian countryside fueled by the economic depression and with the increasing influence of communism and socialism, which manifested itself with the creation of the PSR (*Partido Socialista Revolucionario*), with the formation of peasant leagues, and with the holding of Labor Congresses pressured the Liberal governments of the 1930s to act.[11] The government of Olaya Herrera founded the *Banco Central Hipotecario, Caja de Credito Agrario*, *Caja Colombiana de Ahorros*, and the *Instituto of Accion Social* to bolster the appeal of the Liberal Party and to make the Liberal central government relevant. Indeed, the founding of these national institutions brought the central state into the lives of ordinary Colombians.

López Pumarejo's government went further. During his first period of government, known popularly as *La Revolución en Marcha*, (1934–1938), López Pumarejo sought to establish the legitimacy of the Liberal central government in the eyes of the Colombian rural folk as well as to undermine the appeal of communism and socialism. Richard Stoller states, "López proclaimed a programme of fiscal, institutional and social reforms. Among those most frequently cited are the 1935 tax reform; the 1936 Constitutional reform, which defined property as a 'social function'; and Ley 200 of 1936, an ersatz agrarian reform which pressured large landowners to exploit their properties or face expropriation"[12] (Stoller 1995, 1). The creation of institutions geared toward popular classes and the promulgation of laws created the belief amongst small holders and settlers that the central state sympathized with their political and social objectives.[13] Law 200 of 1936 in particular favored the rights of settlers over those of landowners who held a title but did not cultivate the land.

CENTRAL STATE IN THE LOCAL CONTEXT OF THE 1930S AND 1940S

Central State and Its Agrarian Policy

The Liberal government created Agrarian Leagues in the north of Cauca to organize indigenous rural folk.[14] As seen in the previous chapter, a significant sector of Cauca's elite was Liberal, which had divided the local elite and complicated its alliance with the central state during the Conservative regime.[15] With the Liberals in power, Cauca's Liberal elite sought to modernize Cauca and to benefit from its newfound access to the central state. As seen earlier, the elite of Cauca was frustrated with the mismatch between its past glorious political contributions to the Colombian nation and its present economic status vis-à-vis other departments. The neighboring department Valle del Cauca's economy took off in the early twentieth century, whereas

Cauca's economy stagnated without any significant industrialization or agricultural based development. The elite of Cauca commonly blamed the absence of economic development in Cauca as due to the absence of a viable infrastructure to transport agricultural products and to the continued presence of indigenous *resguardos*. The continued existence of a large number of indigenous *resguardos* (in contrast to the rest of the country) was in large measure responsible for Cauca's backwardness according to both Liberal and Conservative elites.

Francisco José Chaux illustrates how the Liberal elite of Cauca gained a major foothold in the central government in the 1930s and its enthusiasm for modernization. He became the *Minister of Industrias y Comercio*/Industry and Commerce in the 1930s, and since there was no Ministry of Agriculture at the time, he was in charge of agricultural matters. He was also instrumental in drafting the *Ley de Tierras*/Land Act of 1936 as well as for pushing for the dissolution of the *resguardos* of indigenous communities. This two-pronged approach makes perfect sense if one considers that the main objective of Law 200 of 1936 was to ensure that land was productive. Although it did affirm the importance of social use of land, its other objective was the productivity of land. Francisco José de Chaux considered the land of *resguardos* to be unproductive since he and other Caucano elite held the mistaken and racist assumption that Indians were by nature lazy and not "forward thinking." This conception of an indigenous person ignored the reality of indigenous people who were members of an indigenous *resguardo* but were also settlers of land plots outside of the *resguardo*. The representation of indigenous people as obstacles to progress and as parasites of the local economy permeated the local press and the minds of many in Cauca. So, for the Minister of *Industrias* what could better achieve the objective of making land productive in his region than dissolving the *resguardos*?

Francisco José Chaux's allies for the modernization of Cauca were (in particular for Tierradentro) the missionaries of the French Lazariste order who resided in Tierradentro.[16] As seen in the previous discussion of laws that governed indigenous communities, the French order of Pere Lazaristes along with the Vincentinos had arrived to Cauca in 1905. The missionaries argued that roads and economic development were essential tools to "civilize" the indigenous people of Tierradentro; this was a discourse that aligned itself with Francisco José Chaux's ideology. Missionaries in Tierradentro saw themselves as key agents of a mission *civilisatrice*, which (of course) justified their continued presence in Tierradentro.

Ironically, the opponents to Francisco José Chaux's program were often Liberals. However, these Liberals were often outsiders to the region who wrote extensively about indigenous communities and were sent to Cauca as part of the Liberal government's cultural program. Jesus Otero, Juan Friede, Gregorio Hernández de Alba, and Milciades Chaves were all examples of prominent intellectuals who argued for the maintenance of *resguardos*. For these intellectuals and *indigenistas,* an indigenous identity was incompatible with private property, and communal landholding was the only way to ensure the survival of an indigenous ethnic identity in Colombia. The voice of Liberals who argued for the maintenance of *resguardos* was present mainly in the articles of the newspaper, *El Liberal*, as well as through the work that the local Institute of Ethnology (affiliated with the Universidad del Cauca and founded in 1946) carried out under the directorship of Gregorio Hernández de Alba.[17] The local state was well aware of the local opposition that it faced from local Liberals around the issue of the dissolution of *resguardos*. In 1937, the governor of Cauca, Enrique Chaux, who stated his unqualified support for the division of resguardos, informed the national government that this policy faced opposition from local Liberals.

Discourse around the Dissolution of Indigenous Resguardos

The discourse around the breakup of indigenous *resguardos* should be viewed in the context of the growing appeal of the Liberal party and its agrarian reform discourse of the 1930s. The following section of this chapter is based on an extensive review of documents sent to the *Ministerio de Gobierno* regarding the possible breakup of *resguardos*. The correspondence I examined spanned from 1922 to 1951.[18] Overall, from 1935 to 1937 the number of *resguardos* went from sixty-one *resguardos* to fifty-seven *resguardos*.[19] Although the subdivision and name of the state agency in charge of the dissolution of *resguardos* changed from the 1920s to the early 1950s, the nature of the required documentation remained the same.

This documentation was voluminous and extensive since the official breakup of a *resguardo* required the following documentation: a census of its inhabitants; the original title from the Spanish Crown; if the title was missing, which was often the case, then a declaration of witnesses stating how and why the original title was missing; an engineer's survey and measurement of the extension of the *resguardo* (if this was not available then an approximate calculation); a description of the boundaries of the *resguardo*; and a list of the members of the *cabildo*. In addition, the notary located in Popayán had to guarantee the authenticity of the documents that were sent to the central government. The ministry also ascertained whether the indigenous council and the indigenous members of the *resguardo* were in favor of the division or not. The municipal mayor where the *resguardo* was located also had to assess the "*estado de cultura*"/"state of culture" meaning the degree to which the indigenous inhabitants were assimilated and how far the *resguardo* was from main roads and cities of the department. Thus, the municipality was involved and notified at the very beginning of this process. The very first step in the process of the dissolution of the resguardos began when the secretary of the Ministry of Agriculture sent a letter to the indigenous council asking it to provide the documentation listed above.[20]

While the central government clearly started the process of dividing up the *resguardos*, the responses from the indigenous communities and *cabildos* varied a great deal. To my surprise, there were some *cabildos* who advocated for the breakup of their *resguardos*. I do not mean to suggest that most indigenous communities favored dissolving their *resguardos*, but rather that the indigenous councils or persons who continued to write after responding the original queries to the national government saw the central government's policy as the most effective method to preserve its landholdings albeit by abandoning their claim to communal landholding.

Also, for outsiders to the indigenous community, there was no need to involve the national government if they wished to take over part of the land of the *resguardos*. Although there was clear and abundant legislation protecting the indigenous *resguardo* land from sale or rental, the reality on the ground was very different. The correspondence between the central government and indigenous communities shows that land was adjudicated to nonindigenous settlers on a routine basis. This was particularly true for areas that had become valuable in terms of coffee plantings and/or where a road was being built. In addition, as we saw in the section on the discussion of the laws governing indigenous *resguardos* in Cauca, an area of the *resguardo* was segregated for non-indigenous people to settle on. For instance, three indigenous *resguardos* and communities located in the municipality of *El Tambo* dissolved without any national or official interference.

As we shall see in the case study below, some very valuable land with coffee plantings was located in the municipality of *El Tambo*. Thus, outsiders could "breakup" a *resguardo* unofficially quite easily unless there was vigorous opposition from the indigenous community and an open conflict. For indigenous communities, the advantage of asking the central state to carry out the division of the *resguardo* lay in that (in theory) the land rights of each indigenous family who belonged to the *resguardo* were protected after the breakup of the *resguardo*. In addition, the petition to dissolve a *resguardo* was often a means to ask for the central state's intervention and help where there was conflict and/or to gain access to state resources and benefits that *resguardo* members could not qualify for.

Before examining distinct case studies, a brief description of the general adjudication of land within the *resguardo* and process of the division of the *resguardo* is necessary.[21] The division of a *resguardo* consisted in allotting the land that each indigenous head of household (who was an official member of the *resguardo*) occupied and cultivated. For a period of fifteen years after the dissolution of the *resguardo* the new property owner/former *resguardo* member could not sell or alienate his property.

The land of *resguardos* in Cauca was adjudicated to households; the elected indigenous council allotted a portion of the *resguardo* to each family according to its size. The descendants of each household were supposed to remain on the same land plot. In the event that a family needed more land, the head of household wrote a petition that first certified that the family members were indigenous, belonged to the *resguardo*, and finally were Catholic.[22] In this petition, the reasons for asking for more land were outlined. The indigenous council had eight days to respond to the petition. Once the outcome of a petition was decided, then the governor ordered the captains to assemble the largest number of people possible (all indigenous from the same *resguardo*) for a meeting, which always took place on a Saturday. According to the informant, this first meeting (if the petition was successful) was held in the house of the *gobernador* where the boundaries of the property were decided. Then, the governor would go to the land plot where the petitioner resided, and in the presence of everyone the allotment of the new land was publicly announced. The public nature of the announcement of land adjudication created transparency and gave the opportunity for any possible opposition to be aired publicly as well.

The same day or the very next day the secretary of the council wrote up the decision of the council, and once all the members of the indigenous council signed the document, the document was sent over to the municipal mayor for approval. According to the informant consulted on this matter (in the 1940s) this petition could be rejected; the possible reasons for this rejection could be incorrect wording or that some legal requirement was not met. However, one can imagine the situation where the municipal mayor might be opposed for other reasons to the adjudication of a land plot. For instance, a municipal mayor could decide to deny certification of the adjudication of the land plot if settlers who were political allies or friends of the mayor occupied this land plot illegally.

Case of Chapa

The case of Chapa illustrates the challenges that the national government faced when processing the division of *resguardos* in Cauca and uncovers the unexpected identity of its allies.

Setting of Chapa

The resguardo of Chapa known as *Parcialidad de Indigenas de Chapa* was located in the municipality of *El Tambo*, which is in the center zone of Cauca.[23] This municipality was only thirty-three kilometers away from Popayán, which made the land valuable because of its easy access to Popayán's urban market. In October of 1937 the governor of Cauca, Enrique Chaux, described the land of the *resguardo* of Chapa as fertile and where coffee was an important crop.[24] Fedecafe's census of 1932 indicated that the municipality of Cauca with the highest number of trees was El Tambo. El Tambo had a total of 1,705 properties of which 1,683 had less than 5,000 trees and only 22 had 5,000 to 20,000 coffee trees. These statistics indicate that land was well distributed and that the number of large properties was small.

As table 3.1 indicates, three other *resguardos* located in El Tambo had "dissolved" without the government's intervention and in the space of two years. As mentioned above the unofficial breakup of *resguardos* was not legal and often meant that nonindigenous rural folk who had settled and/or bought titles in the *resguardo* preserved their landholdings. To this date (since the passage of the Constitution of 1991) indigenous rural folk of El Tambo have only preserved one *resguardo*, Alto del Rey; the remaining four *resguardos* were dissolved permanently in the municipality of El Tambo. This shows that in the late 1930s, communal landownership was under a great deal of pressure in municipalities where export crops made land increasingly valuable.

Process of Division

A letter dated August 12, 1937, from the indigenous council of Chapa (*pequeño cabildo de indigenas de Chapa*) to the Minister of *Industrias* confirms the worsening situation for indigenous rural folk who held land that had increased in value because of coffee and/or because of its proximity to urban markets.[25] The indigenous council of Chapa requested the breakup of the *resguardo* because nonindigenous rural folk had settled on their land and because traditional authorities such as the *cabildo* were unable to stem the flow of outsiders. Lawsuits on behalf of the indigenous community to force out outsiders were described as ineffective, costly, and lengthy. The inability to maintain the integrity of the *resguardo* boundaries did not start in the 1930s. The current state of crisis for this *resguardo* originated with the land gold mining operations in 1909.[26]

For this *cabildo*, the breakup of the *resguardo* was the only effective way for indigenous rural folk and members of the *resguardo* to hold on to their land rights. The advantage of the official breakup of the *resguardo* was that land was only to be adjudicated to members of the *resguardo*. The petition to dissolve the *resguardo* was couched in a language clearly designed to appeal to the Liberal government's ideology. Chapa's indigenous council stated that the division of the *resguardo* would permit indigenous peasants to cultivate a greater amount of coffee, to protect their grazing pasture, and finally to build irrigation canals because their property rights would be protected. The council members advanced the argument that indigenous people were reluctant to invest the work into making their land fully productive because their land rights were so insecure.

This argument of unleashed productivity (once the *resguardo* was dissolved) was echoed by the governor of Cauca's assessment on whether or not the *resguardo* of Chapa should be dissolved.[27] Enrique Chaux's (the governor of Cauca) response is worth considering because it sheds light on the ideological bases of Cauca's elite liberalism. First, the governor rejected Law 89 of 1890 wholeheartedly because it was antiquated and unsuitable for the 1930s. The implication was that modernity and progress could not be achieved in Cauca because of the shackles that this antiquated legislation placed on indigenous people by creating a separate class of people. Second, the governor argued that the desire to own private property and the attachment/love toward the land that developed from this ownership was a universal one amongst all races: indigenous, black, and white.[28] Third, the governor advanced that the indigenous farmer (who belonged to a *resguardo*) lived in a state of insecurity because the indigenous council could adjudicate his lot to any other person or family. In addition, according to the governor, land was not divided up equally amongst the members of *resguardos*, and he stated that more land was adjudicated to the members of the indigenous council whom he depicted as being more ambitious and as taking advantage of the majority of the inhabitants of the *resguardo*. This last remark should elicit a chuckle from the reader; it is supremely ironic that the proponent of Liberalism (hence capitalism) should object to the ambition of some members of the *resguardo* and reproached its leaders for not practicing "socialism."

More importantly, the remarks made by the governor of Cauca showed that he was ignorant (willfully or not) of the very collective nature of most adjudications of property. As described above, the adjudication of property was a public one and one that generally respected long-standing ties to a land plot. This is not to say that indigenous *resguardo* land was always equally divided or to deny the existence of an indigenous bourgeoisie, but to identify the indigenous council as the evil minority that manipulated and abused the majority of indigenous members of the *resguardo* as the original problem was not accurate. The long-term dictatorship of an indigenous council was not a possibility because of annual elections of the council members. In sum, while both the indigenous council of Chapa and the governor of Cauca agreed upon the insecurity of land rights and on the desirability of the *resguardo*'s dissolution, they disagreed fundamentally on the causes of land insecurity.

Stumbling Blocks toward Dissolution

The first logistical hurdle toward the breakup of a *resguardo* was often the measuring of the land that the *resguardo* occupied. The first exchange between the national government and the indigenous *resguardo* about the approximate size of the *resguardo* almost always elicited a response that the indigenous council was unsure of the size of the *resguardo*.[29] To start the process, the indigenous council of Chapa estimated the size of its *resguardo*, but a full two years later after their initial assent to the division of the *resguardo*, they had yet to hire an engineer.[30]

In addition, the indigenous council faced the challenge of a central government that was unaware of previous correspondence and that sometimes requested the same information. For instance, the central government in 1938 did not know that the governor of Cauca had written a lengthy assessment in favor of the dissolution of the *resguardo* in 1937 and was requesting the same information in 1938.[31] The indigenous councils of Chapa continued to write to the central government asking about the status of their request and expressing both their continued support for the measure of dissolution as well as their concern about the cost of the division of the *resguardo*.

Indeed, a major concern for the indigenous councils in favor of the dissolution of the *resguardo* was who would pay for the cost of the division and adjudication of the land. Most indigenous councils requested that the central government pay for the entire cost of this process and asked the Ministry of Agriculture or Industry repeatedly whether or not the national budget had allotted a budget item for the division of the *resguardos*. The fees for the dissolution and adjudication of the land were prohibitively expensive; land had to be surveyed, measured, and adjudicated, which involved hiring an engineer (or some sort of technical expert) and a lawyer. In addition, everything had to be notarized, which also meant hefty fees. The *cabildo* of Chapa expressed this common concern and linked the speedy dissolution of their *resguardo* with Liberalism. They stated:

> To send these documents, first we desire that you do us the important favor of informing us if there is a budget item for the expenses; because if this budget item were not voted for, it would not have the speedy result that this council wishes for. This would signify a step towards the oppression of progress.[32]

Consequences of This Process

In January of 1941, the central government had still not processed the division of the *resguardo* of Chapa; the ministry was still asking for more information.[33] Indigenous members of the Chapa *Resguardo* sent a letter dated October 29, 1942, to the nation's attorney general, which indicated that the process of division had gone awry. The letter writers indicated that they had never met with the engineer in charge of surveying and of measuring the different land plots, which was a serious problem because they were unable to inform the engineer whose plot belonged to whom and about the boundaries of each property.[34]

In addition, they maintained that the lawyer, the engineer, and the governor of the indigenous council were trying to swindle the majority of the *resguardo* inhabitants by allotting the smallest amount of land to the members of the *resguardo* and keeping large amounts for them to sell.[35] The indigenous council members and the lawyer argued that the sale of certain land plots was necessary to finance the costs of the division of the *resguardo.* In addition, the indigenous letter writers suggested that the lawyer and the engineer violated proper procedures several times by adjudicating land plots whether or not the owner of the land plot was present, which meant that the proper boundaries of property were ignored. To add insult to injury, several nonindigenous persons were added to the list of members of the *resguardo* and thus were attempting to gain land fraudulently. Furthermore, the indigenous council members also contravened the spirit of the law by claiming more land for their service to the community.

It is important to note that the original council members who had requested the division of the *resguardo* were no longer in power at the time that the indigenous petitioners wrote their letter outlining the improper procedures that took place. The former president of the indigenous council, Tomas Mambascoy, was one of the petitioners signing this letter to the Attorney General. Thus, we should not explain the desire to divide the *resguardo* as driven by a few corrupt bad apples who had gained control of the indigenous council. Nor should we adopt Enrique Chaux's view, which suggested that indigenous councils never represented the will of the majority and that they were solely out to profit from the political power that their offices gave them. Here, chronology and sequence of events are important to consider. In 1937, the desire to dissolve collective landholding and the corresponding political and legal structures expressed in Law 89 of 1890 was a genuine one and was a choice that came from within the community. However, was it an entirely free choice? Certainly, outside pressures such as land invasion and the growing inability of *cabildos* to act effectively drove the indigenous council and members of the *resguardo* to decide to adopt the ideology of Liberalism in (we can say now) the misguided hope that the Liberal state would protect their land rights in an effective manner. In the late 1930s for some indigenous communities, Liberalism exerted a profound appeal and was not contradictory to an indigenous identity. For these petitioners, an indigenous identity was not based on communal landownership and none of them suggested that acquiring formal private property would signify the abandonment of their ethnic identity.

A 1962 Division of Indigenous Affairs report indicated that the *resguardo* of Chapa had dissolved but that the titles of the former *resguardo* owners were nowhere to be found.[36] In other words, the central state had completely botched the dissolution of the *resguardo* and had left the indigenous ex-members of the *resguardo* completely unprotected and at the mercy of local crooks. Overall, the process of dissolution in this case did not ensure that the land rights of indigenous rural folk of Chapa were protected and instead invited further abuse and conflict.

Case of Cohetando

Setting

The Cohetando *resguardo* is located in Paez municipality and is considered part of the indigenous subregion of Cauca called Tierradentro. The Paez municipality is situated in the far eastern corner of the Cauca department and borders the Huila and Tolima departments. Its contiguous position with a subregion of Huila that had experienced growth in terms of coffee made land in Cohetando more valuable in 1930s. As seen earlier, Tierradentro was and is considered as an indigenous area *par excellence* with its cluster of fifteen *resguardos* in one municipality. The fifteen *resguardos* still exist today.[37] While the population of Cohetando was quite small (244 families and 1,500 inhabitants), its size (60,000 hectares) was significant.[38]

Although the size of the *resguardo* was significant, the development of its agriculture lagged behind other subregions of Cauca. In the Paez municipality, coffee was not as widely cultivated as it was in the municipality of El Tambo (where the *resguardo* Chapa was located). In 1932 there were only 238 coffee properties in the entire Paez municipality in contrast to Tambo's 1,705, and there were no properties with more than 5,001 trees.[39] However, by the late 1940s, coffee cultivation had experienced exponential growth in the subregion of Tierradentro. The intensification of coffee production came about because in the late 1940s the general price of coffee soared, and Tierradentro's coffee had become renowned for its high quality as well.[40] In addition, when the division process began, the road between Garzon-La Plata-Caloto-Cali that was being built crossed the *resguardo* of Cohetando.[41] The easy accessibility of a major road automaticaly increased the value of the land because agricultural products could be easily transported to major markets.

Process of Division

As seen in the case of Chapa, in the first round of correspondence between the indigenous *cabildo* and the central government, the secretary of the Ministry of Agriculture requested not only the relevant documents, but also the opinion of the council regarding the dissolution of the *resguardo*.[42] The *cabildo* expressed its support for the measure of dissolution of the *resguardo* stating that they wished to become owners of the land plots instead of being usufructuary of lands.[43] In a similar manner to the Chapa inhabitants, they wanted the central government to pay for the entire cost of the breakup of the *resguardo* along with the adjudication of land plots and rejected the possible solution of selling a land plot to pay for the cost of the division as art. 34 of Law 89 of 1890 suggested.[44]

It is worth pausing here to consider the discourse that the indigenous petitioners of Cohetando adopted when arguing for the dissolution of their *resguardo*. They sought to define themselves as civilized, which in their mind meant that most had abandoned the "Paez dialect" and that the majority of men and women were literate. On the one hand, one can interpret the abandonment of their native language (which they condescendingly called a dialect) as the internalization of the dominant values (which it was) and as a rejection of their ethnic identity. On the other hand, they did not express the idea that somehow they were no longer indigenous, but rather that they were "civilized" indigenous rural folk. In other words, these indigenous rural folk sought to define indigeneity as separate from language and from belonging to a collective land structure.

This desire to present themselves as civilized stemmed from Law 89 of 1890, which clearly stated that indigenous people who were still "uncivilized" were those who needed the protection of the legal framework of the *resguardo* as well as the continued oversight of religious orders. Cohetando's indigenous petitioners saw the *resguardo*'s dissolution as empowering because it made them of age, and consequently with the ability to manage their legal and land affairs.[45] Indigenous members of Cohetando chafed under the missionaries' legal jurisdiction as a later memorial made evident.[46] The missionaries, specifically Padre David Gonzalez, had closed down their school that had been functioning in the same location in the *resguardo* for the last twenty years. The children were told to attend another school (in La Ceja) that was far away and of difficult access; the indigenous residents had written three petitions complaining about this decision to Padre David Gonzalez as well as to Monsignor Laguere. Much to the disgust of the petitioners they had not even received a response to their missives.

In the memorial addressed to the President of the Republic, the petitioners identified themselves as Liberals who were *Lopistas* (partisans of President López) and emphasized their allegiance to the Colombian president's variant of Liberalism. The decision to close down their school and to send the children of Cohetando to La Ceja was politically motivated; they alleged that the other school belonged to an area where people were *Aranguistas*. The *Aranguistas* were supporters of Arango Velez who represented the Conservative branch of the Colombian Liberal party; Arango Velez had hoped to obtain the nomination to represent the Liberal Party, but was defeated by López.[47] The petitioners went on to state that the teachers nominated by the Rector of the schools in Tierradentro belonged to the Conservative Party; the implication was that those teachers were even less suitable for the children of Cohetando. They requested that their school be reopened and the nomination of a teacher who was a true democrat and Liberal. The above missive was a separate one from the correspondence on the division of the *resguardo*, but in terms of chronology it came after and before the requests that this same indigenous community made for the dissolution of its *resguardo*.

This letter sheds light on the wider context of what the division of *resguardo*/collective landholding meant for these Liberal indigenous rural folk. The appeal of the dissolution of collective landholding lay in part in its association with Liberalism of reform that promised the empowerment of indigenous communities. Specifically, for the indigenous community of Cohetando, the breakup of the *resguardo* was a way to challenge the political and legal authority that the missionary orders held in Tierradentro.

In other exchanges with the national government where the different *cabildos* requested the breakup of their *resguardos* the indigenous petitioners of Cohetando expressed their frustration with being equated with "primitive" human beings and insisted on their right to be treated like other Colombian citizens. While other scholars have rightly pointed out that this discourse accepted the very problematic categories of civilized and not civilized, these indigenous petitioners rejected the notion that they were inferior beings and the embedded notion in Law 89 of 1890 that to be indigenous was to need protection and guidance.

This larger context helps us understand Cohetando's indigenous community's persistence in requesting the division of their *resguardo*. In documents dating from May to July of 1939, the *cabildo* voiced its strong support for the breakup of the *resguardo*, and also supplied the necessary documentation for this process to go forward. The election of a new *cabildo* did not change this viewpoint; in February of 1940 the *cabildo* expressed its need to know when and how the dissolution of the *resguardo* was scheduled to take place.[48] In November of 1941, Cohetando's indigenous *cabildo* not only reiterated its support for the division of the *resguardo*, but also its disagreement with the decree that extended the legislation that governed and safeguarded *resguardos* for ten more years in the department of Cauca.[49]

The national government was also not happy about the decision to postpone the division of the *resguardos* as the secretary of the Ministry of Agriculture implied when he suggested to the indigenous council of Cohetando that it had the legal right to take the governorship of Cauca to court.[50] This exchange is puzzling since the national congress had also extended the legislation of Law 89 of 1890 for another ten years. This may be a case of the executive branch (in particular this agency) expressing frustration with the roadblock mounted by the legislative branch of government.

The biggest stumbling block for both the Ministry of Agriculture and for the indigenous council was the lack of financing available for the dissolution of the *resguardo*. The correspondence between the indigenous council and the national government continued, and the different *cabildo* presidents expressed their frustration at the inexistence of a budget allotment, which would allow the breakup and adjudication of land to go forward. In a response to the indigenous *cabildo*'s request to go forward with the breakup of the *resguardo* despite the new legislation, on October 27, 1942, the Ministry of Agriculture explained that the only way for the dissolution to go forward was with the indigenous *resguardo* providing the funds according to decree 1421 of 1940.

Division

The solution that the central government adopted was Resolution number five for the Cohetando *resguardo*. This Resolution of the Ministry of National Economy/Department of Land/Public Land section dated August 2, 1944, declared the *resguardo* of Cohetando "baldio land"/meaning public land.[51] In order to declare the land of Cohetando public land, the central state defined the indigenous community of Cohetando as a civil community rather than a *resguardo*. This declaration was made possible because the *resguardo* did not possess the original land title/grant and because the declarations of the witnesses did not meet the burden of proof.

The other rationale given for the executive order of Resolution number five was that all parties supported the dissolution of this *resguardo*. The indigenous council, the majority of its inhabitants, the governor of Cauca, and the national state were all in agreement that the *resguardo* should be declared defunct. The stated objective of this resolution was not to take advantage of the *resguardo*'s legal weakness, but rather to make it possible for each indigenous *resguardo* member to obtain a land title for his land plot and full citizenship rights. In addition, the dissolution of the *resguardo* stated specifically that land plots could only be adjudicated to the original indigenous members of the Cohetando *resguardo*.

Since all parties agreed that the indigenous people of Cohetando were "culturally advanced," the central state argued that legal guardianship and the continued minor legal status of Cohetando residents were no longer necessary. Indeed, while indigenous members of the resguardo were considered legally of age for most rights and obligations of Colombian citizenship, they were considered minors when it came to land matters. The central government with this executive decree sought to end the special category that indigenous people belonging to a *resguardo* belonged to.

By 1944, the central state had grown impatient with the commissions and the arbitration tribunals of the division of *resguardos* that in the words of the secretary of the Ministry of Economy "never succeeded in undoing the intricate controversies that give rise and that later are dissolved without achieving the objective of division." The central government encountered a myriad of logistical difficulties that reflected its weak institutional presence in Cauca. The powerlessness of the central state to even obtain notarized copies of the *resguardo* land titles free of charge was but one indication that the central state seriously lacked clout on the local ground. For instance, an extended exchange between the notary Arroyo and the secretary of the Minister of Agriculture (J. V. Garces Navas) showed how local power brokers felt quite free to turn down requests made by the central government. Arroyo of the Primera Notary refused to send certain *resguardo* titles to the central government because they were too onerous (handwriting was small/paper faded) to copy without pay. The secretary of Agriculture reprimanded the notary and reminded him that he was supposed to provide these copies free of charge as the Law mandated, but his admonitions had little effect.[52] The secretary of the Agricultural Ministry even turned to the Justice Ministry for help with this challenge.[53]

This institutional weakness became the fatal flaw when processing the actual division of the *resguardo* and adjudication of land plots. While Resolution number five declared the legal death of the *resguardo*, a document dated October 4, 1963, and signed by J. Osorio S. Jefe de *Resguardos* Indigenas, makes it clear that in practice the division of the *resguardo* never took place. No land plots were ever adjudicated to the *resguardo*'s members; and furthermore the indigenous council was still in place and functioning in 1963.

The case of the Cohetando *resguardo* reveals the power of the Liberal discourse and the limitations of the Colombian Liberal state of the 1930s and 1940s. It makes little sense to assume that the indigenous council and members of Cohetando were somehow forced to write these numerous missives to the central government, and that they were under pressure from local missionaries and nonindigenous settlers. Even though Cohetando's land was becoming valuable because of the building of major roads and because of the rising price of coffee, indigenous petitioners did not complain in their petitions about the invasion of nonindigenous settlers. This was a large *resguardo* with relatively few inhabitants. In addition, the petitioners were not shy about expressing opposition to the missionary order's educational policy as we saw above and manifested a strong sense of allegiance to Liberal Lopismo. The most accurate way to interpret this petition to dissolve the *resguardo* is that for the indigenous *resguardo* members of Cohetando the Liberal ideology was extremely attractive in that it promised landownership and equality. Furthermore, while it is true that the indigenous petitioners had internalized a racist understanding of what civilized meant, they did not seek to abandon their indigenous identity.

This attempt to redefine and reinvent an indigenous identity that allowed for modernity and the maintenance of indigeneity was apparent in the missive sent to central government. In November of 1945 the indigenous *cabildo* of Cohetando was unaware that the decree Resolution Number Five had passed and reiterated its support for the division of the *resguardo*. The indigenous council proclaimed proudly that the Indian race was a hardworking and forward-looking one and that they (the Indians) were the ones who had given value to the land that had been abandoned by the national government.[54] There was no inherent contradiction in asserting their indigeneity as well as their desire for individual landownership and for progress for this indigenous *cabildo*. The importance of land and the unique tie that indigenous rural folk asserted that they possessed in later decades was also evident in this missive. They stated, "In one word, we wish to be the owners of what is our own life and energy; of all that constitutes the patrimony of all our families for centuries."[55] However, in the 1930s and 1940s, this tie with the land did not necessarily have to be based on collective landownership.

The capacity or willingness to reinvent an indigenous identity was not present in the Liberal state of the 1940s, which stemmed in part from the rigid racist categories it was wedded to. The Liberal central government remained obstinately unaware of the reality of many indigenous rural folk who cultivated an individual land plot (even in the *resguardo* land structure) and who managed in most cases to maintain continuity of ownership from one generation to another. In addition, the Liberal state disregarded the tremendous work ethic of indigenous rural folk who worked tirelessly to eke out a living out of the land. Instead, Resolution number five stated,

> Absolute owner of his land plot, the indigenous person becomes more attached to it, he will feel the traditional attachment to what has been his only fountain of life, and he will be careful not to sell or lease his land plot to the mestizo for any pittance, as they have done under the communal land regime in which everything belongs to everybody and nothing belongs to someone, and in which each one longs to free himself by selling his hypothetical right for a few coins that at least give him the pleasure of savoring, though momentarily, the happiness of being the owner of something real and to foresee the possibility of changing them, for him and only him, for the small land plot that does respond faithfully to his efforts and his toil and within which he can indeed stake all those inherent attributes to the human personality within society.[56]

Case of Pedregal de Topa[57]

Setting

The *resguardo* of Topa was a very small one in terms of its population. It only had 117 families; a total number of 682 families lived on the *resguardo*.[58] According to the correspondence, Topa's land was very fertile second only to Turmina in the area of Tierradentro; coffee, sugar cane, and plantains were cultivated.[59] A major road from La Plata to Belalcázar was close by as well, which similarly to the case of Cohetando made land plots valuable. The *resguardo*'s proximity to Huila also placed it in a key economic corridor.

Process of Division

In the first round of correspondence in May of 1939 between the Ministry of Economia Nacional and the indigenous council, the indigenous council rejected the division of the *resguardo*.[60] The entire community summoned in a general meeting had voiced its disapproval of the proposed measure of dissolving the *resguardo*. The indigenous council expressed its dismay that a government that called itself democratic could consider adopting the measure of dissolving the *resguardos* when the disastrous results of this policy could be seen in the Huila and Tolima departments. The indigenous council went on to say that most probably all of the original owners/members of the *resguardos* in Tolima and Huila had been left without land because the "civilized" (referring to nonindigenous people) had taken advantage of the ignorance and weakness of indigenous people.

The members of the indigenous council also stated that while they were uninformed about the approximate size of the *resguardo*, they did know that a significant portion of the *resguardo*'s territory (granted to them by the Spanish Crown) had been declared public land (which was illegal). The implication was twofold: one that the indigenous community of Topa had already suffered a loss of territory, and the other was that the dissolution of the *resguardo* could be problematic.

Five years later in August 1944, the indigenous council of Topa had changed its mind about the proposed dissolution of the *resguardo*.[61] The *resguardo* members did not wish to be considered minors and/or as inferior beings; they argued that they were unfairly deprived of the benefits that were granted to the "common Colombian." The indigenous petitioners' discourse suggested that indigenous people of Topa had accepted the dominant notion of the time that to be "Indian" was to be "inferior" or in any event "primitive." However, they refused to identify with this primitive status, and instead presented themselves as capable citizens who were deserving of the same benefits available to nonindigenous Colombians.

In particular, the benefits available to settlers who (in theory) through Law 200 of 1936 could own land they had settled on were especially attractive to these indigenous petitioners. The council of Topa mentioned how indigenous people of talent who had settled on public land enjoyed free and tranquil possession of their land, house, and crops. This peaceful possession was in contrast to the indigenous *resguardo* member who (according to these petitioners) was at the mercy of the indigenous council who could adjudicate his property to another member at any time. In addition, indigenous *resguardo* members found it difficult if not impossible to obtain loans and technical assistance (because they "leased" the land rather than owning it) from institutions such as the *Caja de Credito Agraria* and the *Instituto de Fomento Territorial.*

When indigenous petitioners presented themselves as settlers of the frontier areas of Colombia, they were not only reinventing the racial definition of an indigenous person, but also challenging the notion that the vigorous and successful settler of public lands was always an Antioqueño. As Appelbaum, Roldán, Sanders, Safford, and Wade have shown, blackness and Indianess were associated with backwardness, whereas the Antioqueño settler was equated with whiteness and progress. The close correlation between the deserving citizen (who could obtain benefits) and his racial status was upended by the claim and reality of indigenous rural folk who settled on public land. For these indigenous petitioners this was not a claim with abstract consequences; the assertion that indigenous rural folk were also settlers of public land was followed by a request that the central government establish research farms on *resguardo* land, furnish seeds for crops, build housing on adjudicated land plots, and provide access to expert agricultural advice. Unfortunately for the indigenous people of Cohetando and for most rural Colombians, the central state would not only fall short in terms of providing benefits during the 1940s, but it would also abandon settlers to their fate when they were violently dispossessed of their land and of all improvements (*mejoras*) made to the land.[62]

While the indigenous council of Topa was attracted to the Liberal state's promises of increased resources and access to land, these letter writers did not intend to use the Colombian Liberal ideology to challenge the local reigning social and economic order. The petitioners requested that the breakup of the *resguardo* leave the division of land plots intact, which signified that those better off within the *resguardo* would maintain their privileged status. The request for leaving the land plot boundaries intact also signaled the possibility that the representatives of the council in 1944 were of a more conservative viewpoint than the council representative of 1939 who opposed the breakup of the *resguardo.*

In 1946 the indigenous council continued to petition for the breakup of the *resguardo* expressing its concern about land invasions and its puzzlement with the fact that other *resguardos* such as Talaga and Guanacas were dissolved but not Topa, which had more fertile land.[63] Several telegrams requesting the processing of the division followed the July 1946 petition for the breakup of the *resguardo.* The delay in the processing of the division of the *resguardo* begs the questions of why was the indigenous council so insistent on the dissolution of communal landownership and why the delay?

Correspondence from the 1950s helps to clarify the answer to the two questions above. One stumbling block was the fact that the *resguardo* boundaries were ignored and that several large land plots were adjudicated (prior to any division of the *resguardo*) to nonindigenous settlers. Two significant terrains where towns were established (Yarumal and San Vincente) were within the official boundaries of the *resguardo*. In theory, once the *resguardo* was divided, its land could only be adjudicated to indigenous members of the *resguardo*, and thus the existence of large land plots belonging to nonindigenous people was problematic to say the least.

The council's inability to police the *resguardo*'s boundaries and to maintain the integrity of its territory was also evident within the *resguardo*. An indigenous council granted a nonindigenous person, Nepomuceno Pineda, membership status to the *resguardo* of Topa and adjudicated a land plot to him.[64] Mr. Pineda, who was a successful merchant, built an "elegant" house with an aqueduct (which was very unusual in those days) and encircled his property named "El Danubio" with barbed wire. Mr. Pineda then sold his property to a Ricardo Peña, who registered the property and the sale in a notary. Later indigenous councils were powerless to force Peña out according to the author of the report.

The date of the latest report was 1951, which meant that Colombia was in the midst of its civil war known as *La Violencia*. However, the report gave no explicit indication that the issue at hand was violence, but merely stated that the council was unable to carry out a judicial order against Peña. Even though the author of the report did not state this, we can deduce that Mr. Peña and Mr. Pineda before him enjoyed the support of the municipal authorities. As we saw earlier, the adjudication of land was first signed off by the indigenous council, but the municipal mayor also had to approve it as well. Therefore, the municipal mayor of Inzá must have approved the transaction between the indigenous council and Mr. Pineda knowing full well that Mr. Pineda was not an indigenous member of the *resguardo*. At the level of the indigenous council, it is difficult to say whether it was coercion or corruption; it was probably both.

In October of 1951 despite the tremendous documented irregularities present in land transactions concerning the *resguardo* of Topa, the Conservative government officially declared the *resguardo* of Topa a civil community settled on public land.[65] The Conservative government had adopted the same mechanism used by previous Liberal governments to dissolve collective landholding advancing that the community had lost its title and that the witnesses's declaration did not meet the burden of proof.

The conservative government not only used the same legal mechanism/executive decree that Liberal governments had utilized, it also adopted a traditional Liberal discourse. Ironically, the prior Liberal governments had stressed that they were not trying to take advantage of the indigenous people's weak legal status, but that they sought to solidify the tie between the indigenous rural folk and his land. Since Law 89 of 1890 was a Conservative law that placed indigenous people in the category of minors needing legal guidance for land matters, one would assume that the Conservative government would stress the role of the state as a protector. Instead, the discourse around the resolution breaking up the Topa *resguardo* compared the end of collective landholding and of the rule of Law 89 of 1890 to the abolition of slavery.[66]

Both the Liberal and Conservative Colombian states coincided on the notion that land ownership and its utilization were effective mechanisms to achieve citizenship. The resolution stated,

> All these compatriots are hardworking owners of land plots planted with coffee, sugar cane, and other crops of the area. They are lovers of bovine cattle raising, wool and equine horses, all these qualities of great value lead me to rule in favor of supporting these inhabitants' right to arrive at the state of freedom, ending the minor status to which law 89 of 1890 consigned them, and so that all may be given or assured of their land plots by way of legal allotment.[67]

CONCLUSION

In the 1930s, the López Pumarejo government made its presence felt throughout Colombia via its powerful discourse of agrarian reform and popular Liberalism. In the 1930s the Liberal nation-state wished to establish a stronghold in the countryside where Conservatives frequently dominated local politics. López Pumarejo's agrarian reform—although it had contradictory results as Catherine Legrand documents—sent thousands of settlers in search for "tierra baldía or public land." More importantly the discourse of agrarian reform sought to legitimize the small holder vis-à-vis the large landowner who was sometimes described as an impediment to progress; the ideal citizen was the settler on the frontier.

In addition, in the late 1930s and 1940s, the nation-state took on a new presence in Cauca when it started the process of the dissolution of *resguardos*. This governmental policy began a direct dialogue between the nation-state and indigenous rural folk. Indigenous councils were asked to pronounce a judgment on whether or not the dissolution of *resguardos* was desirable. In the previous chapter, the conversation between the central state and indigenous communities was very much dominated by Manuel Quintín Lame as well as by the local state. Anthropologists and historians have generally described the relationship between Liberals and indigenous rural folk as an antagonistic one because the Liberal state sought to break up/*parcelar* indigenous *resguardos* into family-owned plots. However, an analysis of this correspondence shows that Liberalism was seen as an effective tool to undermine local structures of power. According to the Liberal central state, the aim and rationale of this policy was to foment ownership amongst the indigenous rural folk, to destroy the colonial structures of the *resguardo* and *cabildo*/council that they perceived to be stifling individual initiative and entrepreneurship, and finally to give indigenous rural inhabitants a stake in the "new modern society" that Liberals hoped to create.

As we have seen, indigenous communities and councils responded to the Liberal state's initiative of dissolution of *resguardos* in a number of ways. Most indigenous communities rejected the division of their *resguardos* whereas others sought to continue the conversation with the central state to gain resources, to redress injustice, and to possibly gain an ally. In the process of this dialogue, indigenous communities also constructed alternative definitions of indigenous ethnic identity that were different from Manuel Quintin Lame's vision of indigenous ethnic identity. The suggestion that an indigenous person was an agent of progress and modernity in the 1930s was a revolutionary concept because it challenged the prevailing racial hierarchy and ideology that maintained that "mestizos" and "whites" were the bearers of progress and modernity.

Overall, the correspondence between the central state and indigenous councils demonstrated that indigenous communities and their councils were under considerable pressure; the presence of settlers, missionaries, and the increased power of municipalities all conspired to diminish the power of indigenous councils as well as to undermine the unity of communities.

NOTES

1. *El Liberal*, Friday, October 13, 1939, 2
2. *El Liberal*, Friday, October 6, 1939, 4.
3. Ibid.
4. Diego Castrillón Arboleda, *De la colonia al subdesarrollo* (Popayán: Editorial Universidad, 1970), 16.
5. Joanne Rappaport, *The Politics of Memory: Native Historical Interpretation in the Colombian Andes* (Durham: Duke University Press, 1998), 92.
6. Joanne Rappaport, *The Politics of Memory: Native Historical Interpretation in the Colombian Andes* (Durham: Duke University Press, 1998), 100.
7. Resolution of Fourth Conference of Indians and Campesinos celebrated in Cauca. August 31 and September 1, 1944 in Popayán. The statement was sent to Justo Diaz Rodriguez, the director of the Department of Tierras. Ministerio del Interior—Asuntos Indígenas—now located in Archivo General de La Nación, Sala Republica.
8. Gregorio Hernández de Alba, "El Instituto Etnologico del Cauca," *Boletín Bibliográfico de Antropología Americana* 10 (January-December 1947), 20–22. The Institute was directly affiliated with the University of Cauca, but collaborated with the Ministry of Education. Its objectives were not solely academic as article 8 of its founding charter made clear; it had an *indigenista* section devoted to the study of indigenous people's social problems and to finding solutions for the inclusion of indigenous people into the nation.
9. Ibid.

10. An initial report listed sixty-one *resguardos* in the department of Cauca according to a letter from the Governor of Cauca, dated May 6, 1935, to the Ministry of Industria y Trabajo. This table is based on the reports of October 5, 1937, that placed the number of *resguardos* at fifty-six and sixty-one in May 6, 1935.

11. See Isidro Vanegas, "International Links to Early Socialism in Colombia," *Latin American Perspectives*, issue 159, vol. 35, no. 2, March 2008 (25–38), for an insightful analysis of the early Left in Colombia. Also see Renan Vega Cantor for an excellent overview of land struggles in the 1920s in Colombia.

12. Richard Stoller, "Alfonso Lopez Pumarejo and Liberal Radicalism in 1930s Colombia" *Journal of Latin American Studies* 27, no. 2 (May, 1995), 367–97.

13. See Catherine Legrand's *Frontier Expansion and Peasant Protest in Colombia, 1850–1936* (Albuquerque: University of New Mexico Press, 1986).

14. Francisco Beltrán Peña, *La utopia mueve montañas. Alvaro Ulcue Chocue* (Bogotá: Editorial Nueva America, 1989), 92.

15. Jose Maria Rojas and Elias Sevilla Casas, "El campesinado en la formación territorial del suroccidente colombiano" in *Territorios, regiones, sociedades*, ed. Renán Silva (Bogotá, Colombia: Cerec, 1994), 173. Sevilla Casas and his coauthor state the Liberal elite of Cauca was at a disadvantage compared to the Conservative elite of the neighboring departments because of their opposition to the central Conservative government.

16. Chaux had attended the Seminario Conciliar of Popayán that was run by the Lazarist order and even considered becoming a priest (earlier in his life) much to his father's disapproval. See Abel Cruz Santos, *Francisco Jose Chaux y su tiempo* (Bogotá: Caja de Credito Agrario, 1981), 85–86.

17. See Troyan (2007) and Troyan (2008a) for a discussion of Gregorio Hernández de Alba's life as well as a discussion of Colombian *indigenismo*.

18. The archive that I researched in 1999 in the Ministerio de Interior in Bogotá had just finished compiling the documents that I looked at and was in the process of transferring files to the Archivo General de la Nación. Consequently, the numbers of the files (which were organized by cajas whose documents did not have page numbers) are not necessarily valid for the *Archivo General de la Nación* where these files are now located. These files are now all located in the AGN and in the Sala Republica and are catalogued based on the names of the *resguardos* or under the Department of Cauca.

19. Report from Governor of Cauca dated May 6, 1935, addressed to Ministerio de Industria y Trabajo and Report from Governor of Cauca, dated October 7, 1935, also addressed to Ministerio de Industria y Trabajo. Caja 2637. *Ministerio de Gobierno/Division de Asuntos Indígenas Archive*.

20. Examples of this "first" letter asking for this documentation can be found in many files of the Resguardos that were "extinguished." It can be found, for instance, in the file on Resguardo Indígena El Pedregal de Topa, which I discuss later. Resguardo Indígena El Pedregal de Topa. AGN SR. Letter sent by Francisco Ruiz departamento de Tierras. Sección de Colonizacion. Republica de Colombia. Ministerio de Agricultura y Comercio. Bogotá April 25, 1939. Addressed to the Sr. Presidente del Cabildo De la Parcialidad de Indígenas de Topa, Inzá Cauca.

21. I gathered the information about the process of division of *resguardos* from my general research of primary documents. Maria Teresa Findji also explains how Paez Indians (now referred to as Nasa) had always cultivated in a family unit. She points out that it was the Spaniards who forced a "collective" tribute on the Paez Indians by asking each *resguardo* to produce a specified tribute. See "Tras las huellas de los Paeces" in *Encrucijadas de Colombia America Amerindia* (Bogotá: Instituto Colombiano de Antropología , 1993) 49–69.

22. Notes on Coconuco. Field Diary. Gregorio Hernandez de Alba archive. Biblioteca Luis Angel Arango, p. 53. All the information that follows about the process of allotting land to a family was taken from this diary. Although the informant was from Coconuco, the process was probably the same regardless of where the *resguardo* was located.

23. Maria Teresa Findji, *Elementos para el estudio de los resguardos indígenas del Cauca-Censo indígena del Cauca* (Bogotá: DANE, 1978), 7.

24. Enrique Chaux, letter dated October 5, 1937. Resguardo Chapa, Municipio de Tambo, Departamento del Cauca. AGN. Sala Republica.

25. Resguardo Chapa, Municipio de Tambo, Departamento del Cauca, AGN, SR.

26. Letter from Cabildo/Tomas Mambascoy (president of cabildo) to Ministro de Industrias, dated August 12, 1937. Resguardo Chapa, Municipio de Tambo, Departamento del Cauca. Archivo General de la Nación. Sala Republica.

27. Letter from Enrique Chaux, Gobernacion del Departamento del Cauca to the Señor Ministro de Industrias de Bogota, dated Popayan October 5, 1937. Resguardo Chapa, Municipio de Tambo, Departamento del Cauca. AGN. SR.

28. Enrique Chaux went as far as to say that indigenous people felt an even greater love for their land even if they were organized in *parcialidades*, which is an argument that was later made by twentieth-century activists for indigenous rights in Cauca that indigenous people had the greatest love and tie to the land. However, in the twentieth-century context, this argument was used for collective landholding.

29. Resguardo Chapa, Municipio de Tambo, Departamento del Cauca. AGN. SR.

30. Resguardo Chapa, Municipio de Tambo, Departamento del Cauca. AGN. SR.

31. Luis Lasprilla to Governor of Caua, June 21, 1938, and requests the same information. Resguardo Chapa, Municipio de Tambo, Departamento del Cauca. AGN. SR.

32. Resguardo Chapa, Municipio de Tambo, Departamento del Cauca. AGN. SR. Letter from *Cabildo* of Chapa to Ministry of Agriculture and Commerce, April 26, 1939. "Para enviar estos documentos, primeramente deseamos se nos haga el importante favor de informamos si se ha designado la partida para atender a la división; pues al no estar votada la partida para los gastos, no tendría un resultado pronto como lo desea este cabildo. Lo que seria tambien abrir un paso a la opresión para progresar."

33. Resguardo Chapa, Municipio de Tambo, Departamento del Cauca. AGN. SR.

34. Resguardo Chapa, Municipio de Tambo, Departamento del Cauca. AGN. SR. Letter sent by indigenous people of Chapa, dated October 29, 1942, addressed to Procurador de la Nación.

35. Resguardo Chapa, Municipio de Tambo, Departamento del Cauca. AGN. SR. All the information about the engineer and the accusation of violation of procedures came from the same letter to the Attorney General.

36. Resguardo Chapa, Municipio de Tambo, Departamento del Cauca. AGN. SR. Efrain Idrobo Rengifo Alcalde municipal del Tambo, dated October 17, 1962. A letter from the mayor indicated that the titles would have been distributed to the landplot owners in response to the government's query about where these titles were.

37. Raul Arango-Enrique Sanchez, *Los Pueblos Indígenas de Colombia 1997: desarollo y territorio* (Colombia: TM Editores, 1998) in the table of Resguardos y Reservas Indígenas por departamentos Poblacion y Area segun año de Constitución, Junio 30 de 1997, no page number in Appendix.

38. Censo de la Parcialidad Indígena de Cohetando del Municipio de Paez, Departamento del Cauca. "Extinción de Resguardo Cohetando Cauca," AGN/Sala Republica. Letter addressed to Señor Secretario del Ministerio de Economía Naciónal, Bogotá, from the *cabildo*, dated May 30, 1939.

39. Findji, 193. Fedecafeteros, Censo 1932.

40. *Notas de Viajes a Tierradentro*. Archivo Gregorio Hernandez de Alba. Biblioteca Luis Angel Arango.

41. Letter from the indigenous council and other members of the resguardo to the Ministerio de Economía Nacional. "Extinción de Resguardo Cohetando Cauca," AGN/Sala Republica, dated May 30, 1939.

42. Correspondence starts on April 25, 1939. From the secretary of Ministro de Agricultura y Comercio/Republica de Colombia, letter to President of Cabildo of Parcialidad of Indigenous of Cohetando. "Extinción de Resguardo Cohetando Cauca," AGN/Sala Republica.

43. Letter from the indigenous council and other members of the *resguardo* to the Ministerio of Economía Nacional. "Extinción de Resguardo Cohetando Cauca," AGN/Sala Republica, dated May 30, 1939.

44. Letter from the indigenous council and other members of the *resguardo* to the Ministerio of Economía Nacional. "Extinción de Resguardo Cohetando Cauca," AGN/Sala Republica, dated May 30, 1939.

45. Letter from the indigenous council and other members of the *resguardo* to the Ministerio of Economía Naciónal. "Extinción de Resguardo Cohetando Cauca," AGN/Sala Republica, dated May 30, 1939.

46. Letter to the President of the Republic, Dr. Alfonso López, dated March of 1943. Precise day of March was not legible from "indígenas of Cohetando." Long list of signatures follow the letter. "Extinción de Resguardo Cohetando Cauca," AGN/Sala Republica.

47. Jorge Mario Eastman, "Eduardo Santos, 1888–1974," *Boletín de historia y Antiguedades* 92, no. 829—June 2005.

48. Letter from the Cabildo of Cohetando, dated February 12, 1940, to the Senor Ministro de Economía Naciónal in Bogotá. "Extinción de Resguardo Cohetando Cauca," AGN/Sala Republica.

49. Letter from Pedro Perez, Gobernador de la Parcialidad to Ministro de Economía Naciónal, dated November 4, 1941. Extinción de Resguardo Cohetando Cauca," AGN/Sala Republica.

50. Letter from Justo Diaz Rodriguez/Jefe del Departamento de Tierras, dated November 7, 1941, to the governor of Parcialidad of Indígenas of Cohetando Paez.

51. "Extinción de Resguardo Cohetando Cauca," AGN/Sala Republica.

52. Letter from Ministro/Secretary J. V. Garces Navas to the Notario, dated March 7, 1939. Two articles stated clearly that notarios are supposed to deliver titles for free; Article 29 of Law 89 of 1890 and art. 26 of Law 19 of 1890 according to the J.V Garces Navas.

53. Extinción de Resguardo Cohetando Cauca," AGN/Sala Republica.

54. Extinción de Resguardo Cohetando Cauca," AGN/Sala Republica.

55. "En una palabra queremos ser propietarios de aquello que es nuestra propia vida y energia; de aquello que constituye el patrimonio de siglos de todas nuestras familias."

56. "Extinción de Resguardo Cohetando Cauca," AGN/Sala Republica. "Dueño absoluto de su parcela, el indígena se arraiga más a ella, volverá a sentir ese apego tradicional a la que ha sido su única fuente de vida, y se cuidará de traspasarla al mestizo por cualquier mendrugo, como lo han hecho bajo el regimén comunal en que todo es de todos y nada es de nadie, y en que cada cual anhela libertarse vendiendo su hipotético derecho por unas cuantas monedas que al menos le den el gusto de saborear, aunque sea transitoriamente, la dicha de sentirse propietario de algo real y de entrever la posibilidad de cambiarlas, para él y solo él, por una pequeña parcela que si responda fielmente a sus esfuerzos y fatigas y dentro de la cual si pueda poner en juego aquellos atributos inherentes a la personalidad humana en la plenitud de sus funciones de relación."

57. Referred to as Topa from now on.

58. Official document of Ministerio of Agricultura y Comercio, dated Bogotá, January 15, 1940. Titulo: "Proceso de Extinción del Resguardo Indígena El Pedregal de Topa," Archivo General de la Nación, Sala Republica.

59. Letter received July 27, 1946, from the *cabildo* of Pedregal de Topa to the Ministerio. Titulo: "Proceso de Extinción del Resguardo Indígena El Pedregal de Topa," Archivo General de la Nación, Sala Republica.

60. Letter from Presidencia del Cabildo de Indígenas del la Parcialidad. Topa, May 25, 1939, addressed to Minister of Economía Naciónal. Titulo: "Proceso de Extinción del Resguardo Indígena El Pedregal de Topa," Archivo General de la Nación, Sala Republica.

61. Letter dated August 18, 1944, to the minister of Economía Naciónal from the indigenous council of Topa. Titulo: "Proceso de Extinción del Resguardo Indígena El Pedregal de Topa," Archivo General de la Nación, Sala Republica.

62. Catherine Legrand, *Frontier Expansion*.

63. Letter from the indigenous council of Topa to the Ministro de Economía Naciónal, July 2, 1946. Titulo: "Proceso de Extinción del Resguardo Indígena El Pedregal de Topa," Archivo General de la Nación, Sala Republica.

64. Inzá, August 6, 1951. Letter to the director of Recursos Naturales of the Ministerio of Agricultura and Ganaderia from Carlos Hurtado/representative of the Comision Divisora de

Resguardos Indígenas de Tierradentro. Titulo: "Proceso de Extinción del Resguardo Indígena El Pedregal de Topa," Archivo General de la Nación, Sala Republica.

65. Resolution number 35, October 2, 1951, using article 14 of Decree-Law 1421 of 1940. Titulo: "Proceso de Extinción del Resguardo Indígena El Pedregal de Topa," Archivo General de la Nación, Sala Republica.

66. "y los indígenas quedaran libertados del imperio de la ley 89 del 1890 y demás normas legales que rigen los Resguardos, recobrando automaticamente todos los derechos inherentes al común de los ciudadanos con el derecho preferencial de adquirir del Estado el titulo de adjudicación . . ./and the indigenous people will be free from the rule of law 89 of 1890 and other legal norms that govern the resguardos, recovering automatically all the rights inherent to the average common citizen with the preferential right to acquire from the State the title of allotment."

67. Todos estos compatriotas son laboriosos dueños de parcelas cultivadas con café, caña deazúcar y otros cultivos de la zona. Son amantes de la cria de ganado vacuno, lanar y caballar, todas estas cualidades de gran valor me dan derecho a conceptuar a que sus habitantes lleguen a un estado de libertad, acabando con el titulo de menores como expresa la ley 89 de 1890 y que a todos se les dé o asegure sus parcelas por medio de adjudicaciones legales.

Chapter Four

The 1950s

La Violencia in Cauca, State Responses, and Riochiquito

NATIONAL CONTEXT

La Violencia is a term used to describe the period of conflict (from 1948 to 1960) in Colombia that resulted in massive numbers of deaths, displacements, and loss of property (in particular land). The distinguishing feature of *La Violencia* was that the opposing camps were organized by partisan affiliation; in other words Liberals fought against Conservatives. Paul Oquist, the first author to provide serious statistical evidence, estimated the number of dead due to *La Violencia* at 200,000.[1] There is no clear agreement amongst historians and social scientists about when *La Violencia* ended; indeed, some historians have argued that *La Violencia* never ended in Colombia, but instead mutated into new forms of violence.

The starting date for *La Violencia* is debated in equal measure. Some historians identify the first rumblings of *La Violencia* as taking place in 1930 when the Liberal government gained control of the central state after thirty years of exclusion. As Mary Roldán has pointed out, the election of Liberals to the central government in 1930 coincided with the growth of the central state, which increased stakes for its control.[2] As a consequence of the increased importance of partisan affiliation, violence along partisan lines erupted in the departments of Boyacá and Santander where Liberals took advantage of their national electoral victory to attack Conservatives forcing them to leave their political posts.[3]

A split in the Liberal Party enabled the Conservative Party and its candidate, Mariano Ospina Perez, to regain control of the central state in 1946 after sixteen years of Liberal rule. Despite President Ospina's moderate stance vis-à-vis the Liberals, partisan conflict did not abate. Radical members of the Conservative Party such as Laureano Gómez and disgruntled members of the Liberal Party engaged in heated and vindictive rhetoric. For instance, Laureano Gómez began to speak of 1.8 million voters with fake *cedulas* (identification cards) casting doubt on the legitimacy of the electoral process. The violence went beyond rhetoric in Boyacá and Santander where Conservatives retaliated against Liberals by physically attacking them and not allowing them to vote.

A defining moment and some would argue the beginning of *La Violencia* came on April 9, 1948, when Jorge Eliecer Gaitán, the charismatic and populist Liberal presidential candidate, was assassinated in Bogotá; an urban mob responded in anger to Gaitán's assassination by destroying the center of Bogotá. Urban unrest spread to other cities such as Cali (Valle del Cauca) and Caloto (Cauca), and to rural areas where Liberals dominated. *Gaitanistas* in Bogotá appealed via radio for the formation of revolutionary juntas throughout the country to create a New Revolutionary Order.[4] Rural and urban popular violence frightened the Colombian elite and signaled a widening of the partisan violence.[5]

The next turning point in the development of *La Violencia* was the presidential election of 1949. The Liberal Party pulled out of that year's presidential contest citing a lack of security for the Liberal electorate.[6] Running an unopposed presidential contest, Laureano Gómez (representing the right wing of the Conservative Party) became the President of Colombia in 1950. From 1950 to 1953 the national government implemented a campaign of forced conservatism, which resulted in the rise of right-wing paid assassins (known as *pájaros*) and to the emergence of peasant self-defense movements.

Moderate elites from both parties became fearful of the growing radicalization of popular violence, which led to their support of General Rojas Pinilla who cut short Gómez's term by deposing his government; General Rojas Pinilla governed Colombia as a military dictator from 1953 to 1957. At first, Colombians breathed a sigh of relief thinking that the military government would end conflict between the Conservative and Liberal Parties and bring about an enduring peace. One of Rojas Pinilla's first measures was to offer an unconditional amnesty to combatants of *La Violencia*.[7] As part of this campaign for amnesty, the military distributed leaflets promising peace and amnesty for the guerrillas who had taken up arms against Laureano Gómez's government.[8] While the government of Rojas Pinilla was successful in demobilizing guerilla armies in Tolima and the *Llanos Orientales*, levels of violence, which had tapered off, surged again between 1954 and 1958 constituting the second phase of *La Violencia*.

General Rojas Pinilla's growing political ambitions prompted the Liberal and Conservative parties to come to an agreement known as *Frente Nacion-*

al/National Front in order to neutralize the political threat posed by the populist general. The pact established that the Liberal and Conservative parties would alternate the presidency and share all other political posts equally. The stated motivation of this pact was to end the violence that was attributed to interparty conflict over political power; the unstated motivation was to stem the elite's loss of control over politics and the concomitant rise of social and economic instability in the countryside.

INTERPRETATION OF *LA VIOLENCIA*

Was *La Violencia* a civil war, a series of peasant uprisings, a "bourgeois revolution," or an elite's reactionary response to social change?[9] The traditional narrative explained *La Violencia* as due to an entrenched enmity between Liberals and Conservatives; partisan affiliation was more than a political choice, it was an identity. The underlying premise to this explanation of *La Violencia* was that the decision to join the Liberal and/or Conservative party was not a rational choice that the voter of the lower classes made by carefully evaluating which party best represented his interest; rather it was family tradition and/or place of origin that determined the partisan affiliation. During the period of *La Violencia*, the partisan identity took on a new importance and led to the indiscriminate killing of partisan rivals. Oral history accounts often confirmed the power of partisan identity and documented how wearing the wrong color (red for Liberals and blue for Conservatives) at the wrong place could mean death in some areas of Colombia during *La Violencia*. Since much of *La Violencia* took place in rural areas, the image of the semi-illiterate peasant fighting in the name of some pre-modern identity was a prevalent one in the traditional narrative about *La Violencia*.[10]

The continuing violence after the Liberal and Conservative Parties agreed to alternate power in 1958, however, undermined explanations that attributed *La Violencia* mainly to partisan enmity. The "New History" of Colombia written in the 1970s and 1980s suggested new ways to interpret *La Violencia*; a series of regional studies of *La Violencia* provided the basis for this new direction. My intention here is not to cover the entire historiography on *La Violencia*, but to discuss the literature that relates and connects the themes of state formation with the development of *La Violencia*.

As Catherine Legrand stated in her seminal article "La Politica y La Violencia En Colombia (1946–1965): Interpretaciones En La Decada de Los Ochenta," Oquist was the scholar who brought the central state into the discussion of *La Violencia*. The author of *Violence, Conflict, and Politics in Colombia* advanced that the Colombian central state expanded during the 1920s and 1930s, but that it suffered a partial breakdown due to conflictive partisan interests and to intense competition over new political spaces. Thus, violence spiraled out of control due to the partial breakdown of the central state.

While Oquist made a major contribution by bringing the state into the discussion of *La Violencia*, Carlos Ortiz and Daniel Pecaut pointed out that Oquist's reading of the Colombian central state was based on the flawed notion that the Colombian central state was a cohesive and homogeneous actor.[11] In contrast, Carlos Ortiz, who wrote a seminal regional study about *La Violencia* in Quindío, suggested that the Colombian state was "immersed in fragmented and heterogeneous power networks, where central points of power multiply themselves and dilate, and where the State and its repressive squads only bring about part of the violence."[12] Ortiz's major contribution was to transform our understanding of the Colombian central state; he argued that the central state was not simply the agent of a ruling class whose aim was to repress grassroots organization and to preserve its economic privileges. Ortiz's earlier work on Quindio also demonstrated the crucial role that intermediaries (often shopkeepers converted into merchants) played during *La Violencia* in the dispossession of land, goods, and coffee.[13] In the case of Quindio, merchants, because they were able to acquire land, goods, and coffee at very low prices from victims of *La Violencia*, constituted a new middle class. Ironically, as a result of *La Violencia*, land tenure patterns became more democratic in this region. Ortiz's regional study showed how the central state did not impose a specific agenda, but rather was shaped and molded by different actors and regional forces.

Pecaut also argued that the Colombian central state's formation was uneven and that in areas outside of Bogotá, political parties were the state.[14] Here it is necessary for us to return to the period of the 1930s when the arrival of new political actors democratized national Colombian politics.[15] As we have seen in the previous chapter, Jorge Eliecer Gaitán transformed Colombian politics with his populist style that drew upon his close identification with "el pueblo." As Herbert Braun compellingly argues, Jorge Eliecer Gaitán challenged the terms of political inclusion and changed the tone of Colombian politics; the effect of *Gaitánismo* was the splintering of the Liberal Party into various factions. If we accept Pecaut's notion that outside of Bogotá, the "state" was the political parties, the splintering and ultimately the assassination of Gaitán led to the collapse of a crucial "network" à la Ortiz in regions and subregions where Liberals predominated.

Another counterargument to Oquist's interpretation of *La Violencia* is that the partial collapse of the central state did not necessarily produce a vacuum of authority at the local and regional levels.[16] In other words, there was not a vacuum of political power, which produced violence, but rather that the regional state (in places where it had a significant presence) acquired a new importance. Roldán examined the case of Antioquia where she showed that violence was significantly concentrated in a small number of municipalities; in the first phase of *La Violencia*, electoral competition caused violence in municipalities and towns where the numbers of Liberals and Conservative voters were roughly equal.[17] In the later stages of *La Violencia*, violence became particularly severe in municipalities that were viewed as culturally distinct by the regional government of Antioquia; Roldán called these municipalities peripheral.[18]

Through an examination of state formation, violence, and ethnicity in Cauca, this chapter will address the debate outlined above. The first part of the chapter examines violence along partisan lines, whereas the second part of the chapter examines how the central state attempted the mitigation of conflict around land through the formation of the Tribunals of Reconciliation and Equity with ineffectual results. Finally, the third part of the chapter examines the central state's response to the *Republica Independiente de Riochiquito*, which was a "self-defense" community composed of both indigenous and nonindigenous rural folk as well as *bandoleros*.

LA VIOLENCIA IN CAUCA

To the best of my knowledge there is no regional study of *La Violencia* in Cauca, thus my description of the overall process of *La Violencia* relies on a limited number of sources. The limited number of secondary sources which cover *La Violencia* in Cauca most likely stems from the relatively low number of reported casualties in the first wave of *La Violencia*. From 1946 to 1957, the number of reported fatalities in Cauca was low compared to other regions; Cauca does not even make the list as one of the ten most affected departments in Oquist's table, "Distribution of Violencia Fatalities for the Ten Most Affected Departments Affected by Violence."[19] The tenth department in this table was Cundinamarca with 4,033 deaths.[20]

However, in the second phase of *La Violencia* (1958–1966), as Oquist's table of Departmental Distribution of *Violencia* Fatalities, 1958–1966 documents, Cauca emerged as the seventh most affected department with 457 deaths.[21] Indeed, other documents produced by the *Tribunal of Reconciliation and Equity* stated that Cauca was considered one of the departments with the worst violence in the country, and therefore was selected to be one of the five departments to receive these tribunals.

The available secondary literature that refers to *La Violencia* in Cauca centers on the subregion of Tierradentro; the number of cases by municipality reported by the Tribunal of Reconciliation and Equity confirms that Tierradentro (made up of the municipalities of Belalcázar and Inzá) accounted for a large number of reported cases.[22] However, the municipality where the most cases were brought forward was Toribio. Here, what might explain the slight disjuncture between firsthand accounts and statistics compiled by the

Tribunal is a question of chronology. The statistics available from the Tribunal of Reconciliation and Equity include cases all the way up to 1961, whereas eyewitness accounts and published secondary sources focus on the early period of *La Violencia*.

Indeed, it was logical that the first wave of *La Violencia* should hit Tierradentro especially hard since the indigenous people of Tierradentro had been intimately involved in partisan politics since the nineteenth century.[23] In 1912, the effect of partisan politics deepened when indigenous men were given the right to vote in the elections of councilmen, deputies, assembly representatives, and congressmen.[24] That, according to Father David González, indigenous people were given the right to vote for these elections, was surprising in a national context where from 1914 to 1936 only men who were literate and who met an income requirement could vote for these elections. National universal male suffrage was only granted in 1936.[25]

To be more specific and accurate, violence hit the municipality of Belalcázar/Páez hardest in comparison to the municipality of Inzá (these two municipalities make up Tierradentro). Nine cases were brought forward to the Tribunal of Conciliation and Equity versus the twenty-nine cases that the Páez municipality received. Sutti Reissig Ortiz who did her fieldwork in San Andres, Tierradentro, confirms that violence hit the municipality of Belalcázar especially hard; she states that a large percentage of the male population of Belalcázar died in a battle during the first period of *La Violencia*.[26] The town and surrounding area where she did her fieldwork, San Andres, was an enclave of liberalism and of peace surrounded by other areas where partisan fighting and banditry were common.[27] The indigenous members of the Mosoco *resguardo* located in the Belalcázar municipality took refuge in San Andres.[28]

Oral history published relatively recently sheds further light on the early stages of *La Violencia*. As seen in the very first stage of *La Violencia*, violence was expressed along partisan lines. Jorge Eliecer Gaitán's assassination in 1948 in Bogotá led to an immediate reaction in Liberal towns and municipalities where there was an attempt to organize Revolutionary Liberal committees and groups to respond to Gaitán's assassination.[29] The Conservative government quickly organized a campaign of terror that aimed at repressing any organizational attempt on the part of Liberals.[30]

A crucial element to this campaign of terror carried out by the government was the firing of all police officers that were Liberals and the hiring of officers who were Conservative and who were mostly from the departments of Boyacá and Cundinamarca.[31] These officers became known as *Chulavitas* because many of these men came from the town of Chulavita in Boyacá.[32]

In his testimony Juan Palechor (one of most prominent indigenous leaders of the CRIC) recounted how he had campaigned for Jorge Eliecer Gaitán and was committed to Gaitánismo liking both Gaitán's political message and his nickname "El Indio." Juan Palechor was able to escape possibly his execution or in any event his imprisonment by staying away from the town of the *resguardo* of Guachicono and by not being at home when "they" (presumably the authorities) came to get him. In particular, the conservative regime attacked the leaders of the agrarian leagues present in the north of Cauca and assassinated José Gonzalo Sánchez (cofounder with Manuel Quintín Lame of the *Supremo Consejo de Indias* as well as right-hand man during the Manuel Quintín Lame movement) in 1952.[33] An integral part of the state campaign of terror was to force everyone to vote Conservative and for Laureano Gómez.[34] Lorenzo Muelas's father (Guambiano/Misak indigenous activist who became a Senator) also participated in the Gaitanista movement; his son explained his father's affection for the Liberal Party as one that was not clearly understood, but that was nonetheless deeply felt. He states, "When the violence of 1948 came, when all the killings of the Paeces in Tierradentro came, when there was also the killing of Guambianos, one of the three Liberal Guambianos were shot in the center of the town of Silvia. My father was also on the list. Because he was trained to be devoted to the Liberals; he said that since he was a child he liked to cheer for the Liberal Party, that he did not know what the Liberal party was but he liked it. And he was a Liberal. And he was a *Gaitanista*, and he said that affected him a great deal, that he regretted the death of Gaitán a great deal. That if nothing had happened to him (meaning Gaitán), Colombia would have been different, that for the peasant it would have been different. I say who knows? Who knows what would have happened if Gaitán had become president? If it would have been different? If it would have been the same? Who knows? That is why my father left, he was in Mondomo, he was hiding out in the mountains, waiting for time to go by."[35]

Senator Lorenzo Muelas's take on his father's partisan affiliation should be viewed in light of his own disaffection with the traditional political system. This quote shows how the prominent leaders of the Misak community who were Liberals were summarily shot no doubt as an example to the rest of the Liberals. Lorenzo Muelas's father was able to escape the assassination attempt by hiding out in Mondomo, which is located in *tierra caliente* and where his father owned a plot of land.

The most chilling events took place in Belalcázar. As seen previously, Sutti Reissig Ortiz mentioned a battle that took place in the town of Belalcázar, but the most commonly referred-to event is that of the massacre that took place in 1949 where 112 people were killed in one day by military troops and police officers/chulavitas.[36] Johnny Delgado Madroñero mentions how there was no press coverage of this massacre unlike other killings and massacres that took place in Valle del Cauca and that the only official document that memorializes this massacre is the Guzman book. Father David González refers to a massacre that took place in Belalcázar, but he described the execution of eleven men (not 112) on the bridge of Cuetando and who were then thrown into the Páez River.[37]

Father David González who was a Conservative depicted how the process of transforming Belalcázar into a conservative district was a horrific one. Various methods of terror were implemented. The first was where "educated men" instructed the "masses" to hunt down Liberals; Father David González states,

> The main speaker, a man with a university diploma, with a high level official position, from a balcony, revolver in hand, harangued: "Conservative people, Liberals must be hunted down like fierce looking animals, we have to squash them like rats, have you heard? Have you understood?"—"Yes Sir, and we shall do it." The angry crowd cried out.[38]

The second tool used by the central state during this time period was to appoint military Conservative mayors regardless of whether the majority of the municipality had voted Conservative or Liberal. In 1949, Santos Rincón, a sinister man from Boyacá, was appointed as head of the Belalcázar municipality; the rationale given to the appointment of mayors was that order would be restored, which would quell the popular uprising in Liberal municipalities after Gaitán's death.[39] The appointment of a stranger to the community who held significant power over the municipality and who had no ties to the region was a disaster and only led to the deepening of hatreds and resentments. The newly appointed mayor, Santos Rincón, harassed and humiliated local Liberal authorities (judge and council representatives) by jailing them and forcing them to sweep the streets.[40] Accompanied by the police force, he then proceeded to visit the home of Liberals to beat the unfortunate residents who had stayed and stole their food along with any possessions. The head of the household was then locked up in a room with no food or drink for two days; after this period, the mayor with a gun in the left hand and a crucifix in the right hand would force the Liberal to swear allegiance to the Conservative party on his knees. The military mayor continued to terrorize the Liberal population by placing sticks of dynamite in their homes and with military parades of recruits who chanted loudly and held machetes under their ruanas.

The campaign of terror that was indiscriminate and that attacked prominent Liberals horrified even Conservatives such as Father David González and led to the request for the removal of Santos Rincon. However, only when eleven men were executed and thrown into the river Páez did the national government send a commission to investigate the events.[41] Initially, the two colonels in charge of the investigation stated that they were unable to apportion responsibility, and it was only with the arrival of Dr. Quintero (described as an honest lawyer) that Santos Rincon's role was revealed and that he was removed from office. However, justice was never served since the poor Dr.

Quintero was the object of many complaints whereas Santos Rincon escaped to Ecuador without ever facing justice.[42]

As horrific as the events were in Belalcázar, worse was happening in the countryside and appears to have been largely left undocumented and unremembered in the official record. Indigenous men, women, and children who were from Liberal areas were rounded up and taken into cars; they were then killed and thrown into the rivers.[43] Juan Palechor pointed out that the Catholic Church, Monsignor Vallejo (one of the highest representatives of the Catholic Church in Cauca), did not protect the indigenous people of the Páez municipality who were under his care; this is not surprising since, as we have seen, the Catholic Church was closely allied with the Conservative party's campaign of imposing conservatism.[44]

Indigenous people of Belalcázar who remained were placed under complete and humiliating control. A permit had to be obtained to buy a basic commodity such as a pound of salt, and a purchase of pants and a shirt had to be reported to the military commander. Benjamin Dindicue, quoted in Palechor, also described how *chulavitas*/police stole indigenous people's livestock, burned their houses, and in some cases killed indigenous *compañeros*.[45] Rape, although not mentioned in the official record, was a commonplace reality and fear for indigenous women, who hid when hearing that the soldiers were coming.[46] Stories about older women being raped instead of their daughters circulated amongst the community.[47] The point here was that not even older women were safe from soldier's attacks; there was also a hint to a racial dimension to the rape that becomes apparent when a soldier is quoted as saying that "old-coca chewing lady was pretty good." Since only indigenous people chewed coca leaves, the racial reference was clear.[48]

Another massacre took place in the *resguardo* of San José. Lieutenant Bustamante and Corporal Henoa were responsible for the killing of thirty-nine indigenous people; the accusation (possibly by Monsignor Vallejo) was made that guerrillas were hiding in or nearby the *resguardo* of San José.[49] Soldiers who were probably frustrated with their unsuccessful search for guerrillas retaliated by rounding up indigenous men. Ultimately, thirty-nine indigenous men were killed with bayonets and then thrown into the river.[50] The *San José* massacre was carried out in 1955, later than the Belalcázar one (1950). By the mid-1950s soldiers and police officers routinely accused indigenous people who resided in areas where guerrillas transited of being men of the mountains meaning guerrillas. Arbitrary arrest and executions of indigenous leaders were carried out; the official claim was made that these indigenous men "tried to escape."[51]

LAND ISSUES

During *La Violencia*, the land of Liberals was transferred not only to Conservatives but also to individuals who sought to take advantage of their neighbor's moment of political weakness. The other complication was that *La Violencia* exacerbated previous land conflicts that were already simmering in the 1930s and 1940s. The case of Caldono illustrates the layering of conflict.

Case of Caldono

The municipality of Caldono, which is located in the north of Cauca, continues to be a site of conflict and violence. The author of a relatively recent article narrates how a car bomb exploded near the police station of Caldono in May of 2011, and how 250 people were displaced due to the ongoing fighting between the army and guerrillas.[52] Even more recently on October 2, 2014, combats were taking place between the FARC guerrillas and the national government in the hamlet of Las Delicias located in the municipality of El Caldono, endangering the civilian population.[53]

In 1955, the indigenous community of the *resguardo* of Caldono sent a letter to the section of public lands indicating that tensions over land in Caldono had worsened in the mid-1950s.[54] The letter-writer stated that more tensions had arisen just as the indigenous community was about to benefit from the division of its *resguardo*. The central government had not carried out the division of the *resguardo*, and as a consequence the indigenous members of this *resguardo* were being evicted from their land plots. The discourse employed by the indigenous petitioner is particularly interesting because it juxtaposes the notion that the indigenous inhabitants of Colombia were the nation's first sons with the notion that the *resguardo*'s division would finally free them from oppression:

> The objective of the Commission sent by the National Government to parcel out our lands was thus to free us from the cruel and excessive oppression, as we who are Indians, are the first born of the Fatherland.[55]

This quote confirms the argument made in the second chapter that an indigenous identity was not always equated with collective property for some indigenous rural folk in the 1930s, 1940s, and 1950s. The following excerpt of the letter also allows us to understand that the process of division of *resguardos* was a disaster:

> The commission in charge of the Division does not fulfill its mission, and so as a result, we find ourselves in the distressed situation of starting to see ourselves stripped of the land that our ancestors left us, where we have worked

> peacefully to earn our daily bread, and where our sons and daughters, the legitimate owners of this land, will work.[56]

The letter-writers were not pleased with the national government's inability to carry out the division of *resguardo*. A series of letters between the different branches (Natural Resources-Public Land Section to the Commission in charge of the Division of *Resguardos*) of the Ministry of Agriculture leads us to understand that one of the stumbling blocks to the breakup of the *resguardo* was a large land plot called "La Llanada" where about one hundred individuals, mostly indigenous, had land plots with houses and coffee trees. According to Carlos Hurtado, these indigenous inhabitants came to see the Commission daily to request the adjudication of their land plots of La Llanada.

The division of this land plot was suspended because of a controversy around the boundaries of the *resguardo*. According to the indigenous inhabitants of La Llanada, this land plot was part of the *Caldono resguardo*, and they had sent the documentary evidence to prove this. Carlos Hurtado claimed that ill-intentioned people were pressuring indigenous settlers/*resguardo* members to sell their *mejoras*/improvements to the land at a low price telling them that they were about to lose everything (land and improvements) because the division was not being carried out. The government representative feared the outbreak of violence and of social conflict because of the suspension of the division due to the confusion around who were the legitimate owners of La Llanada.

One possible interpretation of the division of the *resguardo* during a period of violence is to see the national government in cahoots with the regional elite pressuring the indigenous inhabitants to go through with the division of the land. Juan Palechor (indigenous leader of CRIC) certainly remembers the events surrounding the division of the Caldono *resguardo* in such a manner. His recounting of the events is worth quoting in its entirety:

> After a few years we got news in the *resguardos*, in the *resguardo* of Caldono, for example, outsiders were using *politiqueria* to appropriate the lands of indigenous compañeros, taking advantage of all the power in the hands of the Conservatives. It was said that a national senator by the name of Mario S. Vivas was appropriating lands that belonged to Indians and terrorizing them by hauling them to jail and giving them water torture for three days, forcing them to say that the *resguardo* should be abolished or that land should be divided up and distributed, just wearing them down, forcing them to say that, even if it was out pure fright. Other compañeros left the area; they migrated and dispersed. That's how outsiders were able to grab land and get large properties. That's why there are large landowners in Caldono.[57]

Although Mario S. Vivas (who in the early 1950s was a lawyer) was involved in the process of the division of the Caldono *resguardo*, he was arguing against the process going forward.[58] It was not that he was opposed to the division of *resguardos* in theory; on the contrary when he wrote to Carlos Hurtado, he applauded the national government's intent to modernize the countryside via the breakup of *resguardos*.[59] His insistence that the breakup of the *resguardo* could not go through (as drafted) stemmed from the fact he did not want certain land plots included in this division because he claimed that some of these properties that were considered part of the *resguardo* belonged to him.[60]

Resolution number 36 that decreed the division of the *resguardo* of Caldono was a resolution that extinguished not only the *resguardo* of Caldono, but also Pioya, Pueblonuevo, La Aguada, and Pitayo because all these *resguardos* belonged to one *parcialidad* called *parcialidad* of San Lorenzo of Caldono; this initial resolution was dated November 14, 1953.[61] Mario S. Vivas insisted that the title used to establish the boundaries of the *resguardo* of Caldono was false; it was not possible because the title encompassed 150,000 hectares for only 12,000 indigenous people and not more than 2,000 whites. In case the Ministry of Agriculture was not swayed by his case, he added that the properties of Dr. Alfredo Navia and Dr. Alfonso Medina were within the supposed boundaries of the *resguardo*.

Dr. Alfredo Navia and Dr. Medina were both influential politicians. Dr. Alfredo Navia was a prominent Liberal politician from Santander de Quilichao who became a senator and who was governor of Cauca in the 1930s; Dr. Medina was nominated "abogado del Cauca" by Governor Simmonds in the 1960s.[62] Dr. Mario Vivas listed the names of many other landowners who would be negatively impacted by the breakup of the *resguardo* as drafted. Dr. Mario S. Vivas was not preoccupied that the central government would actually take his land or that of other prominent landowners because he had full confidence in the validity of his land titles and in that the police would protect him.

What concerned Dr. Mario Vivas was the impact of the news that the boundaries of the *resguardo* included the land of such prominent landowners on landless rural folk. The lawyer from Popayán stated that the ambition of all landless rural folk was to own land; he was particularly concerned with the reaction of indigenous people and stated,

> Indigenous people with flighty ideas who exist in great number in the central mountain range will have an incentive to threaten, as Quintín Lame and Pio Collo did a few years ago when they threatened the personal safety and life of the white inhabitants of all towns of the mountain range. Because it is advisable not to forget that in Colombia hatred of the Indian against the white is ancestral because he believes that he owes the loss of his lands and his economic situation to the white man, when the primordial cause lies in his lack of

> willingness to work and in the vices of coca and *guarapo* (a type of alcohol) that have damaged him biologically and spiritually.[63]

Dr. Mario Vivas was waving the threat of racial war with his false assertion that Manuel Quintín Lame's so-called rebellion had taken place recently; in reality in 1954 the events had taken place more than twenty-five years ago. Also ironically, he painted Pio Collo and Manuel Quintín Lame with the same brush, when Pio Collo had worked on behalf of the local government to hunt down Manuel Quintín Lame. Here, we can hypothesize that Pio Collo's liberal partisan affiliation along with his indigenous ancestry led Dr. Mario Vivas, a Conservative, to portray Pio Collo in a negative manner. His overall objective when reminding the national state of the Quintín Lame rebellion was to warn the national state that indigenous rural folk were dangerous and could rebel at any time. In addition, his characterization of indigenous people (which he called *indio*) as a race of lazy, drunk, and coca-addicted people delegitimized any possible claim the indigenous *resguardo* members had to the land.

While Dr. Mario Vivas was fully confident of the power of his political connections and of his place in society, the national government in 1954 was no longer in the hands of Conservatives, and General Rojas Pinilla was in charge. The mention of Dr. Alfredo Navia (as a landowner who was negatively impacted) was meant to defuse the charge of partisanship. In other words, since the north of Cauca was Liberal and in particular Caldono, Dr. Mario Vivas did not want his claims to be tainted with the issue of partisanship. Going back to Juan Palechor's statement, we can see that although Dr. Mario Vivas was racist and did take over land in an illegitimate manner, it was not an all-Conservative complot. This may seem like splitting hairs since the end result was that indigenous people lost their lands to the nonindigenous landowners. However, the crucial issue here is the position of the central state. In other words, the indigenous leader portrayed the central and local state as working in unison to achieve the expulsion of indigenous sharecroppers/members from *resguardo* land, but the reality was more complex in that the central state was not attempting to take land away from indigenous people. It was indeed trying to break up the *resguardo* while respecting the boundaries of the property outlined in the colonial title, but the proposed solution did not benefit the local elites either.

Carlos Hurtado pointed out that even if the boundaries of the *resguardo* were proven to be false (as drawn up), indigenous rural folk still had a claim to the land because they had occupied the land plot (La Llanada) for at least a century and had made significant improvements to the land. The *Ley de Tierras*/200 of 1936 protected the claims of these indigenous rural folk. The head of the commission stated,

> Accepting for the sake of argument that a ruling was made favoring the pretensions of the particular claimants, the compensation for the improvements would be worth more than the land itself; and a lawsuit for the recognition of these improvements would give rise to a considerable number of actions and exceptions since administratively one cannot resolve the validity or nullity of the titles that the parties demonstrate, (thus) one would have to conclude that the litigation would last many years. The sensitive or regrettable issue would be that return of the era of the law of the knife or of the stick used to dislodge the indigenous people of their possessions as it has happened in other days with the complicity of some authorities.[64]

Indeed, violent confrontations over land were already occurring. Indigenous residents of La Llanada had complained to the Commission of Division that they were being pressured into selling their *mejoras*/improvements to the property at a low price since the division had stalled. Carlos Hurtado also mentioned that two indigenous families that resided in Santander and La Aguada were assassinated for holding on to their land. Local authorities were depicted as impotent and ineffective when prosecuting those responsible for crimes; Carlos Hurtado requested that the Ministry of Justice send a special investigator for the crimes committed in Santander (located in the north of Cauca).

Worse yet, the quote above seemed to indicate that Carlos Hurtado thought that local authorities could be complicit in the violent expropriation of land (in other cases). In both Hurtado's and Palechor's versions violence was used as a tool to expropriate indigenous peasants, but the perpetrators of violence were not aided and abetted by the central government in Hurtado's version.

Carlos Hurtado portrayed the commission in charge of the breakup of the *resguardo* as acting on behalf of indigenous petitioners who wanted to go through with the division process; he mentioned that petitioners came daily. However, a full reading of the correspondence between Carlos Hurtado and the director of *Recursos Naturales* reveals a more complicated picture. The central government's representative was pushing aggressively for the division of the *resguardo* to go through. The head of the commission (to divide *resguardos*) mentioned how he had to search to find indigenous inhabitants to convince them of the desirability of dissolving the *resguardo*; he was also a racist calling indigenous people who opposed the division, "*mentes sencillas*/simple minds." Carlos Hurtado may have been trying to impress the central government with his prodigious activity recounting the conferences and meetings that he had organized and of his effectiveness in swaying the opinion of indigenous people; however, it is also likely that he did indeed encounter a great deal of resistance because by 1955 it had become extremely clear that the national government was completely ineffective and unable to adjudicate land in an efficient manner. The mention of "active maneuvers" on the part of the mayor of Caldono to convince indigenous people of the desirability of the process of division also undermines Hurtado's argument that the push for the breakup of the *resguardo* was an organic one.

Does it then follow that the indigenous people of Caldono were coopted and perhaps tortured (as Palechor suggests) into supporting the breakup of the *resguardo*? Palechor's testimony as well as the archival sources suggest that violence was omnipresent both in the form of forced expropriations, "active maneuvers" on the part of the mayor, and with assassinations. The archival record does show, however, that some indigenous people were in favor of the division since they wrote petitions to the national government; here careful attention to the correspondence helps to identify who was behind the petitions. Hurtado specifically mentions the octogenarians of La Llanada who were impatiently waiting for the adjudication of their land. It makes sense that the indigenous residents of La Llanada who had built houses and planted coffee were indeed pushing for the dissolution of the *resguardo* if it meant that they could hold on to the patrimony that generations of families had worked on. These indigenous inhabitants were hoping for an effective central state that would protect their patrimony through Law 200 of 1936. Carlos Hurtado, although a racist, also worked for this adjudication process that he thought would protect the interest of the hardworking indigenous farmer. The central state's representative was eager not only to show his value as an employee, but also to demonstrate that the central state was indeed going to protect legitimate claims to land. He was fully aware that every day that the central state failed to carry out its promises weakened the central state and consequently his position as well.

Conflict around land in Caldono was exacerbated by the increasing presence and value of coffee.[65] In 1932 coffee was only grown on 492.8 hectares whereas in 1960 coffee was present in 2,567.1 hectares; furthermore the best yield for Cauca in terms of coffee was in the municipality of Caldono.[66] The high yield of coffee per hectare signified that land was especially valuable in Caldono because of its fertility. Another key issue was that informal land tenancy arrangements were extremely common. For instance, an indigenous family might rent out a portion of its land to relatives and or to friends in the community. Once coffee trees were planted, the question of how to compensate the person's work and to properly recollect the original tenancy agreement was often difficult to settle. The fluidity of land tenancy arrangements coupled with increased value of coffee created a situation where conflict could arise quickly.

The arrival of the central state with its commission to dissolve *resguardos* complicated the land situation further. The commission's first step for the breakup of the *resguardo* was to measure and carry out a visual inspection of land plots, which immediately created conflict because there generally was no clear consensus over the boundaries of each land plot. Most indigenous rural folk delineated the boundaries of their property with a stone or at best a tree; some were tempted to move the stone or whatever was movable to augment their property.[67] The level of tension was apparent in that the police and the *cabildo* authorities accompanied Hurtado when he was doing his visual inspections and establishing the boundaries. Although the head of the commission stated that he managed to solve controversies around boundaries that predated the attempted division of the *resguardo*, his presence in situ re-opened old wounds and threw into question established boundaries. Ortiz's argument that the central state was shaped by local dynamics of power and that it added another layer to *La Violencia* is particularly relevant here.

State employees were under pressure from their supervisors in Bogotá who were becoming impatient with the lack of progress with the process of the *resguardo*'s division. In his defense, Carlos Hurtado reminded the director of natural resources that since there was little entertainment available in the area (no movies, theaters, parks, etc.), he and the other employees of the Commission spent most of their time working. To add insult to injury, Hurtado pointed out that his pay was very modest. While the work conditions of these state employees may seem on the one hand to belong to a footnote, it is relevant in terms of considering the strength of the presence of the central state in the area as well as the added pressure that existed on these employees to push forward an agenda to break up the *resguardos*.

Social scientists and oral testimony have often characterized conflict around land in Cauca as one that pitted nonindigenous settlers/*colonos* against indigenous inhabitants of a *resguardo*. While it is certainly true that nonindigenous settlers did in some cases (as in Guachicono) push their way into *resguardos*, conflict also existed amongst indigenous people. Boundaries between land plots adjudicated by indigenous councils were often unclear and even murky at times. In addition, some indigenous members of *resguardos* who had invested considerable time and effort into their properties were not opposed to the division of the *resguardo* if it meant they could hold on to their patrimony as seen in the case of La Llanada. The central state first made its presence felt in the 1930s through correspondence and through its interaction with indigenous councils. The process of actually dividing up, which consisted of adjudicating the land of *resguardos* to indigenous inhabitants, coincided with the first phase of *La Violencia*. The presence of the central state aggravated the ongoing conflict with its proposal of change in terms of land tenancy and with its inability to carry out its promised mandate.

Race and ethnicity played an important role in the nature of conflict around land as well; however, not by helping to necessarily determine who belonged in which camp, for the *resguardo* and anti-*resguardo*, but rather in delegitimizing the claims that indigenous settlers made as settlers. Here, Mario S. Vivas's discourse was particularly powerful in that he combined the memory of Manuel Quintín Lame's so-called rebellion with the portrayal of an indigenous person who was unhealthy and unfit (tapping into the eugenics discourse of the time). In addition, it was clear that Mario S. Vivas counted on local authorities (police and municipal mayors) to protect his rights to property as well as to repress and squash any opposition to his land acquisitions. The representative of the central state, Carlos Hurtado, was facing an uphill battle. He was leading the charge for a lost battle—that of protecting the rights of indigenous settlers to their land and improvements in the midst of violence. The representative of the central state did not dare identify who were the "*elementos malintencionados*/malicious elements" who sought to dispossess the indigenous people of their land and coffee plants. The language of anonymity used here speaks volumes about the powerlessness of a poorly paid state employee to enforce the law of the land for land matters. However, the powerlessness of indigenous settlers was even greater in the 1950s as they watched (even though they resisted) others take over the land and improvements that had taken generations of hard work to achieve.

A far more effective response than relying on the central state to carry out its policy was to enlist the help of local amateur lawyers/called *tinterillos* in Colombia to defend their land claims. These *tinterillos* followed Manuel Quintín Lame's footsteps as they took people's cases to court; one such *tinterillo* was Juan Palechor who would later become one of the most important indigenous activists. Juan Palechor narrates how he was able to prevent the expropriation of his wife's relative's land by acting as a "lawyer" when the land transfer was supposed to take place. Although violence and lawlessness prevailed in many instances, law was and is important to understand how some claims were legitimized and others dismissed. The legitimization of these claims may seem irrelevant in the context of violence, but ultimately this legitimization through law will bolster the political space created by the national government in the 1960s.

TRIBUNAL OF RECONCILIATION AND EQUITY/REPUBLICA INDEPENDIENTE DE RIOCHIQUITO/*RESGUARDO* DE ARAUJO

An integral part of *La Violencia* was the emergence of Liberal and communist guerrillas. In response to the Conservative government's widespread repression, liberal and communist peasants formed self-defense units that took refuge in Colombia's remote countryside; some of these units became guerrilla movements.

These self-defense units/guerrillas were different from their predecessors of the War of a Thousand Days in that their membership was heterogeneous; urban workers, fired policemen, and rural politicians joined these groups.[68] Gonzalo Sánchez groups the different guerrilla movements into three categories; he advances that guerrilla movements in the first category emerged in areas of recent colonization where land titles were disputed and where there was a history of agrarian activism. The guerrilla movement in northern Cauca fits this first category.[69]

The full scope and impact of these self-defense movements that became guerrillas only became known after General Rojas Pinilla's coup.[70] In 1953, General Rojas Pinilla offered what Sánchez and Meertens called a "political solution" to the ongoing conflict between guerrillas and the central state by offering a general amnesty to all armed groups, meaning that although General Rojas Pinilla was a military man, he sought to (at first) resolve the conflict with guerrillas through political measures. The central state by engaging politically with these armed groups gave them a national presence. In 1958, the National Front government passed another amnesty that in the words of Sánchez and Meertens "had a twofold objective: to legitimize the bipartisan struggle against Rojas's tyranny and to rebuke, in the name of the National Front the continued existence of that very struggle."[71] In 1961 Álvaro Gómez Hurtado, in the midst of a debate around the agrarian reform, argued that the state had ceded its sovereignty in various areas of the countries where guerrilla enclaves existed; Álvaro Gómez Hurtado called these guerrilla enclaves Independent Republics.[72] Riochiquito, an area in Tierradentro, that included the *resguardo* of Araujo was one of these so-called Independent Republics.

This section of the chapter examines in depth documents produced by the Tribunal of Conciliacion y Equidad/Tribunal of Reconciliation and Equity that the Liberal president Carlos Lleras Restrepo created. The origin of these tribunals was the *National Committee to Investigate the Causes of La Violencia* created on May 27, 1958; this committee traveled around the country interviewing people and the different parties involved in the conflict and also negotiated peace agreements with guerrilla groups.[73] The objective of the committee was to document and to understand the events behind *La Violencia*; the committee's findings led to the formation of the tribunals of Reconciliation and Equity in five departments that were most affected by the second phase of La Violencia (Cauca, Valle del Cauca, Caldas, Huila, and Tolima).[74] The tribunal for Cauca was in place for two years and was composed of two magistrates, two secretaries, and two *citadores* (summoners). To ensure impartiality, partisan parity was in place for the secretaries as well as the magistrates.

The tribunal sent telegrams and bulletins to the municipal mayors and judicial inspectors of the police to announce their arrival and to inform them about the Tribunal and its decrees.[75] The tribunal relied on the municipal mayor to inform the inhabitants of the municipality about its arrival. Once the magistrates had arrived to a specific locale, they often limited themselves to listing the names of the plaintiffs and defendants in their reports. The members of the tribunal also posed questions to the inhabitants to find out if there were claims that could be processed and that were under jurisdiction of the tribunal.

The jurisdiction of the tribunal of Reconciliation and Equity was limited to land issues; rape, murder, and assault were not considered. Decree number 0002 which created the Tribunal of Reconciliation and Equity, limited its jurisdiction to immovable assets and land improvements.[76] Thus, the intent of the tribunal was not to bring perpetrators of serious crimes to justice or to bring about reconciliation between victims and perpetrators of crimes such as rape, murder, and assault. Instead, the Tribunal only sought to bring about an agreement between two living parties regarding land issues. In the words of one judiciary employee, Neftali Narvaez, "They were supposed to encourage conflicting parties to come to an agreement about matters of land and to suggest the advantages of a quick settlement to avoid long, prolonged, and costly trials."[77]

Although the competency of the tribunal was limited, citizens who were seeking justice for the murder of their relatives did approach the tribunal hoping for some resolution. For instance, the magistrates (while they were visiting Guapi) reported the case of Damase Mancilla who came to the tribunal to inform them that police officers had killed his brother, Basilio Mancilla, on January 1, 1954. Damase Mancilla had already attempted to start a judicial process when he went to the local offices of Guapi, the Superior Courts, and finally the *Tercera Brigada* (Third Brigade of the Colombian Army), which all declined to help him.[78] The magistrates of the Tribunal of Reconciliation and Equity also turned him away since the murder was clearly not under their jurisdiction.

The limited jurisdiction of the tribunal was indicative of the central state's weakness and of its unwillingness to confront serious crimes such as murder, assault, and rape. The choice, while understandable, to focus on land was an abdication on the part of the central state. It brings forth the question of how could one address only one component of land dispossession; in other words, since land dispossession was carried out either through violence or the threat of violence, how could the central state heal the profound wounds that *La Violencia* meant for so many rural inhabitants?

One can only imagine the pain and frustration that Damase Mancilla endured not only because of the loss of his brother, but also when all authorities local and central ignored his request for justice. Guapi is a town located on the Pacific Coast of Cauca, which is largely populated by Afro-Colombians; it was also very isolated from the central part of Cauca because no road connected Guapi to Popayán. The arrival of the Tribunal of Reconciliation and Equity was undoubtedly a momentous event for this isolated region cut off from the regional state, but also largely ignored by the central state. Unfortunately, for the Colombian state and for the people of Guapi, the representatives of the central state were impotent and no doubt disappointed those hoping for justice.

These magistrates were not only stymied by their limited jurisdiction, but also by the lack of effective support from Bogotá, which manifested itself in an inability to confront local politics and in poor logistical support. In 1960 the Tribunal of Reconciliation and Equity had its first seat in Santander de Quilichao located in the north of the department close to where most of the violence had taken place. A year later in 1961, much to the displeasure of the magistrates who were not consulted about this relocation, the seat was transferred to Popayán. The former governor of Cauca, Dr. Victor Mosquera Chaux, a Liberal, had installed the commission in Santander de Quilichao, which was heavily populated by Afro-Colombians and Liberal inhabitants.[79] The conservative governor, Dr. Obando Velasco, when asked why the tribunal was relocated, stated that Conservative people feared going to Santander de Quilichao because their lives could be in danger when visiting this Liberal town and because the indigenous people of Tierradentro could not travel to Santander de Quilichao.[80] The magistrates when appealing the decision made by the Conservative governor stated that claims were made by Conservatives while the Tribunal was located in Santander de Quilichao, and that this town was known for its bipartisanship and civility. In addition, seeking to deflect the charge of bias, the magistrate, Tello, who was from Santander de Quilichao expressed its support for the relocation of the Tribunal to any city in the north, but not to Popayán since the center and south of Cauca were left largely untouched by violence. The municipality of Santander de Quilichao also expressed its support for the return of the tribunal to Santander. The transferal of the tribunal evidently made it ineffective; once relocated to Popayán it did not receive a single claim in the first four months.

The other major logistical stumbling block for the Tribunal of Reconciliation and Equity in Cauca was the lack of available funds. In order to encourage and facilitate an agreement between two different parties in matters of land, magistrates offered loans via the *Caja de Credito Agrario Industrial y Minero*/Agrarian Industrial and Mining Bank of Popayán.[81] Indicating some difficulty in the processing of these loans, the magistrates complained that if they did not have the ability to process and obtain these loans on behalf of the claimants, they would lose the faith and trust of the people. Ultimately, the cost of maintaining the Tribunal of Reconciliation and Equity would serve as a rationale for ending its work; a significant budget deficit presented itself in Cauca.[82]

However ineffective the tribunal of Equity and Reconciliation was in ultimately resolving land conflict and in overcoming local dynamics of power, it did start a new conversation between the national government and citizens. Since the turn of the twentieth century, areas such as Santander de Quilichao were a vibrant part of the political and public life of Colombia; in fact it was their very intimate involvement with partisan politics (through their affiliation with Liberalism) that had led in part to a conflagration of violence. In the 1930s the central state also made its presence felt with Law 200 of 1936 as well as with the formation of agrarian leagues, but it was a state that was firmly anchored in its Liberal identity. With the arrival of the Tribunal of Equity and Reconciliation a new type of central state was emerging; one that was supposed to be nonpartisan and that sought technocratic, efficient, and speedy resolutions to conflict.

RIOCHIQUITO

The *Independent Republic of Riochiquito* was located in the north of Cauca on the border with Huila. It is and was a beautiful mountainous and verdant area of difficult access from the center of Cauca; its economy in the 1950s and 1960s was linked to the towns of Pacarni and Nataga in Huila.[83]

The events that took place in Riochiquito, Tierradentro, shed light on the nature of conflict in Colombia and on the multiple and contradictory roles that the central state adopted. In 1960 a total of about three thousand nonindigenous and indigenous people lived in the area.[84] Riochiquito was also the place where the *resguardo* of Araujo was located and that was originally populated with mostly indigenous people. Today, a civil indigenous community of Araujo[85] still exists but it is small; it consists of two hundred hectares and of only ninety inhabitants.[86] The territorial regime listed is that of individual properties.[87]

In 1961 three petitioners described by the magistrates of the Tribunal as peaceful and decent people came before the Tribunal in Inzá, Tierradentro, to complain that they had lost their land plots with the arrival of the guerrillas to the area of Riochiquito. Another twenty men came to see the magistrates of the tribunal when they visited in Belalcázar claiming that they had also lost their land plots in Riochiquito and were displaced by the guerrillas. In their correspondence to Bogotá, the magistrates emphasized how these petitioners were hardworking men who were unjustly displaced by so-called *guerrilleros*, and also stressed their inability to effect an agreement since the area of Riochiquito was under the control of guerrillas.[88]

Although the magistrates expressed hostility toward the guerrillas characterizing them as the "assailants of Riochiquito," they recognized that the Colombian army had occupied the area of Riochiquito first, and that this military occupation had led to the loss of lives in the region as well as to the deactivation of the indigenous council of Araujo. After the army left, the guerrillas arrived and were depicted as finishing the job of dispossessing the legitimate owners of their land that the army had begun.

A timeline of the formation of the *Republica Independiente de Riochiquito* is difficult to glean from the official documents of the Tribunal of Reconciliation and Equity, but according to José Modesto Campos—who wrote the preface to the leader of Riochiquito, Ciro Trujillo's short memoir (*Páginas de su Vida*)—the self-defense movement that was later called a guerrilla army began its formation in 1953. Ciro Trujillo's political trajectory was similar to that of many Liberals who went from participating in Gaitán's political movement to waging guerrilla warfare. Ciro Trujillo explained that because he had participated in the Gaitanista movement, the *chulavita* police came looking for him at his home once the Conservatives were in power. He left his home and stayed away for a year wandering around small towns and farms in search of a peaceful area; he stated that none was to be found during these times of violence.

He returned home and found his house burnt to the ground, but his relatives had stayed on working the land in the day and hiding out at night in the countryside. There in Tolima, he and other peasants of the area decided to organize a self-defense movement to respond to the scorched earth strategy adopted by the Conservative forces in his region. The self-defense movement consisted in arming men who were above the age of fifteen (who knew how to use weapons), and women who wanted to participate. The organization was successful in protecting the families that sought protection; these families were able to continue farming the land and to effectively "neutralize" any bandits that sought to attack them. Conversations with the Communist guerrillas began in 1950; from his memoir written at the end of his life, it is apparent that the process of conversion from Liberal to Communist was a slow one and that only gelled in the 1960s. He migrated from Tolima with his companions to Cauca in 1953 to escape the repression that the government of General Rojas carried out against guerrillas who did not accept his amnesty proposal.[89]

Manuel Marulanda (known as Tirofijo/sure-shot/future leader of the FARC) and Jacobo Prias had decided to establish a self-defense area in Marquetalia, which was located near Riochiquito; Ciro Trujillo who was friends with Manuel Marulanda, established what he would call a *Movimiento Agrario de Riochiquito*/Agrarian Movement of Riochiquito in Riochiquito, Cauca taking advantage of the close proximity of Marquetalia and of the remoteness of the area. This was not his first time in the north of Cauca; he had visited the indigenous territories of the north of Cauca in 1951. Ciro Trujillo described his arrival in 1953 and the formation of a multi-ethnic agrarian movement:

> Once we had recovered we inserted ourselves into the work of rebuilding the lives of people under the umbrella of an agrarian movement that was built with guerrilla families that had not wanted to surrender and with the indigenous

> inhabitants of the area. The work was extenuating because we had to integrate into one movement the local indigenous population and *campesinos* who had arrived from many other regions of the country. Jacobo Prías and his men accompanied us for a couple of months from the time of our arrival and then they left to go to their base. We continued the task taking advantage of the good relationships established by our movement in 1951 when for the first time we had visited the indigenous territories of the North of Cauca. Our first idea was to create unity, the foundation (of the unity) was that we needed a common defense against possible attacks from the offical forces (meaning police and army) against organized assassins especially those organized by the diocesan administration of Belalcázar and Popayán and by those latifundistas who were businessmen of violence. This objective was achieved. Then, it was urgent to identify and pursue (push forward) old and new claims to land and rights that indigenous people had made and to make sure that these claims were ardently defended by campesinos who were not from the area. This would end the wariness that indigenous people felt towards the "rationals" or "whites" as they called them. We proposed to increase the social and economic relationships (and of any other nature) between the two different major groups that we worked with and in a few years we had built a campesino movement that was exemplary because of its organization, for his self-government, for its industriousness, and for its military capacity.[90]

According to this account, Ciro Trujillo had achieved unity amongst different ethnic groups that were separated by ethnicity, regional origin, and cultural customs. Most impressive was his ability to achieve a degree of unity between rural folk from all over Colombia with indigenous people of Cauca. General Alvaro Valencia Tovar (of the Colombian army and opposing side) also asserted that in 1964 the guerrilla's authority was not imposed through violence in Riochiquito, but counted on the active collaboration of the population; he characterized the relationship between the guerrillas and the indigenous people of Araujo as symbiotic.[91] How do we explain the Riochiquito Agrarian Movement successes in achieving intercultural unity and in defusing conflict around land issues?

First, Ciro Castaño was able to defend Riochiquito's inhabitants from attacks from official authorities as well as from *pajaros* that plagued the area as Ciro Trujillo mentioned in the above quote. Ciro Trujillo and his armed group also provided some resolution and justice for the inhabitants of Riochiquito. In a missive responding to the Tribunal of Reconciliation and Equity's inquiry about land dispossession, the guerrillas explained that some inhabitants had left the area because they had committed immoral acts, and because they feared retaliation from their neighbors.[92] It was more likely that these men faced the prospect of guerrilla justice. Two men in particular were mentioned; Leon Medina Campos who was apparently responsible for the deaths of seventy-seven men in San Luis (Potrerillos) as well as Moises Garcia who was allegedly responsible for the betrayal of a popular movement to end Rojas Pinillas's dictatorship.[93] Thus, the arrival of the guerrillas displaced some landowners in Riochiquito, but also provided some rudimentary justice for peasants who were forced to live side by side with a mass murderer.

Second, the *Agrarian Movement of Riochiquito* implemented a de-facto agrarian reform that allowed for both indigenous and nonindigenous peasant families to live side by side in peace. One of the key measures that helped to implement this informal agrarian reform was the expansion of the *resguardo* territory onto "public land."[94] This de-facto agrarian movement also expropriated the land of some powerful Caucano landowners, which was then redistributed.[95] The first objective of this agrarian reform was to ensure that the indigenous people of Araujo had enough land and that land tenure issues were settled. Along with ensuring that indigenous people had enough land, the leaders of the Agrarian Movement of Riochiquito allowed for and probably encouraged nonindigenous people to buy land plots within the community. These land transactions were apparently notarized and official since the new owners of these land plots had titles to prove their legitimate claim to land.[96] The commingling of nonindigenous and indigenous land plots within the boundaries of the *resguardo* was undoubtedly made easier with marriages between settlers and indigenous people of the community.[97]

Third, an essentially Liberal discourse around land ownership legitimized this de-facto agrarian reform. While General Alvaro Valencia Tovar stated that the ideology that governed the Riochiquito agrarian movement was the result of a fusion between communism and indigenous agrarian social organization, the leaders of the Riochiquito Agrarian movement upheld the ideal of individual and private ownership of land. Ciro Trujillo stated specifically that the distribution of land was done to ensure that no one had to be a tenant and that each family could provide for its needs via the crops produced on its land plot.[98] Concentration of land in the hands of few was seen as undesirable, but this was a common notion not only for socialists, but also for Liberals and Conservative Colombians alike.

For the members of the Riochiquito Agrarian Movement, the key to legitimate ownership of land was work. Here the leaders of the Agrarian Reform movement echoed the slogan of the 1961 Colombian Agrarian Reform, "*La Tierra es para el que la trabaja.*" The hard agricultural work that the leaders and followers of the Riochiquito area performed also allowed for the guerrilla leaders to differentiate themselves from the "bandits" and "criminals." As Gonzalo Sánchez and Donny Meertens pointed out, "To be a bandolero meant, above all, to have lost political legitimacy."[99] They stated,

> About our concerns, for us there are only [concerns] [regarding] the strong work that we have done, as many of the authorities that have come to record since it is our personal duty to serve our nation, as true citizens and never as

> criminals, so much so that since we signed a peace agreement in our territory we cannot be accused of being subversives or criminals, but instead as men of work since we have in this territory [a strong body of work to show from our effort]—that we can say is not true of our nearby neighboring communities [effort in agriculture] despite our poverty, but as we are true guerrillas and not bandits because those that are bandits are those that do not do more than wander around killing, stealing, and attacking defenseless people as it happens in Valle [neighboring department of Valle del Cauca] where there are no guerrillas what they are is a group of rogues, rustlers who do not want to work.

Fourth and finally, the leaders of Riochiquito achieved the unification of the rural folk of the area through their relationship with the central state. The leaders of the Agrarian Movement of Riochiquito informed the magistrates of the Tribunal of Equity and Reconciliation that they had signed several treaties with the central government in 1957.[100] One of those treaties apparently stated that there would be no attempt to recover land that was lost in the process of the violence.[101] For indigenous rural folk and displaced rural folk who were harassed and persecuted by Conservative authorities and rapacious landowners, unification under an authority that provided some semblance of protection and peace must have been welcomed. The legitimacy obtained by the leaders of the agrarian movement conferred some degree of legitimacy to the rural folk as well, and meant that they could hope for some compensation for improvements to the land. Ciro Trujillo and his companions ended their missive to the magistrates with the offer to leave their farms despite the peace and tranquility that existed in the area, but that they would expect the national government to compensate them for the improvements made to the land. They added that this would mean a significant sum since there were at least three hundred farms and no less than a thousand people who would have to be compensated.

UNWINDING AND DESTRUCTION OF RIOCHIQUITO

In April of 1964, three years after the Tribunal of Reconciliation and of Equity had visited the nearby area (Inzá), General Alvaro Valencia Tovar obtained permission to visit the area. The national context of 1964 differed from that of 1961. In 1964, the president of Colombia was the Conservative Guillermo Valencia (who was one of Cauca's favorite native sons) and who was one of Manuel Quintín Lame's former archenemies. The other fundamental change was that the Latin American Security Operation was in place; the LASO (Latin American Security Operation) plan was the United States' counterinsurgency program designed to help Latin American governments to combat communism via military tactics and counterinsurgency measures to build up support amongst the civilian population.

General Alvaro Valencia Tovar was firmly convinced that the Riochiquito project was a Marxist one fused with what he called the "organización social comunitaria aborigen/indigenous community organization."[102] Although he saw Ciro Trujillo as a communist and the Agrarian Movement as a Marxist one, he characterized Riochiquito in a different manner than the *Marquetalia Independent Republic*. One of the reasons why Tovar saw the Riochiquito project differently was because of the presence of indigenous people in the area. General Tovar simultaneously saw indigenous people as passive and as rooted in a past that made them instinctively gravitate toward collective landholding thus making them susceptible to the Marxist message of collective/state landholding.[103]

In April of 1964, General Alvaro Valencia Tovar traveled to Riochiquito to meet with Ciro Trujillo in an attempt to reach an agreement since he viewed Riochiquito as distinct from the other guerrilla enclaves. He described the indigenous multitude that met his helicopter as typically passive and as responding to his visit with a mixture of reserve and curiosity. He attributed his success in communicating with the predominantly indigenous crowd to his prior experience in Quinchía, Caldas, an area that also contained a former *resguardo*. It was ironic that General Tovar considered indigenous people who participated in guerrilla activity that challenged the local authorities of Cauca and who transformed the land tenure patterns of the area as passive.[104]

The scene described by Tovar following his arrival to Riochiquito is quintessentially Colombian and surreal. Once the helicopter wings had stopped rotating, the crowd that Tovar depicted as mestizo and indigenous approached the helicopter, but maintained a respectable distance. Five men representing the Agrarian movement presented themselves to General Tovar and to his pilot; the leader of the group, "Pacheco," the happy "costeño" (from the coast of Colombia) greeted Gen. Tovar. In his later memoir of his encounters with famous guerrilla leaders, Tovar emphasized the fact that Pacheco was a mulatto versus the indigenous and mestizo multitude gathered in the plaza. Gen. Tovar adds that he could detect in Pacheco's accent a Don Juanesque tone, meaning that he probably had a way with the ladies. Ciro Trujillo did not come to the first meeting with General Tovar and sent a message stating that he was unwell.[105] Ciro Trujillo's sister, who was the only owner of a small shop/*tienda* in Riochiquito, offered to open a bottle of champagne that she had been keeping since Christmas for a special occasion for the select group. The community leaders, the general, Pacheco, Ciro Trujillo's sister, and the pilot of the helicopter all raised their glasses to toast for peace and to a possible agreement between the army and the people of Riochiquito.

The gathering took place in the square/plaza of the town that was under construction; every self-respecting town in Colombia has a main square where generally the church, important governmental buildings, and the local store are located. The multitude of rural folk who had gathered to watch the general arrive was depicted as looking astonished at the sight of the general sharing a drink with the representatives of the Agrarian Movement.[106]

General Tovar announced to the crowd of Riochiquito that their group had behaved in a civilized "manner" that contrasted with the Marquetalia band and that therefore the government hoped to reach an agreement with the Agrarian Movement as well as respond to the needs of the inhabitants of Riochiquito. According to General Tovar, the crowd gathered its courage and told him that they wanted roads, schools, health, and a solution to land tenure problems that had arisen after the extinction of *resguardo* Araujo.

When General Tovar returned three weeks later, Ciro Trujillo came out to greet him on his white horse. The army general depicted Trujillo as the typical *tolimense* mestizo (mixed race from Tolima) because he was short and stocky. People thronged around General Tovar and Ciro Trujillo; the general was impressed with Ciro Trujillo's interaction and "clear domination" of the people. His rapport with the rural folk was apparent in that he greeted several persons by name and inquired about personal matters. Women approached Ciro Trujillo's horse and greeted him while touching with reverence the horse's reins. The horse was depicted as a stocky and well-built creole horse; curiously the description of the horse was almost identical to Tovar's depiction of Ciro Trujillo.

For General Tovar, effective political leadership derived from regional origin, ethnicity, and machismo. His preoccupation with the regional origin of each leader and person he met in Riochiquito spoke volumes about the way in which political reality was categorized in Colombia. His blinders were on when considering the political participation of indigenous people; he could not see them as active participants and leaders. He thought of the costeño as the happy-go-lucky man who was a womanizer; he reserved his respect for Ciro Trujillo who was a manly *mestizo* from Tolima. Ciro Trujillo behaved in a manner that General Tovar expected him to: he displayed his "dominance" over followers. Peter Wade showed how race in Colombia was embedded in a language of regionalism so that Chocoano (person from Choco) became a synonym for Afro-Colombian while Antioqueño (person from Antioquia) was associated with whiteness and progress. The racial imaginary and categorization had real consequences as Wade demonstrated how Antioqueños benefited from their "white identity" to carve out a privileged economic and political space in Choco.

Not only was the encounter between Ciro Trujillo and General Tovar shaped by their shared understanding of race, ethnicity, region, and gender, but the alternative political project of the Agrarian Movement of Riochiquito was also embedded in the same gendered imaginary. In other words, the political project of the Agrarian Movement of Riochiquito was transformative because of its land redistribution, but it did not challenge the hegemonic gendered hierarchy. Ciro Trujillo's performance of masculinity was integral to his ascent in the guerrilla ranks and to his ability to gain respect from the rank and file. This is, of course, by no means unique to Colombia, but a common characteristic of many leftist movements throughout Latin America.

The Agrarian Movement of Riochiquito did challenge the hegemonic racial imaginary and specifically, General Tovar's myopic vision, by creating a political space where indigenous people and nonindigenous worked side by side in solidarity. As mentioned earlier, Ciro Trujillo stated, "Luego, era urgente encontrar, y levantar viejas y nuevas reinvindicaciones de los indígenas por la tierra y sus derechos y hacer que estas fueran ardientemente defendidas por los campesinos foráneos que habíamos llegado de otras partes/Then, it was urgent to identify and pursue (push forward) old and new claims to land and rights that indigenous people had made and to make sure that these claims were ardently defended by campesinos who were not from the area."[107] However, it would be a mistake to see this strategy adopted by Ciro Trujillo as unique or even innovative. Indigenous communities and activists had a long history of working side by side with Leftists, and radical Liberals since the 1920s. It was no coincidence that Ciro Trujillo visited the north of Cauca and indigenous communities before settling in Riochiquito; this area was known for its history of agrarian activism and interethnic cooperation.

The larger argument here is that the Agrarian Movement of Riochiquito was not pushing for so-called Independence or for a re-envisioning of Colombia, but for inclusion in a Colombia that was already existent in the Colombian imaginary. Hard work, land ownership, and education were key points in the Riochiquito Agrarian Movement's agenda. The Agrarian Movement of Riochiquito had founded sixteen new schools in the area. The demands that the people of Riochiquito made to General Tovar were hardly radical: schools, roads, and help with the resolution of land issues; they signaled a desire for inclusion into the Colombia of "progress" and "modernization."

The desire for inclusion and the moderate demands made by the Agrarian Movement of Riochiquito made the final outcome of this chapter in Colombian history especially sad. Two important factors conspired against a successful agreement in Riochiquito. The first was that from the very beginning the local state and landowners of Cauca were extremely hostile to the Riochiquito project. From the very first meeting in the main square of Riochiquito, General Tovar stated that the Riochiquito inhabitants expressed their hostility toward the authorities of Cauca, but spoke with respect about Huila's local government; in addition, he identified the local state of Cauca as a key stumbling block to achieve peace.

General Tovar ignited further hostilities when he managed to get Ciro Trujillo's brother out of Popayán's jail much to the local government's displeasure.[108] Although the communist lawyer retained by Ciro Trujillo's brother was described as incompetent and as the one responsible for preventing the judicial process from functioning properly, it was more likely that Ciro Trujillo's brother was languishing in jail because of the political pressure exerted by antagonistic local politicians and landowners. As a result of the brother's liberation, the Ministry of War had to defend General Tovar from accusations. Tensions between the local powerbrokers and the national army in regard to the situation in Cauca were evident in other ways. The governor of Cauca, Arquimedes Angulo, and the leadership of both the Liberal and Conservative parties of Cauca requested repeatedly that the Colombian army invade and take over Riochiquito.

However, it would be simplistic to lay the blame of the unwinding of the Riochiquito project entirely on the local authorities and powerful landowners. The writing was on the wall for Riochiquito once the Colombian army invaded and attacked the nearby guerrilla enclave, Marquetalia, on June 14, 1964. While General Tovar did view Riochiquito in a distinct way to Marquetalia, he was also probably attempting to craft a possible alliance with Ciro Trujillo to make sure that Manuel Marulanda (Tirofijo) would not find refuge in Riochiquito and to ensure that the rural folk of northern Cauca would not support Manuel Marulanda and his troops. This military objective failed miserably since Manuel Marulanda and his troops who managed to elude death and capture by the Colombian army went to Riochiquito where they later held the first guerrilla conference of the southern block.[109] Most historians coincide in that in this precise historical moment the "Independent Movement of Marquetalia" transformed itself into a guerrilla army, *Fuerzas Armadas Revolucionarias de Colombia*/FARC.

While General Tovar continued to push for peace and for an agreement with Ciro Trujillo (despite incriminating correspondence confiscated in the Marquetalia raid between Manuel Marulanda and Ciro Trujillo that suggested that Ciro Trujillo was planning to kidnap General Tovar), events in Cauca polarized the conflict and provided the legitimization of an attack on Riochiquito. A bus that was traveling from Inzá to Popayán was attacked on March 17, 1965; a guerrilla unit (affiliated with Manuel Marulanda) shot the bus's passengers and removed their valuables.[110] The guerrilla unit went on to loot Emigdio Andrade's property and kidnapped him along with his three children.[111] The guerrilla unit also killed a policeman, a security guard, and the local mayor who encountered them; some official offices of Inzá were looted and 67.000.00 pesos were taken from the national bank branch (Caja Agraria) office.[112] The attack on the Caja Agraria was to become the signature move of all future guerrilla attacks in small rural towns; the Caja Agraria (known originally as Caja de Credito Agrario y Minero) founded in 1931 was one of the most ubiquitous state agencies. Thus, it became a perfect target for those seeking a symbolic statement of opposition to the government.[113]

The bus incident and the attack on Inzá provided new arguments for the Cauca elite to push for military intervention. Already in September of 1964, Senator Victor Mosquera Chaux, the prominent Liberal elite politician of Cauca, advanced that the "bandits of Riochiquito" were victimizing indigenous people of the north of Cauca.[114]

The senator of Cauca portrayed himself as the defender of indigenous people of Tierradentro whose land was being seized by the bandits of Riochiquito. In particular, Senator Victor Mosquera Chaux took aim with the counterinsurgency tactics of winning hearts and minds through the civil-military campaign that General Ruiz Novoa supported; he argued that the central state's military strategy of negotiating peace with the Agrarian Movement of Riochiquito was naïve and that it would not help to contribute to solve the public order problem that existed with Marquetalia.[115]

General Ruiz Novoa, who was later removed from his office as Minister of War, argued in an editorial written in one of the main newspapers of the country, *El Tiempo*, that one of the main issues in Riochiquito was the greed of Caucano landowners that he characterized as feudalistic who wished to take over Riochiquito's fertile land.[116] General Ruiz Novoa also pointed out that Senator Victor Mosquera Chaux had insisted on the need for military action in Riochiquito that would eliminate the settlers of this area and even if necessary kill women and children.[117] In response to Senator Victor Mosquera's statement, Gen. Ruiz Novoa stressed that to end the problem of violence in Colombia, the use of force was not sufficient and not always effective.[118] Instead, Gen. Ruiz Novoa thought that the central state had an obligation to remedy economic and social problems that caused violence in Colombia and to provide a strong state presence that would eliminate the political vacuum that gave rise to movements such as the Riochiquito one.

Appallingly, Senator Victor Mosquera Chaux did not deny his insistence on the removal of settlers and their families in the area, but asked why Gen. Novoa had not objected to this proposed measure at the time that Mosquera Chaux made it. To legitimize his insistence on the removal of settlers (that he mockingly stated that General Novoa was so enthusiastic about) and to demonstrate that landowners of Cauca could not possibly be motivated by self-interest, he pointed out that the land of indigenous people was inalienable and thus could not be legally sold/rented out or settled on. The senator of Cauca was right in terms of the letter of the law, but he knew full well that the reality on the ground was that landowners occupied and bought land that belonged to indigenous *resguardos*. The accusation that the landowners of Cauca were feudalistic rankled the senator of Cauca who, as the reader will remember, was a proponent of progress and modernity since the 1930s.

A delegation of indigenous people of Riochiquito traveled to Bogotá in April of 1965 to meet with the Minister of Government to demand an official inquiry into Senator Victor Mosquera Chaux's false statements about the settlers/peasants of Riochiquito. The delegation went further and accused Senator Victor Mosquera Chaux of instigating violence against indigenous peasants of Tierradentro with the objective of taking their land. Needless to say, this investigation never happened.

Instead, in May of 1965, Ciro Trujillo informed General Tovar that his two sons, Abacú and Jair, were killed along with other compañeros from Riochiquito; Abacu and Jair had accompanied the rural folk of Riochiquito who traveled to the market on Thursdays to sell their coffee, beans, and corn as it was their custom.[119] Given that this was an established routine on the part of the rural folk of Riochiquito, the group was an easy target for the hired assassins of the area. Abacú was shot and then received seventeen cuts by machete; his brother, Jair, bled to death when both his legs were blown off. The savage killing signaled the beginning of the end for Riochiquito and for peace in this subregion of Cauca. As a result of this killing, the only road that connected Riochiquito was closed, which signaled a larger rejection of integration and an understanding that military invasion was on its way.

In September of 1965, the Colombian army invaded and attacked Riochiquito.[120] As a result of this invasion, some indigenous peasants decided to join the guerrillas and left the area along with guerrilla units led by Marulanda and Tirofijo. Other rural folk simply left the area abandoning their land plots and crops while others chose to stay despite the risks they faced.[121] Ciro Trujillo joined Manuel Marulanda in the jungle of Yari, and died in action a few months later in the region between Casanare and Boyacá.[122]

Throughout General Tovar's narrative of events in Riochiquito, his sympathy for Ciro Trujillo was apparent. Despite Ciro Trujillo's alleged plot to kidnap him and his indecision at the final hour (when General Tovar put together a negotiated settlement of peace that would have addressed some of Riochiquito's population's needs), General Tovar expressed admiration for Ciro Trujillo's political leadership and clearly saw him as a political actor, and not as a bandit who was to be hunted down. His numerous trips to Riochiquito and his various attempts to negotiate a peace settlement originated from his belief that the Agrarian Movement of Riochiquito was a legitimate response to the partisan violence and land dispossession that had taken place during *La Violencia*. General Ruiz Novoa shared General Tovar's understanding of Riochiquito and evidently had real sympathy for the settlers of Riochiquito whom he saw as having legitimate claims to land and to state protection.[123] While General Tovar and Ruiz Novoa were an integral part of the central state, they both lost crucial support in the end in terms of pushing their vision of the role that the central state should play and in terms of what should happen to Riochiquito. General Ruiz Novoa who became Minister of

War in 1962 was asked in 1965 to leave his cabinet post by Guillermo Valencia, the then President of Colombia.[124] His dismissal came in response to his public remarks about the government's lack of effectiveness in terms of social and economic reform.[125]

In the aftermath of *La Violencia*, competing narratives from different groups emerged not only about the causes of *La Violencia*, but also about the solutions to end the violence. In seeking to end ongoing violence, each party elaborated a narrative about the different groups involved in the ongoing conflict. For General Ruiz Novoa, the heroes of the narrative (in the case of Riochiquito) were thc hardworking settlers who sought to make a living off the land and who were productive citizens in contrast to the feudalistic landowners of Cauca who only wished to grab the land of productive peasants. General Tovar was careful not to ascribe blame directly on the landowners of Cauca, but he too elaborated a narrative that portrayed the participants of Riochiquito as hardworking peasants (indigenous and nonindigenous) who sought resources and protection from the central state. The army's narrative emerged from a traditional Colombian narrative that lauded the hardworking settler and was very similar to the discourse of liberalism in the 1930s that was being resurrected yet again with the agrarian reform of 1961. In this narrative, indigenous people were at best lumped into the general peasantry category; in Tovar's fundamentally racist narrative, indigenous people were passive and instinctively sympathized with communism because of their so-called *quechua* ethnic origins.

The failure on the part of the central state to reach an agreement with Riochiquito's self-defense agrarian movement and its decision to intervene militarily signified an absence of real political will to address the economic and social concerns of the Colombian peasantry in general. The consequences of this lack of political will and of abdication to the local brokers of power like Victor Mosquera Chaux were the continuation of violence and displacement of rural folk. However, we should be careful not to idealize the solutions and narrative proposed by this branch of the Colombian central state in that it rested on a racial and gendered imaginary that placed indigenous people and women at the very bottom of the hierarchy.

While the Agrarian movement of Riochiquito was certainly not free of gender hierarchy, the narrative and solutions that Ciro Trujillo and his companions implemented to end violence in rural Colombia were empowering and indicative of interethnic solidarity. Ciro Trujillo in his short memoir emphasized how his group had to prove to indigenous people that they were serious about addressing land tenure issues and that they sought to understand and listen to the unique challenges that indigenous communities faced in the area. The very attempt (even if it was not entirely successful) to consider/solve the indigenous peasantry's land issues before addressing the nonindigenous peasantry land problems showed that the leadership of the

Agrarian Movement of Riochiquito genuinely respected the will of indigenous communities. This is not to say that the movement was one of total equality; clearly Ciro Trujillo was an established leader, but he had earned his leadership by gaining the trust and respect of both the indigenous and nonindigenous community. Even if reality was imperfect, and there were cases of indigenous peoples who were displaced by the Agrarian Movement of Riochiquito, Ciro Trujillo's discourse showed that he thought of indigenous people and communities as political players to be reckoned with. In other words there was respect for indigenous people, which in itself was a revolutionary act in a profoundly racist Colombia.

In contrast, contempt for the project and for the rural folk of Riochiquito permeated Victor Mosquera Chaux's discourse. A more disingenuous response to General Ruiz Novoa was not possible; as the reader will remember, Senator Victor Mosquera Chaux was one of the strongest advocates for the dissolution of *resguardos* in the 1930s and 1940s. Yet, there he was in the 1960s suggesting that he was the defender of indigenous people in Tierradentro. His assertion that *resguardo* land was inalienable was of course correct, but it did not mean by any stretch of the imagination that he was respectful of indigenous communities' land rights. So what to make of this change in discourse? No doubt the senator was slightly uncomfortable when General Ruiz Novoa reminded him that he suggested exterminating entire families of settlers, but more importantly he may have understood given the changing international context (which will be explored in the next chapter) that indigenous people's rights enjoyed a newfound legitimacy. The other possibility is that Victor Mosquera Chaux thought that maintaining the status quo of *resguardos* with weak *cabildos* (which they were in the 1960s) was infinitely preferable to a strong agrarian movement, which could possibly challenge his landholdings.

In addition, the Agrarian Movement of Riochiquito challenged Victor Mosquera Chaux not just on a discursive level, but in a military and strategic manner. The agrarian reform carried out by Ciro Trujillo (which the reader will remember took over nearby public land) was protected by his military force. The Colombian central state on the other hand, when it sent in its functionaries of the Tribunal of Reconciliation and Equity as well as its employees of the Commissions for Dissolution of *resguardos*, left them quite simply at the mercy of local forces and with little protection. The magistrates when performing their visual inspections of land plots were accompanied by a couple of police agents, but this was ineffective protection in the case of a large crowd or when faced with possible assassins. Carlos Hurtado, the employee of the Dissolution of Resguardos, did not dare identify who were the perpetrators of violence knowing full well that he would be left alone to face any possible violent retaliation. Therefore, the power of the Agrarian Movement of Riochiquito stemmed in great part from its ability to protect and to carry out in a speedy manner a mini agrarian reform, which the central state timidly and halfheartedly pushed forward. The other crucial legacy of this Agrarian Movement was the understanding for indigenous communities that defense of its leaders and of its inhabitants could not be left in the hands of the central state. To understand the formation of the self-defense guerrilla movement, *Movimiento Armado de Manuel Quintín Lame*, one needs to return to the Riochiquito Agrarian Movement. While some scholars have attributed the emergence of MAQL to Manuel Quintín Lame's movement, I would argue that the roots of the armed movement lie in Riochiquito because it was understood there and in that precise historical moment that the central state could not be relied on for protection and that grassroots self-defense movement were the most effective tactic for physical and political survival. To carry out the objectives of the group and to ensure some protection from the assassination attempts carried out by paramilitaries/*pájaros*, an armed response was crucial in the 1980s.

NOTES

1. Paul Oquist, *Violence, Conflict, and Politics in Colombia* (New York: Academic Press, 1980), 11.
2. Mary Roldán, *Blood and Fire: La Violencia en Antioquia, Colombia 1946–1953* (Durham: Duke University Press, 2002).
3. Mons. German Guzman Campos, Orlando Fals Borda, Eduardo Umaña Luna, *La violencia en Colombia, estudio de un proceso social*, tomo 1, segunda edición (Bogotá: Ediciones Tercer Mundo, 1962), 25.
4. Gonzalo Sánchez, "Violencia, guerrillas, y estructuras agrarias," in *Nueva historia de Colombia* (Bogotá: Planeta, 1989), 133.
5. See Herbert Braun, *The Assassination of Gaitán: Public Life and Urban Violence in Colombia* (Madison: The University of Wisconsin Press, 1985), and Gonzalo Sánchez, "Violencia, guerrillas, y estructuras agrarias," in *Nueva historia de Colombia* (Bogotá: Planeta, 1989).
6. David Bushnell, *The Making of Modern Colombia, A Nation in Spite of Itself* (Berkeley: University of California Press, 1993), 204.
7. Gonzalo Sánchez and Donny Meertens, *Bandits, Peasants, and Politics: The Case of "La Violencia" in Colombia* (Austin: University of Texas Press, 2001), 18.
8. Ibid.
9. There is a similar debate around the Mexican Revolution. See Alan Knight's "The Mexican Revolution: Bourgeois? Nationalist? Or Just a Great Rebellion?" *Bulletin of Latin American Research* 4, no. 2 (1985): 1–37. I have taken direct inspiration from this article and placed quotes around the term "Bourgeois Revolution" to give credit to Alan Knight.
10. See Eric Hobsbawm also for the notion of bandits as a pre-modern identity in *Primitive Rebels: Studies in Archaic Forms of Social Movement in the Nineteenth and Twentieth Centuries* (New York: W. W. Norton, 1965).
11. Ingrid Johanna Bolivar, *Violencia politica y formación del estado, ensayo historiografico sobre la dinámica regional de La Violencia de los cincuenta en Colombia* (Cinep. Ceso. Uniandes, 2003), 17.
12. Carlos Miguel Ortiz, "Historiografía de La Violencia" en *Historiografía al final del milenio* (Universidad Nacional, 1994). "Inmersos en redes de poder fragmentadas y heterogéneas, donde los focos de poder se multiplican y diluyen, y donde el Estado y sus cuerpos represivos apenas agencia parte de la violencia" (cited in Ingrid Bolivar, 17).

13. Carlos Miguel Ortiz, *Estado y subversión en Colombia: La violencia en el Quindío años 50*, Cerece Cider, Uniandes, Bogotá, 1985.
14. Daniel Pecaut, *Ordén y violencia: Colombia 1930–1954* (Bogotá: Cerec, 1987).
15. See Richard Stoller, Herbert Braun, Carlos Ortiz, and Mary Roldán.
16. Ingrid Bolivar, 20.
17. Mary Roldán, *Blood and Fire: La Violencia in Antioquia, Colombia, 1946–1953* (Durham, NC: Duke University Press, 2002)
18. Ibid.
19. Oquist, 6.
20. Oquist, 6.
21. Oquist, 9.
22. The Belalcázar municipality is sometimes referred to as the Páez municipality. My calculations are based on a document titled, "Tribunal de Conciliacion y Equidad del Departamento del Cauca." The list started in the month of May 1960 and listed the number of cases, the names of the parties involved in these judicial proceedings, and the name of the municipality where the alleged incident took place. The ending date for the events listed was June of 1961. Caja 138, Carpeta 1074, Fondo Ministerio del Interior. Also Caja 133, Carpeta 01073, Fondo Ministerio del Interior, Archivo General de La Nación.
23. The most cited source on *La Violencia* in Cauca is Father David González's *Los paeces: o Genocidio y luchas indigenas en Colombia*, which is an interesting source because it is both a secondary one in terms of its narrative on the earlier periods of indigenous history in Tierradentro and a primary source, which narrates his firsthand account of *La Violencia* and its impact in Tierradentro. The third part of his book is a firsthand account of his life as a missionary titled, "Memorias de un misionero que vivio mas de 30 años en compania de los Paeces."
24. Padre David González, *Los paeces: o Genocidio y luchas indigenas en Colombia* (Bogotá: Rueda Suelta, no date), 331.
25. Carlos Augusto Noriega, "Las elecciones en Colombia, Siglo XX," *Revista credencial historia*, no. 50.
26. Sutti Reissig Ortiz, *Uncertainties in Peasant Farming, A Colombian Case* (New York: Humanities Press, 1973), 33. Ortiz does not provide a source for this information, but as she lived in San Andrés, she probably obtained this information from her fieldwork.
27. Reissig Ortiz, 33.
28. Reissig Ortiz, 33.
29. Johnny Delgado Madroñero, *El Bandolerismo en el Valle del Cauca, 1946–1966*. Cali: Secretaría de Cultura/Gobernación del Valle del Cauca, 2011.
30. Sánchez and Meertens.
31. Johnny Delgado Madroñero, 29.
32. Johnny Delgado Madroñero, 29.
33. Victor Daniel Bonilla, "Resistencia y Luchas en la Memoria Misak," in *Nuestra Vida ha sido nuestra Lucha: Resistencia y Memoria en el Cauca indigena* (Colombia, 2012), 135.
34. Juan Palechor, 106.
35. Cuando vino la violencia del 48, cuando vino toda la matanza de los paeces en Tierradentro, cuando hubo la matanza también de los guambianos, unos tres líderes guambianos liberales, ahí en pleno casco de Silvia, ahí fueron fusilados. Mi papa tambien estaba en lista. Como a el lo adiestraron para que fuera adicto al partido liberal; él decia que desde niño le gustaba vitorear al partido liberal, que no sabía que era el partido liberal pero le gustaba. Y fue liberal y fue Gaitanista, y decía que le afectó mucho, lamentó mucho la muerte de Gaitán. Que si no le hubiera pasado nada, Colombia hubiera sido diferente, para el campesino hubiera sido diferente. Quién sabe digo yo, quién sabe qué habria pasado si Gaitán hubiera sido presidente, si habría sido diferente, si habría sido lo mismo, quien sabe. Por eso mi papa se vino, se estuvo por Mondomo, metido entre el monte, para dejar pasar."
36. Guzman, 44.
37. Father David González, 368.
38. Father David González, 133. "El orador principal, hombre de diploma universitario, de elevado puesto oficial, desde un balcón, revolver en mano, arengó: 'Señores conservadores, a

las Liberales hay que buscarlos coma a fieras, hay que aplastarlos coma a ratas, Habeis oido ? Habeis entendido ?'—'Sí señor,y así lo haremos' clamaba la enardecida multitude."

39. Father David González, 334. Ironically, Father David González who was a *Laureanista* , was at first pleased with the appointment of the mayor, but quickly became disillusioned with the man's methods.

40. Father David González, 334.

41. Father David González, 368–70.

42. Father David González, 370.

43. Juan Palechor, 107.

44. Juan Palechor, 107.

45. Juan Palechor, 108.

46. Juan Palechor, 110.

47. Juan Palechor, 110. The women's testimony included in Juan Palechor's testimony is very similar to scenes of rape described by Kimberly Theidon. See, *Intimate Enemies: Violence and Reconciliation in Peru.*

48. Juan Palechor, 110.

49. Juan Palechor, 108.

50. Juan Palechor, 108.

51. Juan Palechor, 110. The two men that were executed/gunned down with a machine-gun were Samuel Cuene and Ismael Casas from Pitayo. One particular soldier, aptly named Snake-face, was described as eager to kill.

52. http://notimundo2.blogspot.com/2011/05/caldono-cauca-por-el-conflicto-social-y.html.

53. Proclama del Cauca | Jueves 2 octubre, 2014 a las 9:19 pm Noticia publicada por ProclamaDelCauca.com: Defensoría exigió respetar a la población civil, tras combates en Caldono, Cauca. http://www.proclamadelcauca.com/2014/10/defensoria-exigio-respetar-a-la-poblacion-civil-tras-combates-en-caldono-cauca.html.

54. "*Resguardo* De Caldono."Archivo del Ministerio del Gobierno/Division de Asuntos Indigenas. Caja number 1532. The documents on Caldono are now located in the *Archivo General de La Nación, Sala Republica.* I don't know the current classification code since I consulted these documents previous to their transfer. Letter sent by the indigenous community to the national government/section of public lands, dated October 3, 1955. The section of public lands sent the document to Carlos Hurtado, who was the head of the commission in charge of the division of Caldono. El fin de la Comision enviada por el Gobiemo Nacional a parcelar nuestra tierras era pues libramos de la opresión cruel y desmedida a nosotros que, como indios, -somos los primogenitos de la Patria. Caja 1532. This document was dated October 3, 1955. The quote came from the transcription of memorials/"quejas formuladas" addressed to the national government that the national government then sent to the head of the commission, Carlos Hurtado, in charge of the division of Caldono.

55. Same letter as note 54.

56. Ibid. "No cumple, pues, la Comision parceladora al cometido del Gobiemo y, en consecuencia, nos encontramos en la situacion angustiosa de empezarnos a ver despojados de las tierras que nos dejaron nuestros mayores, en la que hemos trabajado pacificamente para ganarnos el pan diario y en las que trabajaran nuestros hijos que son los legitimos herederos."

57. Juan Palechor, 106.

58. Document dated February 10, 1954, from the Ministry of Agriculture/Division de Recursos Naturales. This document was addressed to the head of the Commission (Hurtado), who transcribed and sent the memorial that was sent by Dr. Mario Vivas to the Ministry of Agriculture. The quotes and information about Mario Vivas come from this document. Dr. Viva's petition was dated February 3, 1954. Mario Saul Vivas became a prominent politician for the Conservative Party. He was elected as a senator in 1970, defeating the prominent politician Guillermo Valencia.

59. Caldono. Extinción de *Resguardo*. AGN. Sala Republica.

60. Caldono. Extinción de *Resguardo*. AGN. Sala Republica.

61. Ibid.

62. http://periodismodehoy.ning.com/profiles/blogs/valores-humanos-de-quilichao.

63. Los indígenas con ideas disolventes que abundan en la cordillera central tendran un incentivo para atentar, como lo hicieron Quintín Lame y Pio Collo, hace pocos anos, cuando amenazaron la integridad y la vida de los habitantes blancos de todos los pueblos de la cordillera. Porque conviene no olvidar que en Colombia es ancestral en el indio el odio contra el blanco porque cree que este le despojo de sus tierras y que a ello se debe su situación economica, cuando la causa primordial radica en su falta de espiritú de trabajo y en los vicios de la coca y el guarapo que los tienen minados biologicamente y espiritualmente.

64. My translation. Letter from Hurtado to the Director of *Recursos Naturales*, dated March 14, 1955. Aceptando en gracia de discusion que se fallase el asunto de acuerdo con las pretensiones de los particulares reclamantes, las indemnizaciones sobre mejoras valdrian más que el terreno; y como un juicio reinvidicatario da lugar a considerable numero de acciones y excepciones, ya que administrativamente no puede resolverse sobre la validez o nulidad de los titulos que exhiban las partes, se concluye que el litigio durara muchos anos. Lo sensible o lamentable seria, que retomaran los tiempos de la ley del machete o del garrote para desalojar o despojar de sus posesiones a los indígenas como ha occurido en otros dias, a ciencia y paciencia de ciertas autoridades.

65. *Resguardo* Caldono, Section Division of Indigenous Affairs. Letter from Carlos Hurtado to the Director of *Recursos Naturales*, March 15, 1955.

66. Maria Teresa Findji, *Censo Indigena*, 38 and 39.

67. *Resguardo* Caldono, Sección Division de Asuntos Indigenas. Letter from Carlos Hurtado to the Director of *Recursos Naturales*, March 15, 1955.

68. Gonzalo Sánchez, 91.

69. Gonzalo Sánchez, 91.

70. Gonzalo Sánchez, "The Violence: An Interpretative Synthesis" in *Violence in Colombia, the Contemporary Crisis in Historical Perspective,* edited by Charles Bergquist, Ricardo Peñaranda, and Gonzalo Sánchez (Wilmington, DE: Scholarly Resources, 1992), 91.

71. Gonzalo Sánchez and Donny Meertens, 22.

72. Alfredo Molano, "50 años de las FARC," accessed at http://elsalmonurbano.blogspot.com/2014/06/alfredo-molano-50anos-de-las-farc.html. Also see Alvaro Valencia Tovar, *Testimonio de una epoca-Años signados por el conflict en el que han vivido inmersos el Estado y la sociedad colombianos bajo el rotulo de la violencia* (Bogotá: Planeta, 1992), 452.

73. Caja 138, Carpeta 1074, Fondo Ministerio del Interior, Archivo General de la Nación, Sala Republica. Also Caja 133, Carpeta 01073, Fondo Ministerio del Interior, Archivo General de la Nación, SR, Bogotá Colombia.

74. Caja 136, Carpeta 01060, Fondo Ministerio del Interior, Acta numero 21 of Ministro de Gobierno, dated January 21, 1959.

75. Tribunal of Reconciliation and Equity Document about a visit to Guapi. Office Report with no year but for the month of November signed by Magistrates José Antonio Tello and Jorge Arturo Bolaños Muños. Another document dated December 1960 outlined the procedures of notifying their visit to the authorities of Corinto.

76. Asamblea Departamental de Cauca in a resolution number 6, dated November 15, 1961, describes the decree 0002 that was emitted in 1960 by the Presidency. "Que por el decreto 0002 de 1960 emanado de la Presidencia de la Republica, se crearon los Tribunales de Conciliacion y Equidad que funcionan en varios departamentos, entre ellos el del Cauca; que esos tribunales tienen como fin especifico el de estudiar y resolver los problemas surgidos por la violencia politica y que hayan afectado el derecho de dominio sobre bienes inmuebles o sobre mejoras realizadas en los mismos, asi como prevenir la occurencia future de tales problemas." Caja 138, Carpeta 1074. Archivo General Ministerio del Interior.

77. Caja 138, Carpeta 1074.

78. Document by the Tribunal of Reconciliation and Equity about their visit to Guapi. Document available was an office report that had no year on it but indicated that the report was for the month of November. It was signed by magistrates José Antonio Tello and Jorge Arturo Bolaños Muños.

79. Victor Daniel Bonilla points out that Victor Mosquera Chaux had left the country when the violence was at its peak, 106.

80. The magistrates also pointed out that the tribunal had traveled to Tierradentro and had received claims.

81. Fondo Ministerio del Interior, Caja 136, Carpeta 01059. Letter from José Antonio Tello and Guillermo Delgado to Eduardo Santa, head of judicial section of *Ministerio del Gobierno*, dated July 6, 1961.

82. Fondo Ministerio del Interior, Caja 133, Carpeta, 01050. The document available is a transcript of an act of government titled: Acta no 23 by the Ministry of Government and the Commission of Rehabilitation. Act was done during the session of December 13, 1960.

83. General Alvaro Valencia Tovar, *Testimonio de Una Epoca*, 450.

84. General Alvaro Valencia Tovar, *Testimonio de Una Epoca*, 451.

85. A civil indigenous community is slightly different from *resguardos*. The Colombian government defines the difference between these two units in this manner: *Resguardos* Indígenas - caracterizados por una unidad territorial delimitada, bajo el gobierno de Cabildo, en cabeza de un gobernador indígena,las comunidades civiles - que mantienen el Cabildo indígena como forma de gobierno, una propiedad colectiva sobre la tierra pero no delimitada en *resguardos*, y en algunos casos en proceso de titulación. www.crc.gov.co/. . ./1.DIMENSION percent20POLITICA percent2

86. Los pueblos indigenas de Colombia, 1997, no page number.

87. Los pueblos indigenas de Colombia, 1997, no page number.

88. Informe que rinde el suscrito magistrado del *Tribunal de Conciliacion y Equidad del Departamento del Cauca* al señor president de la Republica y al señor Ministro del Gobierno. Caja 138. Fondo Ministerio del Interior. Archivo General de La Nación. Bogotá.

89. Ciro Trujillo, *Páginas de su vida*. No page number.

90. Ciro Trujillo, *Páginas de su vida*, no page number. "Ya respuestos nos incorporabamos a las tareas de reconstrucción de la vida de la gente en las condiciones de un movimiento agrario construido con familias guerrilleras que no habian querido entregarse y con habitantes indígenas del lugar. La labor era extenuante porque se trataba de integrar en un sólo movimiento a la poblacion indígena local y a campesinos trabajadores de muchas otras regiones del país. Jacobo Prías y sus hombres nos acompañaron un par de meses a partir de nuestra llegada y luego se marcharon a su base. Continuamos nosotros la tarea, aprovechando las buenas relaciones establecidas por nuestro movimiento en el año 51 cuando por primera vez visitó los territorios indígenas del Norte del Cauca. Nuestra primera idea fue la de producir la unidad de todos, con base en la necesidad de la defensa comun, contra eventuales ataques de las fuerzas oficiales o los pájaros organizados en especial por la curia de Belalcázar y Popayán y por los latifundistas como empresarios de violencia. Este objetivo fue conseguido. Luego, era urgente encontrar, y levantar viejas y nuevas reinvindicaciones de los indígenas por la tierra y sus derechos y hacer que estas fueran ardientemente defendidas por los campesinos foráneos que habíamos llegado de otras partes. Ello, acabaría con las prevenciones de los indígenas hacia los "racionales" o "blancos" como nos llamaban. Nos propusimos incrementar las relaciones sociales, económicas y de toda otra índole entre las dos grandes vertientes de habitantes con los que trabajabamos y en unos pocos años ya habíamos construido un Movimiento Campesino ejemplar por su organización, por sus formas de autogobierno, por su laboriosidad, y su capacidad militar."

91. General Alvaro Valencia Tovar, *Testimonio de una epoca*, 451.

92. Letter to Drs. Vicente G. Cajiao and José A. Tello, dated March 15, 1961. Riochiquito, Cauca from Ciro Trujillo, José Angel Orejuela, Jairo Ramirez, Fabio Trujillo, Gilberto Lopez, Fidel Ramirez, Manuel A. Triana. Caja 138, Carpeta 1074. Fondo Ministerio del Interior. Sala Republica. Archivo General de la Nación.

93. Ibid.

94. General Alvaro Valencia Tovar, *Testimonio de una epoca*, 451.

95. Ibid.

96. Letter to Drs. Vicente G. Cajiao and José A. Tello, dated March 15, 1961. Riochiquito, Cauca from Ciro Trujillo, José Angel Orejuela, Jairo Ramirez, Fabio Trujillo, Gilberto Lopez, Fidel Ramirez, Manuel A. Triana. Caja 138, Carpeta 1074. Fondo Ministerio del Interior. Sala Republica. Archivo General de la Nación.

97. Ibid.

98. Ibid.
99. Sánchez and Meertens, 22.
100. Letter to Drs. Vicente G. Cajiao and José A. Tello, dated March 15, 1961. Riochiquito, Cauca from Ciro Trujillo, José Angel Orejuela, Jairo Ramirez, Fabio Trujillo, Gilberto Lopez, Fidel Ramirez, Manuel A. Triana. Caja 138, Carpeta 1074. Fondo Ministerio del Interior. Sala Republica. Archivo General de la Nación.
101. Ibid.
102. Alvaro Valencia Tovar, 571.
103. Alvaro Valencia Tovar, 571, and Alvaro Valencia Tovar, 99 (2009).
104. General Tovar had not changed his assessment of indigenous people as late as 2009.
105. Alvaro Valencia Tovar, 458.
106. General Alvaro Valencia Tovar, 458. Anyone who has attended a political meeting in rural Colombia can picture the scene of onlookers eager to find out the latest happening and, of course, to perhaps share a drink.
107. Ciro Trujillo, *Páginas de su vida*, no page number.
108. Tovar, Memoir, 466.
109. "Marquetalia 35 años despues," *Semana*, June 28, 1999.
110. Tovar, 478.
111. Tovar, 478.
112. Tovar, 479.
113. In the case of the town of Inzá (since this was one of the first actions of the newly rebaptized FARC) it appeared to have been motivated also by the desire to obtain money.
114. Arturo Alape, *Tirofijo: los sueños y las montañas, 1964–1984* (Santa Fe de Bogotá: Planeta, 1994), 44.
115. Arturo Alape, *Tirofijo: los sueños y las montañas, 1964–1984* (Santa Fe de Bogotá: Planeta, 1994), 45. Victor Mosquera Chaux called the Agrarian Movement of Riochiquito, the sovereign state of Riochiquito. He was not content with the Independent Republic exaggeration and took it one notch higher.
116. Arturo Alape, *Tirofijo: los sueños y las montañas, 1964–1984* (Santa Fe de Bogotá: Planeta, 1994), 45.
117. Arturo Alape, *Tirofijo: los sueños y las montañas, 1964–1984* (Santa Fe de Bogotá: Planeta, 1994), 46.
118. Ibid.
119. Tovar, 482–83.
120. Ciro Trujillo, *Paginas de su vida*, no page number.
121. Alape, 63.
122. Tovar, 132.
123. General Tovar in 1965 was a lieutenant-colonel.
124. Harvey Kline, *Historical Dictionary of Colombia*, 437.
125. Ibid.

Chapter Five

The 1960s and the Birth of Division of Indigenous Affairs

This chapter discusses the relationship between one branch of the central state, the *Division of Indigenous Affairs*, and indigenous communities in Cauca in the 1960s. The Division of Indigenous Affairs emerged in 1960 as the state agency that mediated and set the tone for the relationship between indigenous communities of Cauca and the central state. The creation of this new agency reflected the overall political agenda of the central state, which was to create new forms of allegiance to the central state via agencies that were technocratic; the first part of the chapter explores the connections between the political context of the National Front and the founding of the Division of Indigenous Affairs. The larger international context and specifically the organization (International Labor Organization) also played a role in the elaboration of the Colombian Division of Indigenous Affairs' practices and discourse. The second part of the chapter focuses on the institutional development of the Division of Indigenous Affairs and the responses of some indigenous communities in the area. The last section of this chapter explores the case of Poblazón, which illustrates what happened at the local level in response to the national state's policies.

Overall, this chapter argues that this branch of the Colombian central state encouraged the formation of an "ethnic identity" based on collective landholding and attempted to strengthen indigenous councils as a response to the ongoing violence in Tierradentro and in the north of Cauca. Thus, the conflagration of social order (documented in the previous chapter) shaped in part one branch of the Colombian state's notions of culture and race.

NATIONAL FRONT CONTEXT OF THE FOUNDING OF THE BUREAU OF INDIAN AFFAIRS

It was only in 1960 that the Liberal government of Alberto Lleras Camargo founded the Division of Indigenous Affairs. The preexisting agency was created in 1958 under a different name: *Jefatura de Los Resguardos Indigenas*/Central Office of Indigenous *Resguardos*; this office was not independent and was attached to the Ministry of Agriculture and Ranching. The central state signaled that it was giving greater recognition and importance to indigenous issues when it transformed the Central Office of Indigenous *Resguardos* into the Division of Indigenous Affairs, which was a dependency of the Ministry of Gobierno. The allotted budget and number of employees also increased with the change of name and affiliation.

In 1958, the Central Office of Indigenous *Resguardos* was miniscule with only three employees in Bogotá, and three teams of technicians in the provinces.[1] It appeared that the administrative unit only had twenty employees at the most and that its budget was limited.[2] The central state's concern with indigenous issues was due in large part to Gregorio Hernández de Alba, an *indigenista* since the 1930s. Gregorio Hernández de Alba was a staunch supporter of indigenous communities and had pushed against the dissolution of *resguardos* since the 1940s;[3] he was also Alberto Lleras Camargo's childhood friend; they both went to the same school in Bogotá. His personal relationship with Alberto Lleras Camargo allowed him to insist that the then President of Colombia create a state agency responsible for the welfare of indigenous people.[4]

Although the friendship between Alberto Lleras Camargo and Gregorio Hernández de Alba facilitated the creation of the Division of Indigenous Affairs, this agency was part of the central state's overall reinvention as a modern, politically neutral, and efficient state. As seen in chapter 4, in 1958, the Liberal and Conservative parties agreed to alternate the presidency and to share all other political posts equally to neutralize the threat posed by General Rojas Pinilla (the populist general) and to end partisan strife. While the National Front agreement allowed for an end to partisan strife, it also meant that the Colombian state could no longer rely on political parties to create an allegiance to the central state. The legitimacy of the central state could no longer originate from the political parties; instead a new type of allegiance was created through the promise of the delivery of state services.

Thus, the Office of Resguardos/Division of Indigenous Affairs was one of many offices created in 1958 to modernize the Colombian central state as well as to foment community-led development, which in theory would prevent grassroots organizations (or worse the formation of guerrillas) that could challenge the central state. For instance, President Lleras Camargo created Communal Action Boards/Juntas de Acción Comunal via Law 19 of 1958;

these boards were civic committees that would organize the building of bridges, roads, and schools in a designated urban neighborhood or rural area.[5] A central office for these boards (*Division de Acción Comunal*) was created; this office was at first a dependency of the Ministry of Education, but in 1960 came under control of the Ministerio de Gobierno/Ministry of Government.[6] The key here was the creation of an organizational linkage between Colombia's citizenry and the central state that would substitute for or circumvent the partisan mechanisms that had historically mediated the relationship between citizens and the central government.

A brief comparison with Mexico allows us to shed light on the connection between state formation in the aftermath of a violent conflict and the creation of state agencies that were dedicated to the welfare of indigenous communities. While the Mexican revolutionary government created a department of education and culture for the "Indigenous Race" as early as 1921, it was also in the context of the aftermath of tremendous bloodshed and of the ending of an old regime.[7] In 1925 a department of rural schools for the Cultural and Social Incorporation of Indigenous people was founded. In 1948, the National Indigenist Institute was established and grew very quickly.[8]

The Colombian nation-state in the 1960s and the Mexican post-Revolutionary state shared similar reasons for fomenting an *indigenista* program. Knight argues that "indigenismo offered a means to delegitimize these elites, to prize the Indians away from their lamentable deference, and to bind them to a new revolutionary state."[9] An obvious difference when comparing Mexico with Colombia was the size of the indigenous population and of its communities; Mexico had a much larger indigenous population relative to its overall population than Colombia, which helps to explain why its *indigenista* programs were much larger. However, if we compare a specific region of Mexico such as Chiapas with Cauca in Colombia, Knight's analysis of the Mexican postrevolutionary state's objectives is very relevant to Colombia. In the second chapter, we saw how Cauca's elite (in particular its landowners) was portrayed as feudalistic and thus antiquated by one branch of the Colombian state, the army. In the aftermath of *La Violencia* and with violence still surging in certain subregions of Cauca, the Colombian central state not only wanted to "prize the Indians away from deference" to their feudalistic landowners, but also wished to make sure that the oppressed Indians did not join guerrilla movements. In other words, to ensure that there would be no duplication of *Riochiquito*, community development that respected ethnic traditions seemed like a most effective strategy in terms of successful state formation.

THE INTERNATIONAL LABOR ORGANIZATION (ORGANIZACION INTERNACIONAL DE TRABAJO/OIT REPORT): ETHNIC IDENTITY AND VIOLENCE

The International Labor Organization's report and analysis of the state of affairs of indigenous communities in Cauca shaped the direction, development, and guidelines of the programs that the Colombian Division of Indigenous Affairs implemented. The OIT report not only established guidelines for state policy, but also contributed to the definition of an indigenous ethnic identity in Colombia. Of course, the OIT did not elaborate its vision in a vacuum, and was heavily influenced by Colombian local and central authorities as well as by the Colombian intelligentsia.

The following discussion is based on "Report to the Colombian Government about the Indigenous Problem in the Department of Cauca," which was published by the OIT in 1959. In 1955 the departmental government of Cauca had requested that the central state start the process to request technical assistance that the OIT had given since 1953 to Bolivia, Ecuador, and Peru, which were all part of the Andean Program.[10] That the request came from the local government indicated that the Cauca government was eager for international assistance, and that it perceived its indigenous population as a "problem." In contrast to the central state, the local elite and state viewed themselves as the bearers of progress and modernity in contrast to the indigenous population, which they believed was holding Cauca back from modernity and development. The international organization came with its own discourse and definitions of integration, modernity, and progress. In contrast to the local elite who believed that integration of indigenous people meant doing away with their cultural customs, integration for the OIT signified modernization while respecting indigenous peoples' cultural customs and traditions.[11]

Integration of indigenous people was supposed to take place with the creation of centers that would offer training in agricultural techniques, health and social assistance, and vocational skills. In addition, the OIT suggested that national technicians and indigenous developers (trainers) teach these skills to indigenous people. In other words, the idea was that "development" and modernization would become organic.

It was only in 1958 that the OIT expert, Mr. Gregoire Koulisher, was able to carry out his investigation of the "indigenous problem" in Cauca.[12] Persistent violence in Cauca had forced the OIT to postpone the starting date of his investigation.[13] The consulting mission of the Andean program worked closely with the Commission of Special Rehabilitation/Office of Rehabilitation created in 1958 by the central state and directed by the engineer, José Gomez Pinzón.[14] This Office of Rehabilitation had a presence in the five departments that were most affected by violence; Cauca was one of the five departments as seen in the previous chapter.[15] The collaboration between the OIT mission and the Office of Rehabilitation meant that violence was an ever-present factor when assessing the state of indigenous people in Cauca.

The number of institutions and personalities involved with indigenous communities in Cauca and consulted by Mr. Koulisher was substantial: Dr. Mariano Lugari (head of planning in Cauca),[16] Prof. Julio Cesar Cubillos (director of Ethnological Institute of University of Cauca in Popayán), delegates of the governor of Cauca, and finally representatives of the Central Office of *Resguardos*. Monsignor Enrique Vallejo (mentioned in chapter 3), who was in charge of the Apostolic Prefecture of catechism and education in the two municipalities of Tierradentro, also accompanied Koulisher on his visit to indigenous communities. This lengthy list of local notables allows us to understand that distinct local agendas influenced the elaboration of the OIT program.

First, the OIT had to determine who were the "Indians" who needed to be integrated into the nation and the department. In order to determine who was to benefit from the OIT program, the international organization had to come up with a definition of what constituted an indigenous ethnic identity in Colombia. The OIT classified the national indigenous population into three different groups: the Guajira Indians, who were distinguished from Andean Indians; the indigenous groups of Tolima, Caldas, and other departments whose communities were dissolved and were viewed as indistinguishable from other poor *campesinos* of the Colombian countryside; and finally the Indians who lived under the regime of *resguardos* while participating to a certain degree in the economy.

Thus, in the Andean area of Colombia (for Cauca) indigenous people who lived on a *resguardo* were classified as indigenous and as needing integration. A territorial basis for the indigenous ethnic classification was necessary because in many areas of Cauca the boundaries between an indigenous and mestizo identity were not clear. Color of skin, language, and/or bloodline was not always a clear marker of identity. For instance, members of indigenous communities such as the Yanaconas and the Coconucos were often monolingual in Spanish. From the 1960s on, the Colombian central state would consider an indigenous Andean ethnic identity as based on collective landholding (*resguardo*). The territorial basis for this definition of an indigenous ethnic identity signified that any policy adopted by the central state would have to address land tenure issues and could not concentrate solely on the linguistic and cultural aspects of this indigenous identity. In other words, the territorial basis of the Colombian indigenous identity meant that the folklorization of an indigenous ethnic identity was not possible; the state would have to tackle land questions.

The OIT estimated that there were 300,000 indigenous people in Colombia who were not integrated into the economic, social, and cultural life of the nation.[17] The central office of Indigenous *Resguardos* estimated that there were eighty-four *resguardos* left in Colombia with a population of 90,000 people.[18] Cauca was chosen as the first location where the OIT program was implemented since fifty-four *resguardos* still existed in Cauca, whereas the other remaining thirty *resguardos* were dispersed in eight other departments. In addition, the indigenous population of Cauca was concentrated in certain municipalities; the indigenous population was estimated at 30,000 in the six municipalities of Toribio, Caldono, Jambolo, Silvia, Totoro, and Purace.[19] The other geographical area of significant indigenous population was located in Tierradentro (Belalcazar and Paez municipalities) where the indigenous population was estimated at slightly below 20,000.[20]

Not only was the indigenous population concentrated in certain municipalities, but also violence was greater in municipalities with a significant indigenous population.[21] The existence of guerrilla fighting, assassinations, and burning of houses and churches were challenges to the OIT's agenda of integration; in 1958 fifteen schools were still closed in Tierradentro due to the violence.[22] Some hopeful signs that peace would return to the area (and thus facilitating the integration of indigenous people) were the agreement signed in Tierradentro between guerrillas and the central state as well as the building of roads.[23]

The OIT portrayed indigenous people as essentially bystanders to the larger conflict that took place in Colombia. The author of the report attributed the high level of violence in municipalities with a high percentage of indigenous population as due to the topography of these entities. In other words, the mountains and the isolated and broken terrain made these areas perfect for guerrillas to hide out in. In addition, the belief was that the majority of the guerrilla fighters were not indigenous but were from other regions. Here, we can speculate that Mr. Koulisher was told of the case of Riochiquito where local authorities insisted that most of the fighters were originally from Tolima.

While it is true that displaced farmers and fighters who migrated from Tolima founded the self-defense Agrarian Movement of Riochiquito, the movement (as we saw in the previous chapter) was not an imported one. Some indigenous people of Tierradentro not only supported the Agrarian Movement of Riochiquito, but also in some cases became guerrilla fighters. Furthermore, violence in Tierradentro predated the period of *La Violencia* and could be traced back to the turn of the twentieth century when Manuel Quintín Lame's movement emerged. However, when the international organization depicted indigenous people as outsiders to the dynamic of violence, it was then able to portray indigenous people as "innocent" and deserving of special assistance. Poverty was identified as a major stumbling block to achieving durable peace; however, there was no mention of how existing social and economic structures set up by the local elite of Cauca exploited and repressed indigenous communities. Instead, Koulisher suggested that proper cultivation of land was the solution to alleviate problems of poverty; he stated that vast amounts of land lay fallow in Nasa *resguardos*. Mr. Koulisher was either unaware or misinformed about land issues; scarcity of land and insecurity around crops and other improvements of the land were the real stumbling blocks for peace.

The "indigenous problem" of Cauca was also attributed to the poor application of Law 89 of 1890; *resguardo* land was sold illegally to pay off debts acquired by indigenous farmers. This diagnosis avoided the uncomfortable issue of who the debtor was and singled out indigenous people as unable to handle their debts. In addition, indigenous government—specifically the indigenous council—was described as in crisis because regulations that governed the election of councils were ignored. In certain *resguardos*, the situation had deteriorated to the point where a clique had taken over, and corruption undermined the process of land allotment carried out by the council.[24]

The OIT report expressed its disapproval of dissolution of *resguardos* because it argued that in most cases former *resguardo* members lost their land and became members of the "agricultural proletariat."[25] The international context of emerging leftist guerrilla movements, and growing skepticism about capitalism in Latin America meant that the term "agricultural proletariat" was heavy with negative connotations. A "proletariat" could be incited to rebel whereas indigenous people who belonged to a functioning community would be protected from leftist agitators. Furthermore, the OIT pointed out that the dissolution of *resguardo* brought about the moral and social degradation of its inhabitants.

In addition to the moral and social degradation of indigenous people, which resulted from the dissolution of *resguardos*, the OIT presented the indigenous inhabitant of the *resguardo* as unprepared for modernity and capitalism. The successful integration of indigenous people into the capitalist system could only happen with assistance and protection. The author of the report stated,

> Surprised by the necessity to buy and sell, by technical progress and by the wage system—practices alien to his traditional manner of living—he has the necessity of technical assistance, of controlled credit, of a commercial organization that will protect him from certain middlemen who lack moral scruples.[26]

To prepare the indigenous communities for a monetary economy, Koulischer recommended the strategy of using "the essential characteristics" of indigenous rural folk (i.e., being organized collectively and performing agricultural activities in a collective manner) to integrate the indigenous people of Cauca. He identified the indigenous council and the *resguardo* as key collective institutions that needed to be strengthened and modernized. Thus, modernity and development were to be channeled through traditional collective practices and authorities. He stated,

> And the same can be said of collective work: fomenting the spirit of "minga" with a technical orientation and adequate professional formation could improve his work and group habits.[27]

Koulisher essentially suggested a rehabilitation of indigenous communities "sui generis"; his principal idea was to maintain the collective nature of indigenous communities, to respect their cultural and social identity, and to prepare indigenous people for modernity and capitalism through collective institutions.[28] The OIT report respected the "indigenous way of life" and saw value in indigenous communities' collective cultural traditions. However, its policy was based on the premise that indigenous people had no prior experience with capitalism, that they lacked know-how in handling monetary transactions, and that they preferred to work collectively. The OIT described indigenous communities as homogeneous entities, which completely underestimated the diversity of experiences within indigenous communities as well as amongst indigenous communities of the Cauca. For instance, the experience of indigenous rural folk in the *resguardo* of Calderas, which was isolated and where coffee was not cultivated, was vastly different from that of the indigenous rural folk of the Caldono *resguardo* where coffee was an important crop and where markets were close by. In other words, some indigenous rural folk did not lack experience with capitalism or knowledge of financial transactions; the issue was that capitalism as developed in this subregion of Cauca was vastly detrimental to indigenous rural folk's interests. This mistaken belief that indigenous rural folk were somehow "innocent" led the OIT to believe that indigenous people did not raise cattle; one of my indigenous interviewees from the Coconuco *resguardo* related to me how his family had an extensive herd of cattle and asserted that this was not unusual for well-off indigenous families.[29]

Although the OIT discourse failed to take into account the social class stratification that existed within indigenous communities as well as the diversity of experiences, it was certainly a departure from the approach that Colombia's Liberal and Conservative elite had traditionally adopted vis-à-vis indigenous people. The idea that modernity and progress could be achieved through indigenous institutions such as the council and the *resguardo* was anathema to most Liberals (who pushed for the dissolution of *resguardos*) and to Conservatives who thought that indigenous people had to assimilate into *mestizaje* in order to achieve modernity and progress.

The sui-generis approach suggested by the international organization was adopted by the Central Office of Indigenous *Resguardos*. As seen in previous chapters, a discourse that upheld the collective institution of *resguardos* already existed locally in Cauca and was propagated through articles and editorials in both the local and national press by Colombian *indigenistas* such as Gregorio Hernández de Alba, Juan Friede, and Antonio Garcia Nossa. It would be a mistake to attribute too much importance to the OIT report; however, it did signal a key shift in the international context and gave local *indigenistas* some leverage to push their agenda of protecting indigenous communities. The Central Office of Indigenous *Resguardos* received crucial support from the OIT when it was recommended that this office be in charge of the rehabilitation of indigenous people in Colombia, and specifically in Cauca. In other words, the state agency perceived to be most capable in addressing the enduring violence in indigenous communities was the Central Office of Indigenous *Resguardos*. This meant that for one branch of the central state the issue of violence would be seen through the lens of ethnicity and cultural traditions. OIT also recommended that the Central Office of Indigenous *Resguardos* have an office and a representative in Popayán; this recommendation was implemented.[30]

The OIT report and recommendations were offered at the same time that the Colombian government enacted new guidelines regarding indigenous political and territorial institutions; this new policy via administrative decrees and laws strengthened indigenous collective institutions. A presidential decree created the *Instituto Indigenista Nacional de Colombia* in December of 1958, which was affiliated with the Agriculture Ministry.[31] Law 81 of 1958 suspended the division of *resguardos* that had colonial titles, and established that indigenous settlers should be given preference for the adjudication of land when a title for the *resguardo* could not be found. From that moment forward, the official policy of the national state was to suspend the division of *resguardos* and to protect the territorial integrity of *resguardos*. An administrative unit in departments that had more than ten *resguardos* was created to ensure that Law 89 of 1890 was respected and that the economic, social, and cultural development of these *resguardos* was fostered.[32] In 1961, Law 135 permitted INCORA (Agrarian Reform Institute) to create new indigenous territories and *resguardos* so that indigenous communities could maintain their agricultural practices based on collective traditions.

A memorandum drafted by Gregorio Hernández de Alba on November 5, 1959, sheds light on the motivations and goals of this branch of the Colombian central state vis-à-vis indigenous people.[33] The director of the Division of Indigenous Affairs promoted his vision of indigenous people as forgotten and persecuted throughout history and stated clearly his opposition (and consequently that of the office that he led) to the breakup of *resguardos*. He saw the treatment of indigenous people as a national disgrace that needed to be changed urgently.[34] Despite his laudable concern Gregorio Hernández de Alba's discourse was patronizing toward indigenous communities and peoples; he characterized the majority of them as being "primitive" and "backward," and as such needing the central state's special attention.[35] He stated that the division of *resguardos* and adjudication of land plots led to the loss of land for most indigenous families. Two factors led to the loss of land: indigenous people's ignorance about real estate laws and the preying upon indigenous people by nonindigenous people who forced indigenous people to either sell their land at low prices or simply seized their land violently. After the territorial despoliation, land was concentrated in the hands of a few landowners, and cattle ranching replaced intensive subsistence agriculture. Even if indigenous ex-*resguardo* members managed to hold on to their land plots, they were then faced with the problem of not having enough land to cultivate (*minifundismo*) to provide for their families. Tensions and conflicts around land erupted in this scenario, which (Gregorio Hernández de Alba argued) further eroded the unity of the indigenous community.

The director of the Division of Indigenous Affairs also linked the loss of communal land with moral degeneration. Once the *resguardo* was broken up, respect for the indigenous council dwindled and led indigenous people to disregard laws and norms that had previously governed the community. Gregorio Hernández de Alba added that some indigenous rural folk when faced with loss of land became "social problems" and illegally occupied cattle ranching land. In 1959, when "banditry" and violence were commonplace in Cauca, the argument that communal landholding prevented the development of such ills was a powerful one. When the director of the Central Office of Resguardos wrote this memorandum outlining the motivations behind the cessation of *resguardo* dissolution, he attempted to persuade other branches of the national government that this was the best policy to achieve the pacification of areas with endemic violence. While the director of the Central Office of *Resguardos* adopted a revolutionary discourse in terms of upholding the value of communal landownership, his discourse and policies were quite conservative. Stressing the specificity of the situation of indigenous rural folk allowed him to ignore the larger structural problems of social and economic inequality in Colombia, which affected most subaltern actors.

Loss of land and displacement were problems that many rural folk of Colombia faced in the aftermath of *La Violencia*. For the most part, rural folk lost their land plots not due to some lack of sophistication and/or absence of training in real estate legislation, but because the balance of power was simply stacked against them. Faced with negligent and/or corrupt local officials and with a not always autonomous police force, the best solution was often to simply leave and hope that the next place would offer better opportunities. This was true for indigenous rural folk as well. In other words, it was not that indigenous people were unprepared for private ownership of land (which happened with the breakup of *resguardos*), but rather that the collective mechanisms of support and of resistance to land encroachments disappeared simultaneously with the indigenous council's claim to authority.[36] However, Gregorio Hernández de Alba's construction of a discourse that framed indigenous land issues as stemming from cultural traditions allowed this branch of the state to address land issues without directly confronting the elites and power brokers of Cauca.

To bolster his agenda of maintaining collective landholding, Gregorio Hernández de Alba maintained that indigenous communities welcomed these new measures of protection for their *resguardos*; he asserted that indigenous rural folk from extinct *resguardos* were requesting the reconstitution of these entities. Having laid out his case for the new policy, the director of the Central Office of Resguardos advanced that his agency needed more money and personnel to effectively carry out its new mission of protecting communal landownership.

IMPLEMENTATION OF DIVISION OF INDIGENOUS AFFAIRS/OIT POLICIES IN CAUCA

Directives from Bogotá

While there were many administrative offices that offered services to the indigenous population of Cauca, the Commission for Protection and Assistance was the only entity that offered exclusive assistance to indigenous rural folk. This entity was affiliated with the Division of Indigenous Affairs and was created as a result of the OIT Andean Program.[37] An agricultural educator headed the Commission for Protection and Assistance; two indigenous artisan teachers (a carpenter and a weaver), and a secretary were the other members of the Commission. Subsequently, a home improvement specialist (*mejoradora del hogar*) and an experienced farmer were added to this commission. In addition, funds from the Rehabilitation Program and National Service of Social Assistance were disbursed for the founding of five vocational schools for indigenous people.[38]

An examination of the correspondence between the Division of Indigenous Affairs and local authorities during the 1960s allows us to explore how this state agency attempted to implement its new policy of protecting *resguardos* and of strengthening indigenous councils. First, Gregorio Hernández de Alba, the director of Division of Indigenous Affairs promoted the legal defense of indigenous *resguardos* by informing the governors of Cauca, Nariño, and Cundinamarca of the central state's new policy, which ended the breakup of *resguardos*. He also asked regional governors to instruct their employees to defend the land of indigenous communities; he expected them to stop employees from accommodating non-Indians who wanted to divide the *resguardos*. He exhorted regional authorities to use existing legislation to prevent the extortion of indigenous people, and he recommended the general improvement of their quality of life (culture, housing, technology, and housing).

Gregorio Hernández de Alba prepared local officials for the arrival of his employees; for instance, he wrote to Humberto Valencia Paz (head of the Agricultural Division of Cauca) to explain Dr. Laurentino Otero Rios's purpose and function as a lawyer in Cauca for the Central Office of Resguardos.[39] The director of the Central Office of Resguardos envisioned a lawyer who was scrupulously honest and who would convince indigenous people to turn to the central state for protection rather than to amateur lawyers. Gregorio Hernández de Alba stated that the Central Office of Resguardos lawyer would be an heir to the Spanish colonial tradition of protection for indigenous people. While the notion of the Spanish state being a protector of the rights of indigenous people may elicit an ironic smile from the reader, the director of the Central Office of Resguardos was promoting a different type of central state in terms of indigenous people and creating links between the indigenous population and the central state.

Gregorio Hernández de Alba also sought to explain to local officials such as Humberto Valencia Paz that indigenous rural folk were not productive with their land because of the constant fear that a nonindigenous person would seize their land plot once it was cultivated. He reasoned that once indigenous peoples knew that their land plots were secure (with collective landownership and state protection) the local government's tax revenue would increase. Here, the director of the Central Office of Resguardos sought to combat the notion that only with the end of collective landownership tax revenues would go up. In addition, the predominant discourse of Liberalism in the 1930s argued that private ownership was the way in which rural folk of all ethnicities could truly become productive; here Gregorio Hernández de Alba countered this discourse.

Reports from the Field/Reactions in Cauca

Dr. Laurentino Otero Rios narrated in his reports the results of his visits with the members of indigenous councils of Calderas, Santa Rosa, San Andrés, and Yaquiva.[40] This representative of the central state thought that indigenous people of Cauca were in a deplorable state; he described indigenous people of Tierradentro as degenerated by their heavy consumption of chicha or guarapo (homemade alcohol). He also stated that most of the indigenous inhabitants of Inzá were "ignorant, drunk, and illiterate." The economic situation was also depicted as dire with indigenous people working on the land of whites and ignoring their own land plots. In addition, indigenous people of this area had lost all respect for their councils and had even attended meetings in a state of intoxication. In response the lawyer gave instructions to the indigenous councils to send their children to school, to stop drinking, and to work on their land plots.

While Dr. Laurentino Otero Rios's discourse was reminiscent of the racism of Cauca's elite, there was an important difference in that the representative of the DAI saw the degeneration of indigenous inhabitants as due to a loss of cultural values. Nonindigenous actors whom he called "whites" were depicted in an unflattering manner; he claimed that white people in Tierradentro exploited indigenous people and stole their land. He instructed all indigenous councils,

> To all these *resguardos* instructions were given about the negative impact of drinks, making them see the degree of degeneration in which they find themselves, a state that whites take advantage of, to abuse them. It was made clear to them the obligation that they have to send their children to school and to teach them the farming of land.[41]

Indigenous councils responded to Dr. Laurentino Otero Rios's instructions to return to the cultivation of their land with a request for tools, seeds, and cash assistance. They also demanded that the central government build schools. Evident in this dialogue between indigenous councils and this particular branch of the central state was that indigenous councils must have been frustrated (to say the least) with Dr. Laurentino Otero Rios's naïve and condescending approach to solving "their problems." Indigenous councils and inhabitants needed real structural reform and concrete assistance from the government; the moralizing discourse of giving up drinking, although well-meaning, was somewhat absurd.

Dr. Laurentino Otero, while mentioning that during *La Violencia* whites and indigenous inhabitants had seized land that belonged to others, stressed that the "whites" were the most culpable in this whole process. The actual description of violence that took place in the area made it clear that ethnicity was not always the determining factor helpful to establish who was the victim of land theft. He mentioned that indigenous inhabitants of the Avirama *resguardo* and "whites" who had rented out land plots stole land from indigenous people of the Chinas *resguardo*.

Indigenous councils and inhabitants who came to see Laurentino Otero Rios demanded a solution to land tenure issues. For instance, the indigenous council of Belalcázar came to complain about its boundary problems with the *resguardo* of Araujo. Here, given the time frame, we can infer that it was the Agrarian Movement of Riochiquito that had expanded into the *resguardo* of Belalcázar. Some indigenous people from extinguished *resguardos* (Guanacas, La Laguna, Turmina, and Topa) requested that Dr. Laurentino Otero Rios intercede on their behalf with the Ministry of Agriculture so that they could proceed with the adjudication of land plots. The indigenous council of

Alto del Rey in the municipality of El Tambo also visited Dr. Laurentino Otero Rios's office to request the dissolution of their *resguardo* because some members of the *resguardo* had sold their land plots while others wanted a title to their land plots.

Dr. Laurentino Otero Rios, who was supposed to uphold collective landholding and indigenous councils, faced an uphill battle in many cases. In the case of Alto del Rey, he was told that the members of this *resguardo* refused to obey the council's orders. The same situation was present in the *resguardo* of Totoro where sale and renting out of *resguardo* land were prevalent as well as the disregarding of instructions given out by the indigenous councils. In the case of Poblazón, the indigenous council had divided into two bands. In response to this state of affairs, Dr. Laurentino Otero Rios attempted to foment unity in the community and instructed indigenous inhabitants to respect their indigenous councils.

The representative of the central state did more than deliver lectures on the importance of sobriety and of unity; he attempted to address land quarrels within indigenous communities as well as provide protection for the threatened parties. For instance, two indigenous individuals from Vitonco and Mosoco requested protection from another individual who had stolen their land plot and then sold it to another. The lawyer requested that the municipal authorities provide protection to the threatened individuals. In addition, in August of 1960, Dr. Laurentino Otero Rios canceled rental contracts and exchanges of land in Guambia, Quichayo, and Pitayo, all located in the municipality of Silvia. This type of work called *saneamiento*/cleaning up of *resguardos* was important because it provided protection to the legitimate owners of the *resguardos* and prevented the slow transition of *resguardo* land into private landownership.

The Central Office of *Resguardos* also provided agricultural training; it consisted in teaching indigenous rural folk how to use fertilizers and how to grow a variety of crops. The training took place in the Agricultural Institute located in Silvia; there was also a workshop where cabinetmaking was provided in Guambia.

The other type of technical training that was offered was theory and practice of textile industry for adults of both sexes in the indigenous community of Guambia. The person in charge of teaching this workshop was a Guambiano, Francisco Tumiña, a long-term friend and protégé of Gregorio Hernández de Alba. In 1959, Francisco Tumiña was sent to Cuenca, Ecuador, to be trained in semi-mechanical weaving (manejo de la rueca de hilar y de telares semi-mecanizados).[42] The workshop taught students all the stages of traditional weaving and the semi-mechanical process. In the month of August (year is not specified), there were thirty-three women and sixty-three men attending the weaving workshop. There was a certain irony in that the Guambiano indigenous people who were known for their skill in weaving and for wearing their traditional clothes (unlike other indigenous groups in Cauca) were taking this workshop funded by the central state. This workshop exemplified the approach that both the OIT and the Central Office of Resguardos adopted in that they sought to revitalize a traditional skill (weaving) while modernizing it through its semi-mechanization.

Local officials expressed support for the OIT Andean Program's mission. The OIT consultant stated, for instance, that the mayor of Silvia expressed his support for the maintenance of *resguardos* and for their integration. We can hypothesize that while the Silvia local authorities were not necessarily keen on maintaining the *resguardos,* they were glad to receive an influx of money to their municipality. At the regional level, Reinoso claimed that the governor of the department, Dr. Miguel Angel Zuñiga, was actively collaborating with the implementation of the Andean Program; the Andean program was provided with offices in the governorship building. The local state provided a telephone line and funds for gas, transportation, telegrams, mail expenses, and maintenance of cars reserved for the Andean Program. These expenses were then reimbursed by the national government. Based on Reinoso's report, one would think that the local elites and the Catholic Church had changed their position vis-à-vis *resguardos* and had converted to the OIT worldview. However, one should take into account that local authorities were unlikely to express their reservations about a program that provided funds and technical training. After all, the stated objective of the Andean program was to "integrate" the indigenous population; the local elite may have focused on the objective of integration and ignored the emphasis on achieving integration through indigenous and collective structures.

While local authorities publicly expressed their agreement with the OIT policy/Central Office of *Resguardos*' directives, conflict and violence about collective landholding and indigenous councils were very much present. One particular case was that of the *Poblazón resguardo*/civil community; an attempted murder and arson of the police station had taken place in July of 1959. According to the director of the Central Office of *Resguardos*, members of the *cabildo* of Poblazón were afraid to advocate in favor of Law 89 of 1890, and relevant documents (presumably for the maintenance of collective landownership) had been burnt in the city hall.

A Case Study of Poblazón: Responses from the Ground

Correspondence dated May 2, 1968, between Dr. Arcesio Lopez Narvaez[43] writing from Popayán and the Division of Indigenous Affairs Office sheds light on how local notables responded to the central state's push for the revitalization of indigenous identity in Cauca.[44] Dr. Narvaez, a conservative lawyer, wrote directly to the Minister of Government, Dr. Misael Pastrana Borrerro, to request the elimination of the indigenous council of the *resguar-*

do Poblazón located nearby Popayán. Dr. Misael Pastrana Borrerro was a Conservative, but was Minister of Government for the Liberal President, Carlos Lleras Restrepo.[45] Dr. Arcesio Lopez Narvaez, who was a well-known conservative, probably thought that his partisan affiliation and status warranted the Minister of Government's direct attention. However, his correspondence ended up with the Division of Indigenous Affairs.

Dr. Narvaez sought to bolster his case for why the indigenous council of Poblazón should be terminated by giving a historical and legal account of the process of division of *resguardos* in Cauca. He started off describing the legal status of indigenous people who were affiliated with *resguardos*:

> of these backward shrunken groups and conglomeration of rustic beings perpetually assimilated to minors and excluded from the ordinary civil legislation of the Republic, except in regards to popular votes and electoral suffrage, for which they are considered legally of age.[46]

This conservative lawyer's derogatory language used to describe indigenous people stood in contrast to the Division of Indigenous Affairs' discourse that sought to revitalize indigenous cultural values. Dr. Narvaez thought of indigenous people in *resguardos* as held back and trapped in the past because of their cultural values. Dr. Narvaez went on to remind the central state that Law 89 of 1890 was meant to be a temporary measure and that the objective of this law was slow and measured integration of indigenous communities into the larger nonindigenous rural society. In addition, Law 89 gave a term of fifty years for *resguardos* to remain in place; the term of fifty years could be extended if the governor of the department where *resguardos* were located wished to do so. During those fifty years, indigenous councils were supposed to perform a census with the collaboration of municipal authorities. The municipal council had to approve the census and resolve any claims made by interested parties in terms of unjust exclusions from the census. Once the municipal council approved the census, then it went to the Prefect of the Province (whose equivalent in 1968 was the secretary of justice for the local state) for its study, and then finally to the governor of the department. Only then could the governor of the department decree the census. The division and allotment of land was supposed to conform to the census. As long as the *resguardo*'s legal structure was in effect, its members had usufructuary rights to their land plots. Once the division of the *resguardo* was carried out, the indigenous council ceased to exist. As Narvaez reminded the central state, Law 89 of 1890 went into effect on February 9, 1891, and its fifty-year term ended in February of 1941.

For Cauca, four important acts regulated the legal situation of *resguardos* and *parcialidades*: departmental Assembly's Ordinance number 10 of 1922, decree number 35 of 1951, law 81 of 1958, and finally the executive decree 2413 of 1961.

Ordinance number 10 of 1922 inventoried and classified all the *parcialidades* and *resguardos* in Cauca; the total number of *resguardos* and *parcialidades* was assessed at fifty-nine in nineteen municipalities. Dr. Narvaez explained that the local state was eager to dissolve *resguardos* that were located in the center of Cauca next to Popayán, the city that Dr. Narvaez called, "Procera, culta o ilustre ciudad de Popayán"/"heroic, cultured, or illustrious city of Popayán." Popayán, whose status as a civilized and cultured city was undeniable, was seen as diminished by the surrounding indigenous communities, which led to the push to dissolve these *resguardos*. In 1922 according to Dr. Narvaez there were six indigenous *resguardos* in the municipality of Popayán. He listed and located the *resguardos* in their different municipalities.

Popayán= 6 Toribio=3 Santa Rosa=2 Almaguer=1
Tambo=6 Timbio= 2 Cajibio=1 Tunia=1
Caldono=4 Purace=2 Morales=1 Inzá=7
Totoro=3 San Sebastián=2 Bolivar=1 Paez (Belalcazar)=10

While racism did promote the dissolution of Popayán's nearby indigenous *resguardos*, the high value of land around Popayán certainly played a role. Close proximity to a major urban market as well as the growth of the city made this land valuable. The six *resguardos* near Popayán, which were liquidated without any trouble with the exception of Poblazón, were Calibio, Julumito, Puelenje, Santa Barbara and Yanoconas. Dr. Narvaez added that Poblazón was never called a *resguardo* and was instead a multiracial community with Indians, blacks, and mestizos who coexisted together. While Dr. Narvaez saw the multiracial character of this community as an indication that it was not a *resguardo*, this was not necessarily the case since many *resguardos* over time became racially integrated especially if they were located nearby a city and if the land was fertile.

An account of how the community of Poblazón formed gives us an insight into the relationships between white elites and nonwhite groups of the area in terms of land and labor. The genesis for the formation of Poblazón came from the establishment of a large *hacienda* in the area. Dionisa Perez Manrique, a member of Bogotá's elite as the Marquis of Santiago's daughter, married the Marquis of San Miguel de la Vega. When Dionisa Perez Manrique became a widow, she became the sole owner of this immense *hacienda* or *latifundio* located next to Popayán. This large property was adjacent to the community of Poblazón, which held communal land. The advantage for the widowed Marquise to have a large *hacienda* near this community was that she could easily use the nearby labor. Dr. Narvaez stated that some of the *hacienda* workers and their families settled in the Poblazón community. The most likely scenario was that the *hacienda* both used nearby workers and imported some who ended up settling in Poblazón. Eventually, the Marquise's property was divided up into multiple *haciendas* that Popayán's elite came to own. When Dr. Narvaez suggested that the *hacienda* workers originated from the San Isidro region of Paniquita's parochial district (that was never part of Popayán's district), he attempted to make the case that the indigenous people who lived in Poblazón were not from the area and that therefore the Poblazón *resguardo* was not their ancestral land. This argument was somewhat irrelevant because many *resguardos* were formed and delimited by Spanish colonial authorities and were not necessarily based on ancestral indigenous land patterns.

In 1922, Dr. Narvaez suggested that the commission in charge of the breakup of *resguardos* must have considered Poblazón a civil community since it apparently did not conduct a census, whereas it apparently did carry out censuses in the *resguardos* of Calibio, Julumito, Puelenje, Santa Barbara, and Yanaconas. Again this argument was tenuous since, as we saw in the previous chapters, the completion of a census was a difficult matter if there were any sort of land tenure controversies. The *resguardos* that were dissolved apparently enjoyed peace and prosperity, and each indigenous family received its land plot. Dr. Narvaez went at great lengths to say that no strangers took over the land and to deny that there was any violence in the area. He also depicted the properties as "scientifically cultivated." The overall impression he conveyed was one of order and prosperity. Evidently this local magistrate wished to counter the idea that the breakup of *resguardos* led to loss of land and violence for indigenous communities.

In contrast to the rosy picture the Conservative lawyer had painted of the land of dissolved *resguardos*, Dr. Narvaez portrayed the land of Poblazón in 1968 as left fallow while its inhabitants were malnourished and stagnant. He insisted that he was not representing the interests of the neighboring landowners of Poblazón since they could not possibly be interested in expanding their properties toward this "inhospitable hill" where Poblazón was located. Dr. Narvaez added that the neighboring landowners benefited from Poblazón's *resguardo* status since they could use this cheap and vulnerable labor pool to whom they did not even pay minimum wage and did not provide any food or lodging to these "serfs." The civil community (which is what Dr. Narvaez insisted Poblazón was) was allegedly run by four keen-witted exploiters (gamonales); the Conservative lawyer was incensed that the municipal council (which had veto power) had tolerated the formation of this council. The question that emerges is that if Dr. Narvaez was not interested in representing the landowners of the area, what was his motivation? Why was he so intent on proving that this *resguardo* was not a *resguardo* and that its council should be dissolved? While we find out at the end of the lengthy missive that it was because he represented a group of Poblazón community members, racism was definitely part of his mind-set and determination to rid the center of Cauca of Poblazón. He stated, "Only the stain of Poblazón remained," referring to the presence of indigenous people and of an indigenous institution near Popayán.

The rest of the missive documented the evolution of the dissolution of *resguardos* in Cauca. As we have seen, five *resguardos* were liquidated in the Popayán municipality, then five in el Tambo, one in San Sebastián, one in Bolivar, one in Timbio, and one in Tunia. *Resguardos* with the most fertile land and access to urban markets were the first to be dissolved. However, *resguardos* during this time period were not only dissolved, some were newly recognized and legalized. Four new *resguardos* were created in the Inzá municipality and five in the Paez municipality (both municipalities were part of Tierradentro). Although many missionaries later held an anti-*resguardo* discourse, we can hypothesize that with the Catholic missionaries's growing domination of Tierradentro, they wished to consolidate their hold with the establishment of new *resguardos*. In addition, these *resguardos* in Tierradentro in the 1920s were isolated, and coffee in this area only took off as a major crop in the 1930s and 1940s. As we saw in chapter 2, the departmental government of Cauca extended the term of *resguardos* for another ten years with decree number 35 of February of 1941. In February of 1951, a new decree (number 38) extended yet again the deadline for the dissolution of *resguardos* for another ten years. Dr. Narvaez concluded his account of the legislation pertaining to indigenous *resguardos* with a summary of Law 81 of 1958 (which was discussed at the beginning of the chapter) and with an explanation of Decree number 2413 (passed in September of 1941), which gave *resguardos* five more years. He also insisted that the *resguardos* that did not have a title should revert to public land as the legislation indicated it should. The overall purpose of this legal account was to show that Law 89 of 1890 was never meant to be permanent and that countless extensions had prolonged a law that was no longer helpful or adequate.

Dr. Narvaez's missive then returned to the heart of the matter troubling him: the case of Poblazón. Evidently, he sought to further his objective of terminating the legal prerogatives that the council of Poblazón enjoyed by arguing that *resguardos* that did not have a title (which was the case of Poblazón) should be returned to public land. He stated that no title was ever found despite an exhaustive search for it, but he never made it clear who was looking for the titles. He also did not mention the incident (referred to in another document) of the burning of the city hall where such documents might have been located. Instead he referred to a report made by a lawyer, Dr. Victor Gutierrez who came to Poblazón (years ago/probably the 1950s) as a visitador de *Resguardos* Indigenas. Dr. Gutierrez had come to the conclusion that Poblazón was a civil community and not a *resguardo*; to affirm this conclusion he stated that the people of Poblazón were "civilized" and that they enjoyed the peaceful and prosperous cultivation of their land plots. Dr. Gutierrez mentioned that the land was fertile and that potatoes, wheat, barley, and vegetables were grown. Although Dr. Narvaez quoted Dr. Gutierrez, he seemed to ignore the contradictions between his portrayal of Poblazón as a place that no one wanted to acquire and Dr. Gutierrez's description.

Dr. Narvaez's motivation in insisting that Poblazón was not a *resguardo* was revealed at the end of his lengthy missive; he represented certain members of the community who wished to dissolve the *resguardo* and had previously sent a lengthy memorandum in 1967. He argued that these inhabitants of Poblazón, because they were considered part of a *resguardo*, did not have the same protection in terms of their patrimony (land/wealth) that other Colombian citizens enjoyed.

However, the Conservative lawyer admitted that the council now present in Poblazón opposed the division of the *resguardo*/civil community; hence his original request that Poblazón dissolve the council. As the reader will remember, many lawyers who argued the case for dissolution stood to benefit if the dissolution of the *resguardo* went through as they were often paid with land plots. We can speculate that Dr. Narvaez was incensed after investing many hours of his time (which may not have been immediately remunerated) that he would not receive a penny if the dissolution of the civil community/*resguardo* did not go through. He went on even further to agree that the majority of the community of Poblazón supported the council that sought to argue that their community was a *resguardo*. His racism did not let him see that he was undermining his very case; he characterized the people of Poblazón as obtuse and easily dominated by three or four *caciques*/*gamonales*. He expected the central state to unilaterally dissolve the council. The Division of Indigenous Affairs agreed with Dr. Narvaez's conclusion that indeed Poblazón was a civil community, but they pointed out that since Poblazón was a civil community, they had no authority to intervene, and furthermore, only the majority of the people of the civil community had the authority to dissolve the council.[47]

In general, the conservative lawyer ridiculed the *indigenistas* of the area. In addition, Dr. Narvaez was mystified that the municipal authorities of Popayán had done nothing to start the process of dissolution of the *resguardo* and/or community. In short, Dr. Narvaez was disgusted with what he viewed as irrational support that the community of Poblazón enjoyed in terms of maintaining its *resguardo* status.

He maintained that those who opposed the dissolution of Poblazón as a *resguardo* regarded Poblazón as the "most precious and beautiful pearl of the indigenous necklace of IndoAmerica," which Dr. Narvaez was trying to seize. Dr. Narvaez reserved his greatest ire for one of the Division of Indigenous Affairs employees, Marco A. Paz. He pointed out that Marco A. Paz was colluding with the council members of the Poblazón community and was encouraging them to argue/maintain that Poblazón was a *resguardo*. Particularly annoying to Dr. Narvaez was that Marco A. Paz was giving this advice even though he was not a lawyer and had no legal training. He attributed the resurgence of Poblazón's indigenous identity (a fictitious one he argued) to Marco A. Paz's intervention.

> It should be enough to remember that until recently and during many years this council was eliminated because the mayor had cancelled the elections without calling for new elections. And that was the best period of tranquility and peace for the community members. This was changed and ended because a high placed bureaucrat of the *indigenista* division came and said that Poblazón was the ideal place to create an experimental pro-Indian reservation, not only in Cauca and Colombia, but even perhaps in Andean South America. This bureaucrat gave the order and an election was held that the mayor then approved of. And we went back to the old ways. Very beautiful is and will be the evocative and romantic literature about the remote Pre-Columbian and colonial time and some of its institutions and customs. But then what? What do we do with the other guardian principle of our substantive and established legislation in various Codes such the political and municipal Regime (art. 56) and primarily in articles 8 and 9 of our civil code that say: "Custom shall in no case compete with Law."[48]

Dr. Narvaez was a racist who thought that the existence of Poblazón as an indigenous identity stained the purity and reputation of Popayán's Spanish heritage. More importantly for his legal cause, he failed to understand that the moral order of Cauca had changed; he did not understand that a racist discourse that presupposed the superiority of nonindigenous customs would not be supported. His counterdiscourse, which upheld the value of European civilization and the importance of bringing about progress and development, which was hegemonic (although contested) in the 1930s, 1940s, and 1950s no longer worked as effectively in the late 1960s. The Division of Indigenous Affairs and the OIT pushed for progress and development as well for indigenous communities, but a key shift had taken place with the valorization of communal landholding and governance. Dr. Narvaez did not understand the power of the word *indígena* in 1968; in effect what he dismissed as a romanticized and ridiculous attempt to revitalize indigenous traditions was taken seriously both by one branch of the central state and by international organizations interested in indigenous issues.

To attribute solely or to blame as Dr. Narvaez did, the resurgence of an indigenous council in Poblazón to Marco A. Paz (the DAI representative) was an exaggeration. However, we should not underestimate Marco A. Paz's role in the resurgence of an indigenous council. The appearance of a national actor in Cauca who saw richness, beauty, and value in the indigenous character of Poblazón gave legitimacy to those on the ground who supported the resurgence of collective action based on an indigenous ethnic identity. In other words, it was the meeting of desire from the ground, which Dr. Narvaez unjustly dismissed, with the new discourse of an employee representing the central state that gave the indigenous movement in Cauca its initial momentum.

The decade of the 1960s saw a radical change in how indigenous people and communities were represented by one branch of the Colombian central state. The Division of Indigenous Affairs portrayed indigenous communities of Cauca as victims of violence and as ill prepared for modernity. The OIT and the Colombian central state chose to interpret the presence of violence in municipalities where there was a significant indigenous presence due to geographic factors. Thus, the Division of Indigenous Affairs attributed loss of land and destruction of the social fabric as stemming from indigenous people's unique vulnerabilities. Instead of identifying common causes of violence in both indigenous and nonindigenous communities, the emphasis was on how the loss of indigenous traditional cultural values had led to violence and chaos. In other words, it did not identify the role of merchants and of unscrupulous landowners who seized land from peasants regardless of their ethnicity, nor did it posit the need for a central state that would safeguard the rights of all rural folk. Ironically, by ignoring the divisions that existed within indigenous communities and portraying indigenous people as uniformly victimized, the DAI bolstered the formation of a collectivity based on a regional ethnic identity.

In addition, the Division of Indigenous Affairs did not question or challenge the dominant paradigm of capitalism, modernity, and development. The radical and ultimately positive contribution that the DAI in conjunction with the OIT made was to advance that collective landholding and indigenous communal government were the best conduits for indigenous communities to achieve development. In a place like Cauca, which prided itself on its Spanish origins and its white elite, a discourse that celebrated indigenous culture was revolutionary. No doubt the "white" elite did not take this discourse seriously and thought of the OIT and the DAI employees as delusional fools underestimating the power of this discourse in the hands of indigenous communities. The central state's branch, Division of Indigenous Affairs, was not powerful by itself and suffered from the same limitations that the Tribunal of Reconciliation and Equity experienced when implementing the central state's policies on the ground. However, a crucial difference existed in that the Division of Indigenous Affairs created a political and organizational space for indigenous communities to re-create indigenous collective structures. As we shall see in the next chapter, in the next two decades, indigenous communities in alliance with the Left would astutely use this state-sponsored ethnic discourse and collective strategies (based on the revitalization of communal landownership and indigenous councils) to regain lost land and to obtain sorely needed state resources for education and health care in indigenous communities.

By way of conclusion, it is interesting to note that the *resguardo* of Poblazón still exists today and enjoys all the rights and protection that other *resguardos* in Colombia possess.[49] In addition, in December of 2012, the U.S. ambassador to Colombia, Michael McKinley, visited the *resguardo* of Poblazón and heard the concerns of the rural population of Cauca on a territory whose identity was so hotly contested.[50] In the brief article, there was no mention of the long judicial process that Poblazón underwent to become identified and fully recognized by the central state and local state as an indigenous *resguardo*. It is simply referred to as the indigenous *resguardo* of Poblazón. In other words, the discourse and policies advocated by Marco A. Paz and the central state won the day.

NOTES

1. Oficina Internaciónal del Trabajo Programa Ampliado de Asistencia Tecnica. R.6. OIT/TAP/Colombia R.6. Informe al Gobierno de Colombia sobre el problema indigena en el departamento del Cauca. Encuesta Preliminar a la Aportación Eventual de Asistencia Tecnica Dentro Del Programa Andino. OIT. Geneva, 1959, 24.
2. Informe, 24.
3. Brett Troyan, "Constructing a 'Modern Colombia': The Life and Work of Gregorio Hernández de Alba, Director of the Bureau of Indian Affairs: 1930–1970," *European Review of Latin American and Caribbean Studies* 82 (April 2007).
4. Interview with Carlos Hernández de Alba, Bogota, Colombia, November 2000.
5. Javier Ocampo Lopez, "El Maestro Orlando Fals Borda. Sus ideas educativas y sociales para el cambio en la sociedad colombiana," *RHELA* 12 (2009, 18).
6. Ibid.
7. Marie Chantal Barre, *Ideologia indigenistas y movimientos indios* (Mexico: Siglo Veintiuno Editores, 1983), 61.
8. Marie Chantal Barre, 63.
9. Alan Knight, "Racism, Revolution, and Indigenismo: Mexico, 1910–1940" in *The Idea of Race in Latin America, 1870–1940,* edited by Richard Graham (Austin: University of Texas Press, 1990), 83.
10. Oficina Internaciónal del Trabajo Programa Ampliado de Asistencia Tecnica. R.6. OIT/TAP/Colombia R.6. Informe al Gobierno de Colombia sobre el problema indigena en el departamento del Cauca. Encuesta Preliminar a la Aportación Eventual de Asistencia Tecnica Dentro Del Programa Andino. OIT. Geneva, 1959, 1.
11. Ibid.
12. Mr. Koulisher was previously on a similar mission to assess the state of indigenous communities from 1955 to 1956 in Ecuador.
13. Oficina Internaciónal del Trabajo Programa Ampliado de Asistencia Tecnica. R.6. OIT/TAP/Colombia R.6. Informe al Gobierno de Colombia sobre el problema indigena en el departamento del Cauca. Encuesta Preliminar a la Aportación Eventual de Asistencia Tecnica Dentro Del Programa Andino. OIT. Geneva, 1959, 1.
14. Gonzalo Sánchez, "Rehabilitación y violencia bajo el frente nacional," *Análisis politico*, no. 4 (May–August 1988).
15. Ibid.
16. Mariano Lugari was the Italian attorney who invited Lebret (development expert) to come to Popayán and the father of Paolo Lugari. See Alan Weisman, *Gaviotas: A Village to Reinvent the World* (White River Junction, VT: Chelsea Green Pub, 1998), 24.

17. Informe, 7.
18. Informe, 8.
19. Informe, 9.
20. Informe, 9.
21. Informe, 10.
22. Informe, 9.
23. Informe, 10.
24. Informe, 11.
25. Informe, 12.
26. Informe, 12. "Sorprendido por la necesidad de comprar y vender, por el progreso tecnico y por el sistema de salariado—prácticas ajenas a su manera de vivir tradicional, tiene necesidad de asistencia tecnica, de credito controlado, de organización comercial que lo proteja contra ciertos intermediarios poco escrupulosos."
27. Informe, 12. "Y lo mismo se puede decir del trabajo colectivo: fomentando el espíritu de la minga por una orientación tecnica y una formación professional adecuada se podrian mejorar sus métodos de trabajo y equipo."
28. Bilingual education was also promoted in this report for communities that were monolingual in an indigenous language.
29. The example of Manuel Quintín Lame's father is pertinent as well.
30. Informe, 25.
31. Francois Correa points out that the Colombian Institute of *Indigenistas* was created in 1941/formalized in 1943 by a group of investigators affiliated with the newly founded National Ethnological Institute. It was financed by its members. This institute existed for about ten years. "The Modernity of Indigenista Thought and Colombia's Instituto Naciónal Indigenista," *Maguare* (no. 21) 2007, 28. See also Fondo Ministerio del Interior, Caja 1591, Folder 12356.
32. Informe, 12.
33. Fondo Ministerio del Interior Caja 1581, Folder 1536. Archivo General de la Nacion.
34. Fondo Ministerio del Interior, Caja 1591, Folder 12356. Informe/Memorandum de la Division de Asuntos Indigenas. No date. Gregorio Hernández de Alba.
35. Fondo Ministerio del Interior, Caja 1591, Folder 12356. Informe/Memorandum de la Division de Asuntos Indigenas. No date. Gregorio Hernández de Alba.
36. As we saw in the 1930s and 1940s chapter, indigenous councils were increasingly ineffective. The ineffectiveness of indigenous councils to stem land loss led some indigenous *resguardo* members to push for the breakup of *resguardos*.
37. "Bases Preliminares para la aplicación del programa andino entre los indígenas del Cauca, Colombia"/"Preliminary basis for the Application of the Andean Program amongst Indigenous People of Cauca." Fondo Ministerio del Interior, Caja 1581, Folder 12543.
38. Fondo Ministerio del Interior, Caja 1591, Folder 12356. Local infrastructure projects were also funded such as the construction of bridges.
39. Fondo Ministerio del Interior, Caja 1581, Letter to Humberto Valencia Paz, Jefe Zona Agropecuaria del Cauca, Popayán from Gregorio Hernández de Alba. October 29, 1959.
40. Fondo Ministerio del Interior, Caja 166. Informe de Labores del Abogado Tercero de *Resguardos* Indigenas de Caldono, Zona Agropecuaria del Cauca. Sector Popayán. Report corresponding to December of 1960.
41. "A todas esas parcialidades se les dio instrucción sobre el prejuicio de las bebidas, haciéndoles ver el grado de degeneración en que se encuentran, estado que aprovechan los blancos, para abusar de ellos. Se les hizo ver la obligación que tienen de enviar los hijos a la escuela y de enseñarles el cultivo de la tierra."
42. Fondo Ministerio del Interior, Caja 1581. Letter from Gregorio Hernández de Alba to Humberto Valencia Paz, Jefe Zona Agropecuaria de Cauca, Popayán, dated October 29, 1959.
43. Dr. Arcesio Lopez Narvaez was the owner of the Conservative newspaper, *La Razon*, that ridiculed Manuel Quintín Lame and his Liberal allies. http://partidoconservador.info/libro/3-la-republica-liberal.html.
44. Fondo Ministerio del Interior, Caja 166, Carpeta 01370.
45. http://www.biografiasyvidas.com/biografia/p/pastrana_borrero.htm.

46. Fondo Ministerio del Interior, Caja 166, Carpeta 01370. "de esos atrasados reductos y conglemorados de seres rusticos, perpetuamente asimilados a menores de edad y excluidos de la legislación civil ordinaria de la Republica, excepto en lo tocante a votaciones populares y sufragio electoral, para lo cual si se les tiene como mayores de edad."

47. Fondo del Ministerio del Interior, Caja 166, Carpeta 01370. Letter from the Division of Indigenous Affairs to Dr. Arcesio Lopez Narvaez, May 2, 1968.

48. Bastaría recordar que hasta hace poco y durante varios años estuvo eliminado ese Cabildo por haber la Alcadía anulado la elección sin convocar a nuevas votaciones. Y esa fue la mejor época de tranquilidad y sosiego de los comuneros. Que se alteró y vino abajo, porque un alto funcionario de la division indigenista Ministerial vino y dijo que Poblazón era el lugar ideal para crear un "*resguardo*-piloto indigenista", no solo en el Cauca y en Colombia, sino quizá en los Andes Suramericanos. Ese funcionario ordenó, y se hizo una elección de Cabildo al cual posesionó la Alcaldía. Y volvimos a las andadas. Muy bonita es y será la evocadora y romántica literatura sobre las remotísimas epocas precolombina y colonial y algunas de sus instituciones y costumbres. Pero entonces? Que hacemos con otro principio tutelar de nuestra legislación sustantiva y consagrada en varios Códigos, como el de Régimen Político y Municipal (art.56) y primordialmente en los artículos 8 y 9 de nuestro Código Civil, y que dicen: "La costumbre en ningún caso tiene fuerza contra la Ley."

49. http://co.geoview.info/*resguardo*_indigena_de_Poblazón,62089783wD.

50. http://www.incoder.gov.co/Noticias_Incoder/Embajador_EstadosUnidos_Cauca_Indigenas.aspx.

Chapter Six

Ethnic Citizenship in Colombia

The Experience of the Regional Indigenous Council of the Cauca in Southwestern Colombia from 1970 to 1990

Colombia is one of the few countries in Latin America with a long and continuous tradition of electoral democracy. Unlike Argentina, Chile, and Uruguay, Colombia only experienced one brief period of dictatorship in the 1950s.[1] Moreover, in contrast to Peru, Ecuador, and Bolivia, Colombia has allowed all men over the age of twenty-one to vote since 1936 without any literacy, income, or ethnicity requirements. But this exemplary record (for Latin America) of elections and of citizen participation in elections is coupled with the enduring problem of political violence. So here we have what is known as the "Colombian paradox": a democratic country with endemic and pandemic violence.[2]

Operating within this political paradox, the indigenous communities of Colombia and their allies have emerged as a major political force that successfully mobilized to achieve economic and political change. This chapter argues that the success of the indigenous movement was made possible by the elaboration of an ethnic citizenship.[3] I use the term *ethnic citizenship* rather than *ethnic identity* because I focus on the relationship between indigenous groups and the nation-state. Other scholars such as Jimeno (2005) and Barth (1969) have defined ethnic identity in a relational manner as well, but I find the term *ethnic citizenship* more useful given my exclusive emphasis on the political nature of the claims made on the basis of ethnicity.

The elaboration of this relationship between indigenous groups and the nation-state did not occur in a vacuum. Activists, guerrilla armies, and political parties altered and at times shaped the interaction between indigenous groups and the nation-state.[4] Emphasizing certain key moments, I explore how from the 1970s to the 1990s indigenous groups, in conjunction with the nation-state, elaborated a new reciprocal relationship that stressed the ethnic character of the claims made by indigenous groups and at the same time gradually limited the class element of these claims. The repression of broader claims by peasants and the overlooking of the cooperation of nonindigenous social groups in the construction of the indigenous movement were intrinsic to the elaboration of indigenous citizenship.

Colombia is an interesting case for comparison when looking at the interaction between the state and the indigenous movements because it was a formal democracy before other Latin American countries experienced the democratization process. This chapter, while not minimizing the agency of the indigenous communities, argues that, in the case of Colombia, exogenous factors played a crucial role in the formation of ethnic citizenship. These exogenous factors emerged from the violent yet democratic context of Colombia in the 1970s and 1980s. Emergency decrees interrupted and diminished Colombian democracy in the 1970s and 1980s, and human rights violations occurred on a regular basis, but a limited formal democracy existed in that elections took place. Thus, recent studies examining the privileged role of ethnic politics in the general context of political democratization have focused on the decades of the 1980s, 1990s, and 2000s (Brysk 2000; Warren and Jackson 2002). Colombia provides the case study of a formal democracy that experienced the shift from class-based claims to ethnic-based ones in the 1970s and 1980s. During those decades, the left (broadly defined here), while clearly on the wane, had not yet lost its worldwide ideological influence. In addition, the armed left is still very much present in Colombia and posed a real strategic challenge to the nation-state until very recently. In other Latin American countries, no guerrilla army presented a viable challenge to the nation-state at the turn of the twenty-first century.[5]

Scholars of indigenous movements throughout Latin America have noted the shift from class-based claims to demands based on ethnic identity from the 1970s to the 1980s and 1990s (Pallares 2002; Sieder 2002).[6] In her introduction to *Multiculturalism in Latin America,* Sieder (2000, 1) notes that, in the past decade, ethnicity rather than class has become the key focus of political demands in Latin America. Pallares (2002, 34) suggests that in Ecuador a new *indianismo* allows for a "double consciousness" à la W. E. B. DuBois, which allows the indigenous communities to maintain the material demands based on class identity while framing them in an ethnic way. Although I agree with Pallares that class demands are not abandoned but rearticulated, I suggest that this rearticulation has an important ideological and social cost for the majority of Colombian peasants. I certainly do not believe that class consciousness is the only important consciousness or that ethnic identity is some form of false consciousness, but I do think that, in Colombia, the state promoted the move away from a class discourse with the objective of diminishing the power of class-based movements.

Ironically, the indigenous movement in Colombia emerged from a tradition of the left. As this chapter shows, a number of indigenous leaders and nonindigenous activists started off their political activism by participating in leftist organizations. Tate (2007, 73) has shown how the first wave of Colombian human rights activists of the early 1980s arose from the leftist political culture of the 1970s: "For the vast majority of self-defined human rights activists, however, activism was not simply a response to political violence but was profoundly shaped by the political culture inherited from this legacy of radical activism. . . . For both human rights activists and victims' family members who joined the vast majority of organizations, however, activism was defined in the terms of the Colombian left. In their view, Colombian history was an unbroken line of state repression against popular organizations, which justified revolutionary violence and focused on state responsibility."

This holds especially true for the nonindigenous activists who accompanied the indigenous movement in its early stage. The gradual disillusion with the left was brought about in part by the dogmatic approach that one of the armed factions of the left (i.e., Fuerzas Armadas Revolucionarias de Colombia [FARC], or Armed Revolutionary Forces of Colombia) adopted vis-à-vis the indigenous grassroots movement. The other reason for the gradual shift in discourse was the state's nudging toward an ethnic discourse and representation.

As discussed in previous chapters, the Colombian indigenous population has enjoyed unprecedented rights in terms of land and culture since 1991. The vast bulk of that territory is held collectively: 80 percent of the indigenous population owns 408 *resguardos* (collective inalienable land grants created, for the most part, during the colonial era by the Spanish Crown) covering 27,621,257 hectares (Pineda 1995, 13).[7] The nation-state, in the Constitution of 1991, affirmed the inalienable nature of the indigenous collective landholdings (Van Cott 2000, 85). In addition, indigenous communities obtained the right to judicial autonomy within the *resguardos* and to the direct disbursement of state funds to *cabildos*, the *resguardo* council authorities. In the department of Cauca, where the indigenous movement emerged, indigenous communities recovered an impressive amount of land: 74,228 hectares from 1970 to 1996 (Peñaranda 1999a, 92). In recent years, political indigenous leaders have also emerged as one of the most effective voices for peace. The indigenous councils of the *resguardos* reject the presence of armed actors (guerrillas, paramilitaries, and the regular army) in their territory. This rejection of violence and of armed actors is enforced by an army of men who are unarmed except for their *bastones de mando,* or ceremonial canes, which represent indigenous authority.

Scholars such as Rappaport (2005), Caviedes (2000), and Findji (1992) have pointed out the distinct nature of the political practices of the indigenous grassroots group, and more recently the importance of nonindigenous allies. This chapter contends that the indigenous groups, specifically those of the Cauca, reconstructed and reinvented colonial political institutions largely because of the specific historical circumstances of the 1970s and 1980s.[8] I also suggest that at least one branch of the state legitimized this new type of citizenship but sought to limit it to the indigenous ethnic groups.

Indigenous communities and their allies organized themselves in a grassroots association, known as the Consejo Regional Indígena del Cauca (Regional Indigenous Council of the Cauca, or CRIC). The CRIC and the Movimiento de Autoridades Indígenas de Colombia (AICO, or the Colombian Indigenous Authorities Movement—the other indigenous grassroots organization, smaller and with less political clout) constructed an ethnic discourse that eventually privileges nonviolence and deliberately eschews partisan politics. This chapter emphasizes the points at which the indigenous movement constructed a citizenship discourse that sought to democratize Colombian society not through involvement in political parties but through the formation of grassroots associations, the creation of a pantheon of martyrs and heroes, the reinvention of political institutions, and public displays of unity and ethnic identity. This chapter also focuses on the instances when the national state legitimized this ethnic citizenship and thereby ensured its partial success.

The formative moments I will concentrate on are the founding and early development of the CRIC and the formation of the indigenous guerrilla group Movimiento Armado del Quintín Lame (MAQL; Armed Movement of Quintín Lame). These are two defining moments when CRIC members emphasized the ethnic nature of the indigenous peasant's demands and pressed for social change based on the legitimization of their identity as *indígenas.* Thus, the MAQL claimed that it was the direct heir of the armed movement organized by Quintín Lame in the 1910s rather than emphasizing the political context of the 1980s. During these two moments the state ultimately upheld the narrative established by the indigenous movement.

ORIGINS OF THE CRIC

As seen in the previous chapter, in an effort to compensate for the loss of the traditional avenues of political participation, the state promoted new forms of political participation, such as cooperatives, associations, and local civic organizations (*juntas de acción comunal*).[9] For some indigenous leaders, such as Marcos Avirama and Gregorio Palechor, this was an important political space in which they tested their political skills and acquired experience in leadership. For instance, Gregorio Palechor, a former leader of the CRIC, stated: "Entonces ya salió ese órgano que le llaman 'Acción Comunal.' Entonces ya en la comunidad me nombraron como presidente de la Junta de Acción Comunal, porque yo era una persona que prestaba el servicio y era progresista" (Jimeno 2005, 145).

The general context for these initiatives was the agrarian reform of 1961. Law 135 (the central law of the agrarian reform) determined that any unproductive land could be confiscated. It aimed to end unproductive *latifundia* and to distribute land more democratically. Other laws established the automatic renewal of sharecropping contracts for ten years and made eviction more costly. The objective was to modernize Colombia and to foster a middle class of peasants by giving them access to credit, investment, and more land.

Although the United States and the liberal government hoped to avoid a communist revolution by creating a middle class and by encouraging peasants to form an organization in 1966 (Asociación Nacional de Usuarios Campesinos [ANUC], or National Association of Peasants), many organizers from the radical branch of the Liberal Party and Marxists hoped for political change and a radical restructuring of land tenure patterns. Indigenous peasants participated in the agrarian reform in a number of ways. They joined cooperatives, petitioned for fair sharecropping contracts, joined the ANUC, and mobilized politically on the basis of social class. Marcos Avirama (1998), who became the president of the CRIC in the 1970s, told me, "Iba en un proceso político de izquierda del 71 al 73"/"I was involved in the leftist political movement from 1971 to 1973".

ANUC's experience from 1966 to 1973 revealed to the indigenous population the weaknesses of the left and the limitations of the national government's willingness to support a real redistribution of land and resources. While ANUC successfully organized peasants, different factions of the left (e.g., Maoists, Leninists) soon fought among themselves, and some leftists developed a radical and antagonistic discourse toward the state. When repression ensued, in part because of these different factions' revolutionary discourse, some would-be guerrillas left the peasants to face the consequences of state repression alone (Rivera Cusicanqui 1982). ANUC eventually split into two factions in 1972 and lost most of its effectiveness. Thus, the national context of the emergence of the CRIC was one in which the left was splintered into multiple and warring factions and in which the national state had shown its disinclination to support a radical restructuring of resources based on class identity.

The founding of the CRIC is the first moment it started to construct a political space and to elaborate a new language of citizenship. On February 24, 1971, approximately two thousand indigenous peasants came together to found the organization in Toribío, Cauca (CRIC 1981). The majority of the peasants were Guambianos and Nasas, the two largest indigenous ethnic groups in the Cauca department (CRIC 1981). Most of them lived in tremendous poverty. Indeed, statistics placed Cauca's indigenous peasants at the very bottom of Colombia's socioeconomic hierarchy (Findji 1978; Van de Sandt 2007, 109). Also present at that first meeting were nonindigenous government officials from the Colombian Institute of Agrarian Reform (INCORA; Bolaños 1999). Their presence indicates the sympathy that indigenous peasants generated. The meeting also attracted nonindigenous peasants and nonindigenous leftist activists. Afro-Colombians as well as *mestizos* attended the meeting, but their presence is not emphasized in the official literature recounting the founding of the CRIC.

Although most of the discussions addressed unequal land distribution and the need for reform within the framework of the ongoing Colombian agrarian reform, some individuals made long speeches about the imminence of a revolution and the need for revolutionary action (Avirama 1998). Marcos Avirama (1998) stated: "También participan políticos que llegan allá para aprovechar la asamblea para hacer política. Algunos plantean la lucha armada."/"There were also politicians that arrived there (the meeting) to take advantage of the assembly to do politics. Some of them proposed an armed struggle." These revolutionary speeches have been erased from the official record because of the clear repression that ensued from one branch of the state and because they did not fit into the later narrative about the mobilization of the indigenous people. The police and military army members present to gather intelligence about the meeting later arrested many of the nonindigenous and indigenous leaders of this congress (Avirama 1998; *Unidad Indígena* 1975, 2).

The first and principal demand that survived the first congress was for an end to *terraje,* a form of sharecropping. The other demands were that INCORA expropriate farms located on land that had belonged to indigenous communities and distribute that land for free to indigenous families; that the Division of Indigenous Affairs be eliminated; that Law 89 of 1890 be modified, which provided the legal basis for collective landholding; that the *resguardos* be expanded where land had been divided into too-small units; and that indigenous people be allowed to participate in any decisions made about them (CRIC 1981). In addition, a fair amount of discussion had taken place about Law 89, which would turn out to be the cornerstone of the Colombian indigenous movement. The only demand that survived this first meeting was for an end to sharecropping.

The anonymous authors of a history of the CRIC produced by the Centro de Investigacíon y Educación Popular (CINEP) attributed this emphasis on class demands to the presence at the first meeting of mostly indigenous sharecroppers rather than indigenous people who still held land in *resguardos*. The implication is that because the indigenous sharecroppers no longer lived in a community, they no longer had a strong sense of ethnic identity. However, a large number of Guambiano indigenous people who had organized themselves previously in cooperatives (e.g., Cooperativa de las Delicias) did attend the meeting (Bolaños 1999; Muelas 2005, 427). Of all the indigenous ethnic groups in the Cauca, the Guambianos had most retained their indigenous language, clothing, and customs. Ethnic demands were not the most central in this founding meeting (though they certainly were present) because the indigenous sharecroppers adopted the dominant discourse of the time. Furthermore, as Jhon Jairo (1998) stated, "Los marxistas habían hecho el trabajo de base pero no tenían la visión de la especificidad de lo indígena"/"Marxists had done the groundwork but they did not have an understanding of the specificity of the indigenous issue."

This very first meeting of the CRIC is sometimes forgotten or mentioned briefly; when described, it is generally depicted as a temporary aberration in the indigenous movement's linear and continuous progress toward a strong ethnic identity. No mention is made of the presence of the leftist activists and their revolutionary speeches. It was only in my interviews with former participants that I heard of the presence of would-be revolutionaries. The reason these would-be revolutionaries came to this meeting, as well as nonindigenous political actors, lies in the CRIC's origins. The CRIC emerged from the Federación Regional Social y Agraria (FRESAGRO, or Regional Social and Agrarian Federation). Gustavo Mejía and Father Pedro León Rodríguez founded FRESAGRO in September 1970 (Cortes 1988; Jairo 1998). They did not initially intend specifically to organize the indigenous communities, but they wanted to mobilize the lower classes in general. FRESAGRO attempted to organize both the urban and the rural communities in northern Cauca, most of whose inhabitants were Afro-Colombians. According to Marcos Avirama (1998), "El equipo de FRESAGRO estaba trabajando en parte plana con las negritudes. Ellos no respondieron con la propuesta que hacía FRESAGRO de organizar"/"The team of FRESAGRO was working in the flat area (of Cauca) with blacks. They did not respond to FRESAGRO proposal to organize them."

It is worthwhile to consider the backgrounds of FRESAGRO's founders, as FRESAGRO was responsible for founding CRIC. Mejía had just returned to northwestern Cauca from the infamous prison of *La Gorgona* in the Pacific (Jairo 1998). Jhon Jairo attributed Mejía's imprisonment to his participation in the kidnapping of Harold Eder, an extremely wealthy sugar planter. Pedro Cortes (1988) suggested that he had been jailed because he had killed a police officer in self-defense. Mejía's imprisonment in La Gorgona suggested that national and local authorities had taken his crime very seriously. *Unidad Indígena* (the official CRIC newspaper) does not mention any of these details of Mejía's life. When Mejía returned to the Cauca, he came as a member of the MRL, the radical branch of the Liberal Party in the 1960s and early 1970s (Cortes 1988). Once in northern Cauca, he tried to create broad alliances among MRL, the Communist Party, and the Movimiento Obrero Independiente Revolucionario (MOIR, or Workers' Independent Revolutionary Movement). Mejía's background suggests that the indigenous movement started out very much involved in Colombian leftist politics.

The other FRESAGRO founder, Father Pedro León Rodríguez, was a Catholic priest who was part of the radical, Christian Golconda movement (Cortes 1988; *Unidad Indígena* 1982, 3). He was an admirer and friend of Camilo Torres, a priest-turned-guerrilla-leader in the 1960s. Pablo Tattay (1999), a nonindigenous activist and former Quintín Lame guerrilla member, described Torres as follows: "Era un cura de origén conservador. Pero como muchos sacerdotes que actuaron al nivel local se sensibilizó a la situación social. El fue amigo personal de Camilo Torres."/"He was a Conservative Catholic priest. But like many priests that acted locally he became sensitive to the social situation. He had a friendship with Camilo Torres." It was not evident from these beginnings that the indigenous movement would eventually eschew violence as a means of negotiation and mobilization and represent itself as emerging from an indigenous tradition of resistance rather than from the national political context of leftist activism and guerrillas. The silence in the later recounting of the history of the CRIC about certain aspects of Mejía's life allows the indigenous grassroots organization to avoid being labeled by the state as subversive. Mejía's presence also explains why some activists felt that the first CRIC meeting was an appropriate venue for advocating an armed revolution. The police arrests of so many participants in that meeting, among them the CRIC organizers, suggest that they believed that a guerrilla movement was in formation.

This chapter considers the founding meeting as a crucial starting point for the analysis of the Colombian indigenous movement. Two interrelated issues emerge from the examination of this first meeting: the actual policy of the Colombian indigenous movement and the representation and/or narration of the movement. The founding meeting allows us to understand that the ethnic nature of the claims made by the Colombian indigenous movement were not a given. The subsequent twenty years would involve constructing a discourse and policies that would naturalize the ethnic nature of indigenous politics and create a space for ethnic citizenship. It is not that the indigenous people of Cauca were not Indians, but rather that the public nature of their identity had yet to be deployed. Also important here is the state's selective legitimization.

The second CRIC meeting, mentioned most frequently in CRIC accounts of its history, took place on September 6, 1971, in Susana, in northern Cauca (*Unidad Indígena* 1975, 2). The seven demands elaborated at this conference endured for the following twenty years. The nature of the demands is often cited as proof that the ethnic discourse of the indigenous communities of the Cauca emerges from a long historical tradition that goes back to colonial times and was taken up again in the early twentieth century by the Quintín Lame movement. As the reader will recall, Lame was a Nasa Indian who organized the indigenous communities of the Cauca in 1910 and challenged the hegemony of the landowning elite through legal treatises and actions that were later represented as armed ones (Castrillón 1973; Rappaport 1990). By 1918 he was in jail and his political movement had been disbanded (Castrillón 1973). He later moved to the region of Tolima, where for the next twenty years, he again sought to organize the indigenous communities and to recover lost *resguardos*. He died in 1967, isolated and largely forgotten except by a handful of faithful followers (Castillo-Cárdenas 1987).

The seven demands of the second founding conference were almost identical to Quintín Lame's demands of the 1910s. Demands for bilingual education, restoration of the *resguardos*, and preservation of Law 89 signaled a shift in discourse and a step toward the construction of an ethnic agenda within the indigenous movement. The most important aim of the CRIC program was the recuperation of the *resguardos*, which shaped the practices and agenda of the organization for the next ten years. How do we understand this shift? Is this a resurgence of ethnic identity that had been dormant? The second conference took place eight months after the first one, and it is unlikely that a huge shift in consciousness in indigenous communities had taken place in such a short time. This conference took place clandestinely and was much smaller because of the repression that the first one had unleashed (Bonilla 1998).

Víctor Daniel Bonilla (1998), a nonindigenous participant at the meeting, suggested that he had played a crucial role in modifying the demands of the indigenous movement. Jhon Jairo (1998) recounted, "Víctor no era de formación ortodoxa. No ha leído nunca yo creo a Kant, a Hegel, ni seriamente a Marx. Tenia mayor capacidad para captar el entorno. Fue capaz de traducir el discurso de las comunidades."/"Victor was not trained in the orthodox tradition (meaning Marxist). I don't think he had ever read Kant, Hegel or not even Marx seriously. He had a greater ability to understand/perceive the environment. He was able to translate the demands of the communities (meaning indigenous)." Bonilla was a lawyer with a history of intellectual activism; in 1968, he had published the book *Servants of God and Masters of Indians: The State and the Capuchin Mission in Putumayo* about the Catholic missions' merciless exploitation of the indigenous people in the Putumayo area. The book became an international best seller. As a result of the book, Bonilla became a lifelong *indigenista.* In his interview, he described himself as a key player in the construction of ethnic identity in the Cauca. Bonilla (1998) felt that in 1971 the ethnic identity of the Paeces, now known as Nasas, did not exist yet: "Puede hablarse ahora de los paeces casi como una identidad, hace veinte o veinticinco años atrás, no. Uno les decía: 'ustedes los paeces y decían los paeces, Que es eso? Nosotros somos de

Jambalo, et cetera.' Yo tuvé que hacer mucha fuerza para impulsar la identidad."/"Can one talk today about the Paeces almost like an identity, twenty to twenty-five years ago, no. One would say: you the Paeces and they would say the Paeces, what is that? We are from Jambalo, etc." Bonilla (1998) claimed that he played a crucial role at the CRIC's second conference in suggesting that Law 89 should be maintained and in his insistence on the maintenance of *resguardos*. Bonilla (1998) stated: "Yo venía de una tradición diferente a los muchachos jóvenes. Yo quería poner el énfasis en la particularidad del indígena y no me interesaba el discurso homogenizante del marxismo. . . . Para la cuestión indígena no se podía usar la teoría marxista."/ "I came from a different tradition than those young men. I wanted to place the emphasis in the particularity of the indigenous issue and I was not interested in the homogenizing discourse of Marxism. . . . For the indigenous question/issue you could not apply Marxist theory." Bonilla also attributed his understanding of the importance of ethnicity to a conference he attended in Barbados on indigenous people in 1971.

From the second conference, the emphasis on ethnicity endured. Other interviewees claimed that the emphasis on ethnicity came from Mejía, who had spent time in Tierradentro and had been impressed with the level of organization of the indigenous councils (Tattay 1999). When asked about the change from the first to second conference, Tattay replied: "Los que estaban en contra de la ley 89 de 1890 por la cuestión de minoría de edad, eran Trino Morales, quien cambio de posición en lo referente a ley indígena. Para mí el cambio, era que no sabíamos mucho de la ley indígena en la primera conferencia. Estábamos mirando las posibilidades. . . . Gustavo Mejía llego muy impresionado de Tierradentro por el apoyo que los indígenas les daban a los cabildos y a la ley indígena en cuanto a protección y mantenimiento de las costumbres. Creo que su influencia fue importante."/"Those who were against Law 89 because it made indigenous people minors, were Trino Morales, who changed his position regarding the indigenous law. For me the change was that we did not know much about Indigenous Law at the first conference. We were examining the options. . . . Gustavo Mejía came back from Tierradentro really impressed with the support that indigenous people gave to their councils and to Indigenous Law in regards to protection and maintenance of their customs. I believe that his influence was important."

My focus on the advisers so far is not to suggest that the indigenous communities were not organized or that they were not fully involved in the process of mobilization. However, the indigenous communities did not form a cohesive unit, and a future indigenous president of the CRIC emphasized to me that, prior to his political activism in the late 1960s and early 1970s, he had no real understanding of the other indigenous communities in the same department (Avirama 1998). Marcos Avirama (1998) stated: "Cuando viene lo de la reforma agraria en el sesenta y ocho, surge la cuestión de la titulación de los resguardos. Empezamos a reunirnos con gentes de diferentes resguardos. Yo no sabía en este momento que existían estos resguardos, estas comunidades. Empezamos a conocernos y a encontrarnos en este proceso."/"When the Agrarian reform comes around in 1968, the issue around the titling of *resguardos* emerges. We started to meet with people from different *resguardos*. I did not know in that moment that those *resguardos* existed, those communities. We started to get to know each other and to find each other in this process." What I am suggesting here is that within the indigenous communities there was a multiplicity of voices expressed through the different councils, cooperatives organized by agrarian reform officials, and Protestant religious leaders. It was not easy for the communities with few occasions to meet face-to-face to explore the commonality of their exploitation. This was a process that occurred in the 1970s. Because of the physical fragmentation of the indigenous communities and the multiplicity of voices and forms of organization, outsiders who had traveled from one community to another and who came from distinct political traditions seized an existent discourse and articulated it in the first two conferences. A synergy between the nonindigenous activists, the indigenous leaders and rank and file, and finally the leftist grassroots organization took place during this time.

Let us not forget that in 1972 Quintín Lame was essentially a forgotten political leader and his demands were not on the forefront in the indigenous communities of Cauca. Lorenzo Muelas (2001) an indigenous Guambiano senator, told me that his sense of ethnic consciousness had to be awakened in a series of crucial moments. Like many indigenous rural folk who participated in the CRIC's founding meeting, Muelas was a *terrajero,* or sharecropper. Muelas (2001) described himself at the beginning of our interview in these terms: "Yo era terrajero. Mi papá y mis abuelos todos eran terrajeros de la Hacienda de Chimán en Guambia, Cauca."/"I was a *terrajero*. My father and grandparents were *terrajeros* of the Hacienda of Chimán in Guambia, Cauca." Muelas also depicted himself as a rebel with no political conscience. He emigrated to Santander del Quilichao, in the northern part of the Cauca, where his father had bought a plot of land. Being in a place that was very different from his native Guambia, because of the hot climate and food and the presence of Afro-Colombians, gave him a sense that he belonged elsewhere. On a visit back to Guambia, he admired his friends who played the drums and flute, and this further awoke his sense of belonging. A third and very important moment for Muelas (2001) and the members of the Las Delicias cooperative was the publication of Lame's *En defensa de mi raza* (*In Defense of My Race*). Gonzalo Castillo-Cárdenas, a nonindigenous intellectual, was in part responsible for the publication. The 1971 publication of the manuscript gave newfound legitimacy to the ethnic discourse and opened up new political possibilities for indigenous citizens. Here is a very clear demonstration of the importance of nonindigenous intellectuals in locating the manuscript, in finding the funds to publish it, and in bringing it to the forefront of indigenous consciousness.

A crucial stage in the CRIC's formation and in the shaping of the regional consciousness of ethnic identity and the creation of an ethnic citizenship was when the Departamento Administrativo Nacional de Estadística (DANE, or National Administrative Department of Statistics) chose the CRIC to conduct a census of the indigenous communities in the Cauca. The DANE financed the census, which took place in 1972. The national government was adopting a contradictory stance toward the mobilization of the indigenous communities. On the one hand, the police and army arrested several CRIC members after the first conference; on the other hand, indirectly the state had financed this first meeting, as it was the National Institute of Agrarian Reform that had provided the funds for FRESAGRO to organize the conference. The state was essentially establishing the parameters of the mobilization by punishing those who deviated from the parameters. The contradictory actions can be explained in part by the fact that the state is not monolithic but made up of different branches. The armed forces and the police, for instance, were completely different from DANE. However, this contradictory attitude also stemmed from distinct policies: the state was prepared to support indigenous communities that stressed the ethnic component of their agenda, but it actively repressed any organization that it perceived as class based and subversive. This selective legitimization supported the formation of ethnic citizenship.

The census provided the CRIC with the perfect opportunity to disseminate its message among all the indigenous communities in the Cauca (Avirama 1998). During the day, the members of the CRIC would perform the census, going from village to village, and they would make an unofficial nighttime appointment with the entire community of each town (Avirama 1998). During these meetings, the coordinators of the census urged communities to keep fighting to maintain the *resguardos* and to stop the titling of their land (titling signified the privatization of land). In some cases, these coordinators also informed indigenous communities that landowners were in fact illegally occupying *resguardo* land that should be restored to the communities. Marcos Avirama (1998) stated, "Buscabamos que la gente entendiera la importancia de los *resguardos*."/"We wanted people to understand the importance of *resguardos*." The emphasis was always on the restoration of collective land ownership. Without the state's financing of the trips of the census coordinators, it would have been difficult for CRIC to spread its message as effectively as it did. Some of the coordinators were indigenous, such as Marcos Avirama, later a CRIC president, but some were not, such as Luis Ángel Monroy, an Afro-Colombian.

This dissemination of CRIC's message was particularly timely because during these years INCORA was offering to buy certain areas of the Cauca and to redistribute the land in individual plots to indigenous families. Some indigenous people were interested in the offer. The nightly meetings where, in Avirama's (1998) words, the census organizers sought to make people understand the importance of arguing for the maintenance of their resguardos, came at a crucial time in the planning and implementation of agrarian reform. The recovery and maintenance of the *resguardos* entailed more than just collective landholding. It also meant a return to political structures that were created during the colonial period of Colombian history. So the *cabildo*, or council, had to become an important tool in the mobilization of indigenous people, as legally this was the political structure that governed over the land of the *resguardo* and its people. The CRIC coordinators' travels through the Cauca to "raise consciousness" among the rank and file about the importance of the *resguardo* and the *cabildo* ensured that collective landholding and the *cabildo* would be viewed as possible effective mechanisms to obtain political representation and land.

THIRD CRIC MEETING

The third meeting of CRIC took place in Silvia, Cauca, on July 15 and 16, 1973 (*Unidad Indigena* 1976; see also CRIC n.d.). This meeting was a public one and was highly publicized, unlike the second conference, which took place in secret. It also differed from the first one, which had been very embryonic in terms of separating from the left. This third meeting is important because, by then, much of the discourse and practices of the CRIC had crystallized. At that same assembly, the first national meeting of indigenous organizations took place; indigenous representatives from Tolima, Caldas, Nariño, and Putumayo attended (*Unidad Indígena* 1976, 2). Several hundred indigenous peasants from Tierradentro walked all the way to Silvia, in the center of Cauca, right next to the capital. The authorities of Tierradentro had erected roadblocks in an attempt to prevent the indigenous peasants from attending the event. The indigenous communities, which were ferociously repressed by the area's Catholic missionaries and landowners, successfully defied authorities and marched together, carrying flags that proclaimed their ethnic identity and resolve to resist (J. Avirama 1998). This was a remarkable turnaround because Tierradentro's indigenous people had endured some of the worst economic and social conditions (Bonilla 1998; Sevilla Casas 1986).

What did this public meeting of the CRIC signify? From then on, as both Avirama brothers pointed out, the indigenous communities and their leaders took on the leadership roles, and the founding nonindigenous members became advisers. The cultural change and formation of consciousness was accompanied by the growing effectiveness of the CRIC. From 1971 to 1974, twenty-eight peaceful demonstrations took place (CRIC n.d. [1979]). The recovery of land also increased as a result of the marches and legal suits to reclaim *resguardos*. In addition, the indigenous councils were reconstructed and re-created in Caldono, La Aurora, Los Quingos (Morales), La Cilia (Miranda), Medianaranja and Santa Elena (Corinto), and Huellas (Caloto) (CRIC n.d. [1979]). By 1974, *terraje* had been virtually eliminated in the Cauca (CRIC n.d. [1979]).

These remarkable gains were achieved through a radical shift in the discourse and practices of citizenship. For indigenous communities who had traditionally voted and participated actively in both the conservative and liberal parties, this mode of practicing citizenship was largely over. Instead, joining a political association that brought people together around an ethnic identity was the order of the day. The indigenous people of the Cauca voted with their feet and with the political marches that put them on public display. They all came out—men, women, and children—to walk with flags and with a uniform message of CRIC's seven points, inspired by an indigenous leader who had fought for an almost-identical agenda. This mode of participation allowed for the entire community to take part in the practice of citizenship, whereas before the 1950s (when Colombian women obtained the vote), the practice of citizenship by bearing arms, fighting for one or the other party, or voting was restricted to men. Another important element of constructing this new mode of citizenship was to return to pre-republican and/or colonial methods of political representation while radically altering them. The indigenous communities argued that their right to land lay in pre-republican Colombia and in the institutions of *resguardos* and *cabildos* that the Spanish Crown had instituted. This reaching back to a pre-republican mode of political participation allowed the indigenous communities to represent their rights as timeless and as an integral part of their culture. Left out of this narrative of citizenship was that many of the indigenous councils of the Cauca had become beholden to the local elites and to the municipal authorities (Jairo 1998). Since the turn of the twentieth century, the elections of the council members had to be approved by the nonindigenous mayor or priest of the municipality where the community was located. In practice, this meant that the councils were not always responsive to the community's needs and instead were pressured into accommodating local politicians. The use of the existing legal framework allowed them to mobilize legally and to press claims on the basis of ethnicity, thus gaining the partial support of the nation-state. The genius of CRIC was to conserve the institutions, which had a solid legal basis, and yet radically alter them by ensuring that corrupt councils were replaced and that the members of the council were responsive to the community rather than to the local nonindigenous politicians.

The press, as always a key method in disseminating this new vision of citizenship, also played an important role in affirming the rights of indigenous communities. Sympathizers such as Bonilla wrote articles in the leading Colombian newspapers about the marches and how the exploited and repressed citizens of Colombia confronted the police and the army unarmed. Marcos Avirama stated that the leaders of CRIC (himself included) strategically placed older women, pregnant women, and children in the first row of marches, hoping to prevent the police from physically stopping the marches. Although this had no effect on the police, as they beat anyone, man, woman, or child, photographs of older women and children being attacked by the police helped to generate support for the indigenous cause. Thus, a narrative of citizenship was born at that very moment. The nonindigenous advisers became less important in reality but, just as important, they faded from the national consciousness of what constituted a Colombian indigenous movement. The partisan ties that had existed and that had to a certain degree allowed for the founding of the indigenous grassroots organization also faded from public consciousness, and the indigenous communities appeared in the imagined nation as emerging unified and untainted by the bonds of partisan affiliation.

During this same period, Manuel Quintín Lame was proclaimed as a founding hero of the indigenous resistance and was presented to the public as one who was remembered and celebrated. Eventually this representation became reality as the indigenous organizers of CRIC brought Lame's story to indigenous communities and as some indigenous people read his book. A perfect example of this process is Lorenzo Muelas's discovery of Quintín Lame's work.

FORMATION OF A SELF-DEFENSE ARMY: *MOVIMIENTO ARMADO QUINTÍN LAME*

Violence had accompanied the gains in land and political recognition for the indigenous movement in the Cauca. In 1974, Gustavo Mejía was assassinated in Corinto, and it was widely understood that the landowners in northern Cauca had instigated his murder. Mejia's killing was the beginning of the unleashing of a wave of violence from the landowners of northern Cauca and from some branches of the state that lasted until the mid-1980s.

The kidnapping of Eric Leupin, a Dutch consul, in Cali in 1975 worsened this repression. This kidnapping was attributed to FARC. The police began to intervene in all the areas where land was being recovered in northern Cauca. Northern Cauca is and was much more conflictive than other areas of the Cauca because its local elite had economic and political clout. In response to the growing organization of the indigenous communities, the landowners formed the Consejo Regional de Agricultura del Cauca (CRAC, or Regional Council of Agriculture of Cauca). The CRAC invited Cornelio Reyes, the minister of the interior, to the Cauca. Shortly after this meeting, attacks attributed to paid assassins intensified in the northern part of Cauca in Toribio, Caldono, Jambalo, and even in the center of the Cauca, which was usually quieter. In 1975, the following indigenous people were assassinated: Marco Aníbal Melenge, Ángel Mestizo, Manuel Dagua, Avelino Ramos; there were also two assassination attempts on CRIC's president Marcos Avirama.

The increasingly dire situation of CRIC's leaders and members convinced Pablo Tattay (a CRIC cofounder) and others to create a self-defense army, as the state was not fulfilling its most elementary duty of providing safety to its citizens. Tattay's first concern was to stop the assassinations that were destroying CRIC leadership of the northern Cauca.

Pablo Tattay, of Hungarian descent, was a key founder of MAQL (Jairo 1998). He had arrived in the Cauca in September 1969 after studying engineering at the University of Antioquia, where he had become involved with radical Christian groups (Tattay 1999). His sympathy with radical Christianity was cemented by his time in Belgium at the University of Louvain, a hotbed of liberation theology. Tattay started working in the north of the Cauca as a consultant for INCORA. There he became involved with the organization of the indigenous communities (Jairo 1998; Tattay 1999).

The formation of a self-defense army started in 1977 (Tattay 1999). Tattay and others needed weapons and training for this self-defense army. They decided not to approach FARC for help, as FARC was known to impose its ideology on allies, and the army wanted to preserve its autonomy. Tattay got in touch with a group within the Ejército de Liberación Nacional (ELN, or National Liberation Army) that was known as *Corriente Socialista Renovadora* (Renewing Socialist Thought). This group was less militaristic than others and more interested in political and social change, according to Tattay. Military training started during Holy Week of 1977. The group that provided the training had a good relationship with another guerrilla group, the Movimiento del 19 de Abril (M-19, or April 19th Movement).

The *Corriente Socialista Renovadora* dissolved, and the M-19 took over the provision of support and training to self-defense groups dedicated to helping the indigenous movement. Tattay (1999) stated, "En general el M-19 se manejó bien. Ellos siempre fueron muy respetuosos con las comunidades. Se ponían al servicio de las comunidades, no eran como la FARC."/"In general the M-19 handled itself well. They were always very respectful with the communities. They served the community; they were not like the FARC." Unfortunately for the emerging self-defense army, the M-19 carried out a spectacular action that involved stealing weapons from an army battalion via a tunnel. Furious at the public humiliation, the armed forces responded by arresting anyone with leftist connections. The army arrested a whole group of CRIC members (whether or not they were involved with the self-defense groups) and some of its advisers.

All those arrested were tortured. The army charged CRIC advisers and members as being members of an illegal organization, the M-19. Tattay insisted that they had not been members of the M-19, but it was true that a relationship existed. Most of the people arrested in 1979 were released from jail in 1981 because of either lack of evidence or political amnesty. The experience of jail and torture, far from discouraging the arrested members of CRIC from defending themselves, seemed to have had the opposite effect. The people I interviewed who were arrested and tortured felt that their experience proved that the state operated illegitimately and that armed resistance to protect one's life was justified in those circumstances (Avirama 1998; Bolaños 1999).

However, the self-defense army that evolved into a guerrilla army became public only in January 1985. The MAQL went public shortly after the assassination of a local indigenous Catholic priest, Álvaro Ulcué, in November 1984. It carried out a traditional guerrilla action, attacking the local police barracks of Santander del Quilichao. Why the long silence about this self-defense army, and why the announcement of the guerrilla army on this date? Ricardo Peñaranda (1999, 76) attributes MAQL's decision to go public to the increased state repression in the mid-1980s and to MAQL's desire to let other guerrilla armies know that the indigenous movement wished to remain autonomous from other guerrilla movements.

One of the reasons was obviously to avoid further state repression, but another, I think, equally important one was to legitimize the armed actions of this self-defense army. By controlling its "discovery," the guerrilla movement could control its first initial portrayal. The self-defense army did not take the name of Quintín Lame by chance. By calling itself the Movimiento Armado de Quintín Lame, it took a publicly indigenous character even though some members were not indigenous. The coordinator of the first mobile unit of the guerrilla army was Luis Ángel Monroy, an Afro-Colombian, who had been savagely tortured by the army. The act of going from self-defense units to a mobile one is an important one militarily and strategically. The act of mobility allows the guerrilla unit to carry out strategic attacks rather than to just react. Monroy had a long trajectory of accompanying the indigenous movement; he had been one of the first census coordinators in CRIC's early days. By claiming an indigenous character (most members were apparently indigenous but some leadership was not), MAQL also claimed an identity separate from that of other guerrilla armies. Harking back to the armed resistance of the Quintín Lame movement minimized the subversive nature of MAQL: the armed struggle was not about the lower classes or ordinary citizens responding to the threat of violence; rather, it was the resurgence of a pre-republican and age-old tradition of indigenous people. In the context of a polarized political system and the still-existing competition between communist and capitalist ideology, the ethnic character of the armed movement was crucial to its legitimization.

The self-identification of MAQL as a guerrilla army that had no intention of taking over the state and that drew its roots from earlier indigenous resistance shaped the relationship not only between the Colombian public and MAQL, but also between the indigenous communities and the armed movement. Much of MAQL's activity was *ajusticiamiento,* or executing and killing paid assassins or whoever was responsible for killing members of CRIC or of indigenous communities (Tattay 1999). The MAQL also ensured basic law and order within the communities by punishing cattle rustling and other crimes. Another unforeseen role was eventually to provide protection from FARC to indigenous leaders and communities, especially in northwestern Cauca. The FARC distrusted CRIC and its ethnic movement and sought to violently repress leaders who expressed their independence of thought and action (Jairo 1998). In 1990, MAQL demobilized and played a key role in the constituent assembly that eventually enacted the Constitution of 1991 that enshrined indigenous rights.

The success of MAQL and the legitimacy it enjoyed, and to a certain degree still enjoys in the historical memory, came from its responsiveness to the communities but also from its ethnic discourse. When MAQL members gave up their weapons en masse in public, they stated that they wanted all their weapons to be melted down and transformed into a statue of Lame to be placed in Bogotá (Unidad Álvaro Ulcué 1991). The representatives of the state agreed. The symbolic meaning of this gesture could not be clearer: MAQL members saw their actions as part of a historical continuum of indigenous resistance. However, many people from different walks of life and ethnic and social groups participated in MAQL even if the majority of the fighters were indigenous. What is interesting as well is that the state upheld this narrative of MAQL as an ethnic self-defense movement. So while the state knew perfectly well that some members of MAQL were not indigenous and that it had collaborated with the M-19, it chose not to point out the discrepancies at the time. This is because a certain branch of the state hoped to legitimize itself by showing that it would negotiate with a self-defense movement and that it was respectful of ethnic groups. Endorsing MAQL's self-representation also allowed the state not to address issues of social class and the issue of tremendous inequality of land tenure throughout Colombia. Moreover, the state wanted to gain allies in a region where it clearly was not in control. As is often the case, the state did not foresee some of its consequences and the challenges to the status quo that this new type of citizenship could raise.

CONCLUSION

The ethnic indigenous discourse in Colombia revealed itself to be immensely powerful and has transformed the department of Cauca. The lands that belonged to the indigenous *resguardos* in the colonial era have been recovered. A real agrarian reform took place in this department. The structures of political power were also changed because indigenous politicians shaped policies not only at the council level but also at the department level. The people of Cauca even elected an indigenous governor, Floro Tunubala, in 2000.

However, this discourse and ethnic practices have their limitations. They do not allow for a full acknowledgment and celebration of how other ethnic and social groups participated in the construction of this indigenous movement. In the course of representing the indigenous movement as a purely indigenous one and not a multicultural one, the Afro-Colombian and *mestizo* peasants who participated in many of the land recoveries were gradually set aside once the class discourse became less important. This representation was forced on the indigenous movement in that the state, and in particular the army, brutally repressed any attempt at classwide solidarity and the national state encouraged the formation of indigenous ethnic identity. In other words, CRIC did not have much choice in terms of trying to survive politically and physically but to represent itself solely as an ethnic movement.

The second limitation is that indigenous organizations, in particular CRIC, have not been able to discuss openly and freely how they confronted the issue of violence. This was, of course, extremely difficult during the political context of the Uribe government, where even human rights groups were tainted with the label of being subversives. However, the shadow of violence on indigenous leaders and their communities still very much exists. The creation of the peaceful guards who brandish the *bastón* (stick) representing their ethnic and symbolic identity can do only so much. This is especially true in terms of the paramilitaries, many of whom do not share the conception that indigenous people have a special place in the Colombian nation.[10] The state in the 1980s and early 1990s, weakened by its fight with the guerrillas, had its own reasons to negotiate willingly with the indigenous communities and MAQL. A tradition of *indigenismo* since the 1930s within the central state considered the indigenous communities as deserving special recognition, but the opportunity to neutralize one sector of the peasantry and its allies was also attractive.

By elaborating this new discourse of citizenship that linked the indigenous citizen to a pre-republican past and to an ethnic armed movement of the 1910s, the indigenous movement was able to avoid the subversive label and to achieve the recovery of land in a nonthreatening way for the Colombian state. Other peasant communities have adopted the indigenous way of building a movement and have attempted to create new symbols, but these symbols and practices are often less effective because these other nonindigenous groups do not occupy a special place in the Colombian imaginary.

The CRIC emerged at a specific historical moment in the decade after *La Violencia* had officially ended and when citizenship based on partisan affiliation offered few to no opportunities to change the local economic and political structures of power. The organizations of the left at first presented an agenda and practices that were attractive to most indigenous peasants who wanted land and a more equitable distribution of resources. However, the splintering of the left into factions that attacked one another viciously and the emergence of the FARC guerrilla army, which was dogmatic and that sought to impose its point of views unilaterally, soon made this option less attractive.

In addition, the nation-state, which had its own agenda, encouraged the formation of ethnic identity, seeing it as a way to diffuse and undermine the class discourse in the context of the cold war. The state did not act in a cohesive and unified manner but rather its different branches operated seemingly at cross-purposes. Employees of INCORA, DANE, and the Division of Indigenous Affairs sought to help indigenous communities that they perceived as at risk. The international discourse of the 1970s, 1980s, and 1990s emerging from organizations such as the United Nations that privileged indigenous peoples over the ordinary peasant also played a role in prodding the Colombian state to legitimize claims based on ethnic identity. After 1973, when ANUC was essentially shut down, the Colombian state sought to delegitimize the organizations that sought a restructuring of power on the basis of the notion that land was concentrated in the hands of a few elites and that it should be redistributed to all.

Furthermore, the Colombian state was not in a position to bargain with elites with significant economic power. Although it could and did buy out many landowners in central Cauca in response to the pressure of indigenous sit-ins, it was at first unable and unwilling to force the elites of northern Cauca to accede to an agrarian reform (Cortes 2004). By the 1980s, the indigenous movement had acquired enough political and cultural strength to force the issue and managed to overcome the resistance of some elites. However, the continuing violence in northwestern Cauca and the reappearance of police and army barracks in indigenous territory occurred partly because of the FARC's continuing operations jeopardizing indigenous communities again. The indigenous communities have responded with large marches, have notified human rights organizations, and have brought out the indigenous guards armed with their ceremonial canes.

Although the indigenous communities through CRIC and other organizations have achieved a democratization of Colombian society by gaining political representation in all of Colombia's political institutions and by implementing agrarian reform in the Cauca, the nation-state has yet to recognize the claims of all Colombian peasants as valid. Until the Colombian state legitimizes the demands of all peasants and opens up the discussion to the larger society, violence in Colombia's rural areas will endure. While the Colombian state opened a restricted political space for peasants with claims based on ethnic identity, it has ignored the claims of those who are simply hungry, without land, and aggressed by armed factions of both the right and the left. Intellectuals who have understandably celebrated the indigenous movement as a resurgence and a direct continuation of age-old ethnic politics predating Colombian independence have unwittingly helped the state to focus solely on indigenous communities' claims based on ethnic identity. It is of utmost importance to Colombia and to the indigenous communities who live in rural Colombia for indigenous and nonindigenous intellectuals who play a key role in the legitimization of these communities' demands to focus on the wider demands of the indigenous movement to transform Colombian rural society.

NOTES

This chapter was previously published in LARR, Vol. 43, no. 3 (2008). I wish to thank Marcos Avirama, Jesús Avirama, Graciela Bolaños, Víctor Daniel Bonilla, Jhon Jairo, and Pablo Tattay for their incredible generosity and honesty. I would also like to thank the anonymous LARR reviewers for their helpful comments. The writing of this article was funded in part by the Latin America Program of the Woodrow Wilson International Center for Junior Scholars. This chapter is largely based on a series of interviews that took place from February 1998 to July 2001 for my dissertation research, with the exception of one interview in October 2004. My first contact with the indigenous communities in Cauca Department took place in July 1997, when I accompanied a human rights delegation as a graduate student. I returned to Cauca in February 1998 to begin my dissertation research. I started interviewing the indigenous leaders and nonindigenous activists of the Consejo Regional Indígena del Cauca (CRIC) as a result of my previous contacts with this organization. I taped or took notes during these interviews. The interviews took place in the interviewees' homes, offices, and in cafes or bars both in Popayán and in Bogotá. After interviewing one person, that person would inform me that I should really interview another person. My questions changed as I learned more from each interview. Most of the interviews lasted at least several hours.

1. The period of military dictatorship lasted from June 1953 to 1957.

2. The latest historical scholarship on citizenship in Colombia has concentrated on the nineteenth century. Lasso (2003, 228) argues that, in the period after independence, Afro-Colombians played a crucial role not only in fighting for independence but also in shaping republican politics. For a brief period after independence, the republican discourse seemed to offer Afro-Colombians full participation in the political system. However, the Creole elite rejected this full inclusion and proceeded to use the republican discourse to silence issues of racial inequality (Lasso 2003, 240). Sanders (2004) suggests that partisan politics expressed through elections, political clubs, and participation on the battlefield allowed Afro-Colombians' real participation in the political system in southwestern Colombia in the nineteenth century.

3. For an excellent explanation of how political scientists have used the term *ethnic citizenship,* see Van De Sandt (2007, 22–23).

4. Jasmin Hristov (2005) also explores the importance of the political and economic context in her analysis of Cauca's indigenous movement.

5. The Zapatista army in Chiapas that emerged in 1994 does not threaten the existence of the Mexican state. In Peru, *Sendero Luminoso* (Shining Path), a significant threat in the 1980s, has been essentially neutralized since the capture of its leader Abimael Guzmán.

6. In the 1970s, both Bolivia and Ecuador, two countries with strong grassroots indigenous movements, were under intermittent military rule.

7. Estimates vary. Pineda gives a figure of 603,000, which would represent 2 percent of the population. The 1997 Colombian census estimated the indigenous population at 701,680. The latest population figures for the indigenous population of Colombia indicate a significant increase in terms of number and percentage of indigenous people. The DANE 2005 census estimated that there were 1,392,623 indigenous people, or 3.43 percent of the total population.

8. Jackson (1995, 2002) has also underscored the importance of the national state in the politicization of ethnic identity for the indigenous population of the Vaupés. On the importance of sympathetic national actors, see also Gros (1991). For an excellent overview of the national Colombian indigenous movement, see Laurent (2005).

9. As Sabato (2001) has pointed out, recent scholarship indicates that increasing participation in the electoral process, which begins in the nineteenth century for most Latin American countries, did not bring about a democratization of most Latin Americans Elections and their processes did create a political space in which subaltern groups were included, albeit through the conduit of clientelism and through caciques (Sabato 2001). Scholars have attributed the growth of civil society to the emergence and proliferation of associations and volunteer groups such as artisan groups. Thus, the focus has moved from examining the purely electoral process to the formation of civil society. In Colombia, elections did offer an important way for subalterns to participate, but the agreement of the Frente Nacional along with La Violencia made this form of political participation less effective and less attractive. Statistics on electoral participation in Colombia show that during the Frente Nacional era, participation decreased.

10. On the racial ordering of Colombia see Wade (1995).

Chapter Seven

Conclusion

The day prior to the violent events of November 12, 1916, eyewitnesses stated that Manuel Quintín Lame entered the town of Inzá with indigenous women and a band of musicians marching in first. It does not take too much imagination to almost hear the sound of the Andean flutes and drums and to see the dismayed faces of the nonindigenous inhabitants of Inzá when Manuel Quintín Lame arrived. His entry into town with indigenous women and with ethnic music in the quintessential Spanish square of the town symbolized his rejection of European cultural superiority. For the local authorities and nonindigenous inhabitants of Inzá who saw themselves as living on the frontier of civilization, indigenous people defiantly and proudly broadcasting their ethnic heritage in their "European compound" was too much to bear. As seen in chapter 2, Manuel Quintín Lame presented a cultural, political, and economic challenge to the local state and to the municipal authorities of Tierradentro. When the indigenous leader imagined a new path to Colombian citizenship for indigenous people of southwestern Colombia, he challenged the hegemonic understanding of Colombian citizenship. In 1917, the productive use of land, allegiance to a *patria chica* (town/municipality), Catholicism were the key ingredients of Colombian citizenship. The productive use of land was the sine qua non of Colombian citizenship; the indigenous leader's legal claim (based on colonial documents) to properties in the hands of nonindigenous people upended the cultural, economic, and social order of Cauca. In other words, Manuel Quintín Lame argued that legitimate ownership of land was based on pre-Republican documents and not necessarily on productive use of the land, which was close to heresy for nonindigenous settlers of frontier areas.

In 1916, the central state, which sought to legitimize the recent political centralization of Colombia, corresponded with the indigenous leader and the local state thereby presenting itself as the ultimate political arbiter. In the process of presenting itself as the ultimate political arbiter the central state elaborated a discourse about citizenship and the role of the central state. It recommended prudent and cautious behavior toward indigenous communities to the local authorities seeking to gain the monopoly on violence. The Colombian central state also encouraged the local state to carefully evaluate the claims of indigenous communities establishing its role as protector.

The central state and Manuel Quintín Lame engaged in political theater in the decade of the 1910s to further their respective causes. The indigenous leader's decision to enter the town of Inzá with the musicians and with women in front was typical of his choice to showcase his political agenda. Manuel Quintín Lame showed his papers from the national government (and no doubt aggrandized the positive nature of this correspondence) and wore a military uniform that was not one earned by his military service, but that was donated to him. The indigenous leader who was an astute politician understood all too well that in politics perception is reality. In order to win followers, he needed to persuade his indigenous public that he enjoyed a special relationship with the central state.[1] Here it is important to remember that Manuel Quintín Lame had to gain the allegiance and support of indigenous councils; as the reader will remember, indigenous councils of Cauca (especially) gave him the power of attorney and donated money to his political cause.

But, he was not the only one engaging in political theater. The central Colombian state revealed itself to be a poor ally and an ineffective guardian of order, let alone capable of maintaining a monopoly on violence. When important and economically powerful local elites such as Ignacio Muñoz declared that the indigenous movement of Cauca was dangerous and when violence was perpetrated against its indigenous citizens in Inzá, the central state did worse than just watch the violent events unfold, it sent troops. Here it is important to note that the Colombian armed forces were not responsible for the killing of the seven indigenous people, but that they arrived after the fact. The slowness and inability of the Colombian armed forces to arrive to Inzá also showed the structural limitations of the Colombian central state of 1916. Thus, the political theater element resides in that the power of the Colombian state was largely discursive.

Deprived of state protection, Manuel Quintín Lame did not achieve his aim of recovering land for indigenous communities, nor was he able to establish himself as the intermediary between the central state and the indigenous people of Southwestern Colombia. Nonetheless, his discourse on ethnic citizenship and his strategy of an alliance with the central state was later taken up both by the central state and indigenous communities in the second half of the twentieth century.

In the short term, indigenous communities and their councils in Southwestern Colombia endured widespread repression and renewed attacks on their political and economic autonomy. Throughout the 1920s and 1930s, indigenous councils faced new challenges to their political and legal authority; they had lost the ability to veto nonindigenous settlement and faced increasing interference from municipal authorities. Land claims based on ethnic identity and citizenship through collective landownership were not politically viable. Popular Liberalism offered a new pathway to citizenship and new possibilities for obtaining land and state resources.

The analysis of the correspondence between the central state and indigenous communities revealed that certain indigenous councils chafed under Law 89 of 1890, which placed them firmly under the control of the municipality and of Catholic missionaries. Indigenous petitioners who requested the breakup of their *resguardo* often sought a more flexible and malleable definition of indigenous identity that did not oblige them to cultivate land within a collective framework. The discourse of these petitioners was revolutionary in that it challenged the notion that an indigenous person could not be a productive farmer and in that it suggested that the celebrated settler on the Colombian frontier could be indigenous. This discourse upended the racial ordering of Colombia in that it undertook to unlink productive use of the land with certain racial categories. However, the 1930s Liberal discourse that emerged from these petitions accepted the hegemonic discourse of the day that the path to Colombian citizenship was through the productive use of land. The economic underpinning of this discourse lay in the growth of the coffee crop and the increasing value of land planted with coffee trees, which both created economic opportunities as well as increased tensions.

There were of course many variants of popular Liberalism in Colombia; this book only examines the dominant strand of Liberalism that was advocated by the central state. For instance, José Gonzalo Sánchez and others sought to push the Liberal Party to the Left and to create a variation of Liberalism that promoted communal landownership and that was closely affiliated with Leftist political movements. My motivation in concentrating on state-sponsored Liberalism lies in that this was the liberalism that shaped land policies of the central state in the 1930s and 1940s.

During the period of *La Violencia*, indigenous communities faced massive loss of land and widespread conflict. Questions of land ownership and tenancy intersected with partisan disputes and with ethnic tensions. Indigenous councils who were already weakened by decades of repression and of inability to stem the arrival of nonindigenous settlers (especially in areas where coffee was planted) were often powerless to protect members of its communities from violence. The political experiment of Riochiquito consisted in creating a multicultural community that offered sufficient land to all its inhabitants and ensured their protection for a brief period of time. As we saw in chapter 4, the discourse of Riochiquito was not revolutionary, its leaders celebrated the idea that land ownership was tied to its productive use and that Colombian citizenship should ensure access to education and basic services. When the Colombian army (despite the initial support of some of its members for this political experiment) invaded Riochiquito, it signaled the end of the viability of a multicultural popular Liberalism.

In the late 1950s and early 1960s the Colombian state faced the challenge of creating new forms of inclusion and legitimization in the rural areas of Colombia; in the wake of *La Violencia* (the initial conflagration of violence was based on party affiliation) partisan affiliation could no longer function as a mechanism of political inclusion. In Cauca, the Commission of Rehabilitation and the Division of Indigenous Affairs were two state agencies that sought to create allegiance to the central state. The Commission of Rehabilitation and the tribunals of Equity and Reconciliation had the charge of elucidating the causes of violence and of solving cases of land expropriation. The situation in Cauca was dire; indigenous communities had suffered massive land losses and the authority of their councils was seriously eroded. Indigenous people of Tierradentro that the literature of the nineteenth century depicted as stocky and of normal height were in the 1960s of extremely short stature because of the tremendous food insecurity; Cauca also had one of the highest rates of tuberculosis in the world. The Division of Indigenous Affairs and its employees in conjunction with international organizations advanced that collective landholding and the strengthening of indigenous communal government were the best policies to achieve the modernization and integration of indigenous people. This was a return to Manuel Quintín Lame's discourse on indigenous citizenship, but it was not an indigenous leader who pushed it forward but one branch of the Colombian state. Once again, progress, land, and modernity could be achieved through claims based on ethnicity.

This state-sponsored discourse that advocated for indigenous ethnic citizenship emerged simultaneously with the Agrarian Reform discourse of 1961 of "La tierra es para el que la trabaja"/"The land is for the one who works it." In other words, the central Colombian state had a dual approach in regard to the indigenous communities of Cauca; a strand of popular liberalism (in the form of establishing who is worthy of the land) survived in its short-lived Agrarian reform program. The Agrarian Reform was important for Cauca and its indigenous communities because it brought many future advisers of the CRIC to Cauca where they witnessed firsthand the tremendous oppression that indigenous communities endured. However, the Agrarian Reform was a failure because the central state lacked the political will and the power to push forward a real restructuring of land patterns in Colombia. It also failed because the grassroots organization, ANUC, in charge of fomenting support for the state-sponsored initiatives of agrarian reform, suffered from internal Leftist squabbles (Maoist versus Marxist-Leninists) that plagued the Colombian Left. In addition, many members of the ANUC adhered to orthodox Marxism and considered ethnic consciousness as false consciousness and as an impediment to achieving class-based organization and solidarity.

In contrast, some members of the CRIC realized that the most effective way to recover land that belonged to indigenous communities was through ethnic-based claims. This emphasis on ethnicity did not happen overnight, and a class-based discourse continued to exert a powerful attraction not only on members of the CRIC leadership but also on the rank and file. The return to Manuel Quintín Lame's political agenda and understanding of Colombian indigenous citizenship happened at the CRIC's second conference, but his political strategy of an alliance with a central state was adopted much more gradually. In fact, the Manuel Quintín Lame experience of the 1910s showed the limitations of an alliance with the Colombian state. The small nonindigenous group of advisers and the indigenous leadership of CRIC profoundly distrusted the central state, but their most immediate problem was to deal with the growing threat of hired assassins who were decimating the indigenous leadership. In an effort to respond to this locally orchestrated campaign of violence, some members of the CRIC and some nonindigenous advisers formed a self-defense army/MAQL. This initiative brought about an immediate repressive response from the central state in the form of arrests, imprisonment, and torture. The local state also responded in a repressive and brutal fashion to land sit-ins when indigenous communities sought to recover land that legally belonged to them. The experience of so many indigenous rural folk who faced police and army repression in their just and legal recovery of land has meant that the very identity of CRIC was fashioned in opposition to the central state. However, the central state did legitimize many of these land recoveries and through the INCORA established new *resguardos* even in areas where no colonial document could be found.

In 2003, a reader of my recently completed dissertation told me that I needed to decide whether I wanted to write a book about an indigenous ethnic movement or a book that would essentially be a regional history of Cauca. My response was silence because while I knew intuitively that Cauca's unique history played an integral part to the emergence of an indigenous movement, clearly this argument was not fleshed out in my dissertation. Indeed, an integral part to the story of the indigenous movement in Colombia is Cauca's history, which I hope this book has successfully shown. Here I return to the question posed in my introduction: why Cauca? First, indigenous communities of Cauca had a long history of grassroots activism and a tradition of political leadership. Second, Cauca remained underdeveloped and rural in the second half of the twentieth century unlike the rest of Colombia; its elite and bourgeoisie could not represent themselves as the bearers of progress and modernity. Thus, the local elite was unable to utilize a discourse on citizenship that excluded indigenous communities. It also allowed for the central state to have more influence and weight than it did in other regions. Third, Liberal intellectuals and the Liberal governments of the 1960s sought to delegitimize the hold that Catholic missionaries had in Colombia; Cauca presented a perfect opportunity to show the absurdity of the Colombian state abdicating its authority to the Catholic Church. In a nutshell, it was only in Cauca that indigenous people could become the bearers of progress and modernity in contrast to its decaying elite and to a Catholic Church that was seen as retrograde.

From 1910 to 1991, Cauca was radically transformed. Indigenous organizations achieved Manuel Quintin Lame's political agenda of the maintenance of collective landholding, bilingual schools, respect for indigenous culture, and an end to sharecropping. Cauca's local elite racist and profoundly contemptuous discourse and practices were defeated; this was a hard-earned battle. Countless indigenous leaders and nonindigenous activists gave their lives up for this struggle; others endured torture, rape, and permanent exile. Thus, this story of conversations between the central state, indigenous communities, political leaders, and the local state is one of hope and of political empowerment amidst violence and repression.

NOTE

1. Joanne Rappaport discusses the performative aspect of Manuel Quintín Lame's meetings. She emphasizes how a national framework/context was created through the indigenous leader's "rituals." See Rappaport, *The Politics of Memory*, 136–37.

Select Bibliography

PRIMARY SOURCES

Archives

Many of the sources that I consulted in the 1990s were transferred from the Division of Indigenous Affairs to the *Archivo General de la Nación* and reorganized. In addition, a number of sources were not yet catalogued or numbered. Employees of various governmental offices gave me access to the documents before their classification; this is why some of the documents have no available citation. This was also the case for the Gregorio Hernández de Alba archive that I consulted before it was catalogued.

Archivo General de La Nación, Bogotá, AGN, República, Fondo Ministerio de Gobierno, Seccion 4 varios, Tomos 49–186.

Archivo General de la Nación, Bogotá, AGN, República, Fondo Ministerio del Interior, Cajas 100–193.

Archivo General de la Nación, Bogotá, AGN, República, Fondo Ministerio del Interior, Despacho del Ministro-Ordén Público, Cajas 21, 30, 33–182.

Archivo General de la Nación, Bogotá, AGN, República, Fondo Ministerio del Interior, División de Asuntos Indigenas, Cajas 190–3191.

www.proyectoQuintínlame.org

Consejo Regional Indígena del Cauca

Biblioteca Luis Ángel Arango /Archivo de Gregorio Hernández de Alba

Press

El Bolchevique (Bogotá)

El Tiempo (Bogotá)

El Espectador (Bogotá)

Tierra (Bogotá)

Unión Conservadora

Opiniones (Popayán)

El Liberal (Popayán)

Revista De Misiones (1927–1934)

Unidad Indígena (Popayán)

Avirama, Jesús (former president of CRIC). Personal Interview by the author, Popayán, February 1998.

Avirama, Marcos. Personal Interview by the author, Popayán, February 1998.
Bolaños, Graciela (activist and member of the Colombian Agrarian Reform Institute in the 1970s). Personal Interview by the author, Bogotá, November 1999.
Bonilla, Víctor Daniel. Personal Interview by the author, Cali, July 1998.
"Congresos del CRIC." *Unidad Indígena* 1 (1975).
Consejo Regional de Indígenas del Cauca (CRIC). "Como nos organizamos." Pamphlet, n.d.
———. *CRIC, Diez años de lucha, historia y documentos.* Bogotá: CINEP, 1981.
———. *La repression contra los indígenas del cauca.* n.d.
Cortes, Pedro. Personal Interview by the author, Bogotá, October 2004.
García, Antonio. *Pasado y presente del indio.* Bogotá: Ediciones Centro, 1939.
Hernández de Alba, Gregorio. "Alfonso López y los indígenas colombianos. Manuscrito." Bogotá: Biblioteca Luis Ángel Arango, 1960.
———. "Arte y Persona de José Antonio Tumiña. Manuscrito MSS 1334." Bogotá: Biblioteca Luis Ángel Arango, 1948.
———. "Aspectos Guajiros." *Revista Pan* 4 (1935).
———. *Diarios varios, 1939–1942.* Bogotá: Biblioteca Luis Ángel Arango. Archivo Gregorio Hernández de Alba.
———. "El Instituto Etnológico de la Universidad del Cauca y sus contribuciones a la antropología Colombiana." Manuscrito. Bogotá: Biblioteca Luis Ángel Arango, 1948.
———. *Etnología Guajira.* Bogotá: Editorial ABC, 1936.
———. "Informe Correspondiente a las albores cumplidas en la comisión argueológica de Tierradentro. Manuscrito-MSS 1197." (1948).
———. "Investigaciones Arqueológicas en Tierradentro." *Revista de Indias* 9 (1938): 29–32.
———. "Las parcelaciones y las comunidades indígenas." *Tribuna.* (1959).
———. "Lo indígena como expression Americana." *América Indigena* 3 (1944): 223–25.
———. *Notas de Viaje. Manuscrito.* Bogotá: Biblioteca Luis Ángel Arango, Archivo Gregorio Hernández de Alba, 1948.
Jairo, Jhon. Personal Interview by the author, Popayán, February 1998.
International Labour Office. *Informe al gobierno de Colombia sobre el problema indígena en el departamento del Cauca; encuesta preliminar a la aportación eventual de asistencia técnica dentro del marco del Programa andino.* 1959.
Lame Chantre, Manuel Quintín. *En defensa de mi raza.* Bogotá: Rosca de Investigación y Acción Social, 1971.
———. *Las luchas del indio que bajó de la montaña al valle de la "civilización."* Bogotá: Rosca de Investigación y Acción Social, 1973.
Muelas Hurtado, Lorenzo. Personal Interview by the author, Bogotá, July 2001.
———. *Fuerza de la gente: Juntado recuerdos sobre la terrajería en Guambía, Colombia.* Bogotá: Instituto Colombiano de Antropología e Historia, 2005.
Rowe, John. "Apuntes de la Excursión Antropológica de Septiembre de 1947." Cauca: Smithsonian Institution/University of Cauca, 1947.
Sánchez, Enrique, and Hernán Molina Echeverri. *Documentos para la historia del movimiento colombiano contemporáneo.* Bogotá: Ministerio de Cultura, 2010.
Tattay, Pablo. Personal Interview by the author, Bogotá, November 1999.
Valencia Tovar, Alvaro. *Testimonio de una época.* Santafé de Bogotá, D.C., Colombia: Planeta, 1992.
———. *Mis adversarios guerrilleros.* Bogotá: Planeta, 2009.
Trujillo Castaño, Ciro, and José Modesto Campos. *Ciro, páginas de su vida.* Bogotá: Ediciones Abejón Mono, 1974.

SECONDARY

Alape, Arturo. *Tirofijo: los sueños y las montañas, 1964–1985.* Santa Fé de Bogotá, Colombia: Planeta, 1994.
Alonso, Ana María. *Thread of Blood: Colonialism, Revolution, and Gender on Mexico's Northern Frontier.* Tucson: University of Arizona Press, 1995.

Angel, Miguel. "Los negros Caucanos en el siglo XX." *Semana*. May 22, 2012. Accessed February 17, 2014. http://www.semana.com/opinion/expertos/articulo/los-negors-caucanos-en-el-siglo-xx/323107.

Appelbaum, Nancy P. *Muddied Waters: Race, Region, and Local History in Colombia, 1846-1948*. Durham: Duke University Press, 2003.

Aprile Gniset, Jacques. *Los pueblos negros caucanos y la fundación de Puerto Tejada*. Colombia: Gobernación del Valle del Cauca, Gerencia para el Desarrollo Cultural, 1994.

Arango, Raúl, and Enrique Sánchez. *Los pueblos indígenas de Colombia 1997: Desarollo y territorio*. Colombia: Departamento Nacional de Planeación, Unidad Administrativa Especial de Desarrollo Territorial: TM Editores, 1998.

Arboleda Valencia, Julio. "Perfil cultural del Cauca." In *Homenaje al Cauca*. Bogotá, Colombia: Villegas Editores, 1991.

Archila, Mauricio. *Idas y venidas, vueltas y revueltas: protestas sociales en Colombia, 1958–1990*. Bogotá: Instituto Colombiano de Antropología e Historia, 2003.

Arocha, Jaime. "Antropología en la historia de Colombia." In *Un siglo de investigación social: antropología en Colombia*, edited by Jaime Arocha, Nina S. de Friedemann, and Xochitl Herrera. Santa Fe de Bogotá: Etno, 1984.

———. "Afro-Colombia denied." *NACLA Report on the Americas* 25, no. 4 (1992): 28–47.

———. "Inclusion of Afro-Colombians: Unreachable national goal?" *Latin American Perspectives* 25, no. 3 (1998): 70–89.

———. "Los negros y la Nueva Constitución Colombiana de 1991." *América Negra* 3 (1994): 39–56.

Avirama, Jesús, and Rayda Márquez. "The Indigenous Movement in Colombia." *In Indigenous Peoples and Democracy in Latin America*, edited by Donna Lee Van Cott, 83–106. New York: St. Martin's Press, 1995.

Barre, Marie Chantal. *Ideologías indigenistas y movimientos indios*. México, D.F: Siglo Veintiuno Editores, 1983.

Barth, Fredrick. *Ethnic Groups and Boundaries: The Social Organization of Culture Difference*. Boston: Little and Brown and Co, 1969.

Baud, Michiel. *Intelectuales y sus utopias/Indigenismo y la imaginación de América Latina*. Amsterdam: Centro de Estudios y Documentación Latinoamericanos, 2003.

Beltrán Peña, Francisco. *La utopía mueve montañas: Alvaro Ulcué Chocué*. Bogotá: Editorial Nueva América, 1989.

Bergquist, Charles W., Ricardo Peñaranda, and Gonzalo Sánchez G. *Violence in Colombia, 1990–2000: Waging War and Negotiating Peace*. Wilmington, DE: SR Books, 2001.

Bolívar, Ingrid Johanna. *Violencia politica y formación del estado, ensayo historiográfico sobre la dinámica regional de La Violencia de los cincuenta en Colombia*. Bogotá: Universidad de los Andes, Facultad de Ciencias Sociales, Centro de Estudios Socioculturales e Internacionales, 2003.

Bonilla, Victor Daniel. "Resistencia y Luchas en la Memoria Misak." In *Nuestra Vida ha sido nuestra Lucha: Resistencia y Memoria en el Cauca indígena*, edited by Ricardo Peñaranda, 121–65. Bogotá: Centro de Memoria Histórica, 2012.

———. *Siervos de Dios y Amos de Indios, El Estado y la Misión Capuchina en el Putumayo*. Bogotá: Ediciones Tercer Mundo, 1968.

Botero, Clara Isabel, and Jimena Perry Posada. *Pioneros de la Antropología: Memoria visual, 1936–1950*. Bogotá: Colcultura, 1994.

Braun, Herbert. *The Assassination of Gaitán: Public Life and Urban Violence in Colombia*. Madison: The University of Wisconsin Press, 1985.

Brysk, Alison. *From Tribal Village to Global Village: Indian Rights and International Relations in Latin America*. Stanford: Stanford University Press, 2000.

Bushnell, David. *The Making of Modern Colombia, A Nation in Spite of Itself*. Berkeley: University of California Press, 1993.

Campo Chicangana, Ary R. *Montoneras, deserciones e insubordinaciones: Yanaconas y Paeces en la Guerra de los Mil Días*. Cali: Secretaría de Cultura y Turismo, Municipio de Santiago de Cali, 2003.

Castillo-Cárdenas, Gonzalo. *Liberation Theology from Below: The Life and Thought of Manuel Quintín Lame.* Maryknoll, NY: Orbis Books, 1987.
Castrillón Arboleda, Diego. *El indio Quintín Lame.* Bogotá: Tercer Mundo, 1973.
———. *José Tombé (novela).* Bogotá: Instituto Colombiano de Cultura, 1974.
———. *De la colonia al subdesarrollo.* Popayán: Editorial Universidad, 1970.
———. "Trazo etnohistórico." In *Homenaje al Cauca,* edited by Gustavo Wilches-Chaux. Bogotá, Colombia: Villegas Editores, 1991.
Caviedes Pinilla, Mauricio. "Antropología y movimiento indígena." Thesis, Universidad Nacional de Colombia, 2000.
Correa Rubio, François. "La modernidad del pensamiento indigenista y el Instituto Nacional Indigenista de Colombia = Modernity of indigenista thought and Colombia's Instituto Nacional Indigenista." *Maguaré,* no. 21 (2007): 19–63.
Corrigan, Philip Richard D., and Derek Sayer. *The Great Arch: English State Formation as Cultural Revolution.* Oxford, UK: Blackwell, 1985.
Cortes, Pedro. "Indian Social Movements: A Case Study in Cauca, Colombia from a Marxist Perspective." PhD dissertation, Ohio State University, 1988.
Cruz Santos, Abel. *Francisco José Chaux y su tiempo.* Bogotá: Caja de Crédito Agrario Industrial y Minero, 1981.
Curry, Glenn. "The dissolution of the Resguardos Indígenas of Cundinamarca, Colombia, 1800-1863." PhD dissertation, Vanderbilt University, 1981.
Davis, Robert H. *Historical Dictionary of Colombia,* 2nd Ed. Metuchen, NJ: Scarecrow Press, 1993.
Dawson, Alexander. "From models for the nation to model citizens: Indigenismo and the 'revindication' of the Mexican Indian, 1920–1940." *Journal of Latin American Studies* 30 (1998): 279–308.
Delgado Madroñero, Johnny. *El Bandolerismo en el Valle del Cauca, 1946–1966.* Cali: Secretaría de Cultura/Gobernación del Valle del Cauca, 2011.
Eastman, Jorge Mario. "Eduardo Santos, 1888–1974." *Boletín de Historia y Antiguedades* 92 no. 829 (April–June 2005).
Echeverri, Marcela. "El proceso de profesionalización de la Antropología en Colombia. Un estudio de caso en torno a la difusión de las ciencias y su institucionalización." *Historia Crítica* 15 (1997), pp. 67–79.
Escobar Mesa, Augusto. *Naturaleza y realidad social en César Uribe Piedrahita.* Medellín: Consejo de Medellín, 1993.
Espinosa Arango, Mónica Lucía. *La civilización montés: la visión india y el trasegar de Manuel Quintín Lame en Colombia.* Bogotá, D.C., Colombia: Universidad de los Andes, Facultad de Ciencias Sociales, Departamento de Antropología, Centro de Estudios Socioculturales e Internacionales-CESO, 2009.
Eustasio Rivera, José. *La Vorágine.* New York: Editorial Los Andes, 1928.
Findji, Maria Teresa. *Elementos para el estudio de los resguardos indígenas del Cauca-Censo indigena del Cauca.* Bogotá: DANE, 1978.
———. "From Resistance to Social Movement: The Indigenous Authorities Movement in Colombia." In *The Making of Social Movements in Latin America: Identity, Strategy, and Democracy,* edited by Arturo Escobar and Sonia Alvarez, 112–35. Boulder: Westview Press, 1992.
Friede, Juan. *El indio en lucha por la tierra, historia de los resguardos del macizo central colombiano.* Bogotá: Ediciones Espiral, 1944.
———. *La explotación indígena en Colombia bajo el Gobierno de las Misiones: El caso de los aruacos de la Sierra Nevada de Santa Marta.* Bogotá: Punta de Lanza, 1973.
Friedemann, Nina S. de, and Jaime Arocha. *Herederos del jaguar y la anaconda.* Bogotá: C. Valencia, 1985.
Gamarra Vergara, Jose R. "La economía del departamento del Cauca: concentración de tierras y pobreza." *Documentos de trabajo/Economía regional,* 95. Cartagena: Banco de La República-Centro de Estudios Economicos Regionales (CEER), 2007.
García, Antonio. *Pasado y presente del indio.* Bogotá: Ediciones Centro, 1939.

García, Maria Elena. *Making Indigenous Citizens: Identities, Education, and Multicultural Development in Peru*. Stanford: Stanford University Press, 2005.

Gilroy, Paul. *"There Ain't No Black in the Union Jack": The Cultural Politics of Race and Nation*. Chicago: University of Chicago Press, 1991.

———. *The Black Atlantic: Modernity and Double Consciousness*. Cambridge: Harvard University Press, 1993.

Green, John W. "Left Liberalism and Race in the Evolution of Colombian Popular National Identity." *The Americas: Quarterly Review of Inter-American Cultural History* 57, no.1 (2000): 95–124.

Goff, James E. *The Persecution of Protestant Christians in Colombia, 1948–1958, With an Investigation of Its Background and Causes*. Cuernavaca: Centro Intercultural de Documentación, 1968.

González, David. *Los paeces: o, Genocidio y luchas indígenas en Colombia*. Bogotá: Editorial la Rueda Suelta, n.d.

Gow, David D. *Countering Development-Indigenous Modernity and the Moral Imagination*. Durham and London: Duke University Press, 2008.

Gros, Christian. *Colombia indígena, identidad cultural y cambio social*. Bogotá: Editorial Cerec, 1991.

———. *Políticas de la etnicidad: identidad, estado y modernidad*. Bogotá: Instituto Colombiano de Antropología e Historia, 2000.

Guzmán Campos, Germán, Eduardo Umaña Luna, and Orlando Fals Borda. *La violencia en Colombia, estudio de un proceso social, tomo II*. Bogotá: Ediciones Tercer Mundo, 1962.

Hamilton, John Potter. *Travels through the Interior Provinces of Colombia*. 1827.

Helguera, José León. "Coconuco: Datos y documentos para la historia de una gran haciendo caucana 1823, 1842 y 1876." *Anuario Colombiano De Historia Social Y De La Cultura*; No 5 (1970); 189–203. Universidad Nacional de Colombia, 1970.

Hernández de Alba, Gregorio. "El Instituto Etnologico del Cauca." *Boletín Bibliográfico de Antropología Americana (1937–1948)* Vol. 10 (January- December 1947), 20–22.

———. *Etnología Guajira*. Bogotá: Imprenta Nacional, 1936.

———. "The Highland Tribes of Southern Colombia." In the *Handbook of South American Indians Vol. 2. Andean Civilizations*, edited by Julian Steward. Washington, DC: United States Government Printing Office, 1946.

Herrera Angel, Marta. *Ficha bibliográfica de Manuel Quintín Lame*. http://www.banrepcultural.org/blaavirtual/biografias/lamemanu.htm

Hooker, Juliet. "Indigenous Inclusion/Black Exclusion: Race, Ethnicity, and Multicultural Citizenship in Latin America." *Journal of Latin American Studies* 37, no. 2 (2005): 285–310.

Hobsbawm, Eric. *Primitive Rebels: Studies in Archaic Forms of Social Movement in the Nineteenth and Twentieth Centuries*. New York: W. W. Norton, 1965.

Hristov, Jasmin. "Indigenous Struggles for Land and Culture in Cauca, Colombia." *Journal of Peasant Studies* 32, no. 1 (2005): 88–117.

Jackson, Jean. "Culture, Genuine and Spurious: The Politics of Indianness in the Vaupes, Colombia." *American Ethnologist* 22, no. 1 (1995): 3–27.

Jimeno, Myriam. *Juan Gregorio Palechor: historia de mi vida*. Bogotá: Consejo Regional Indígena del Cauca, 2005.

Jimeno, Myriam, and Adolfo Triana Antoverza. *Estado y minorías étnicas en Colombia*. Bogotá: Cuadernos del Jaguar: Fundación para las Comunidades Colombianas, 1985.

Jimeno, Myriam, Andy Klatt, and Joanne Rappaport. *Juan Gregorio Palechor: The Story of My Life*. 2014. http://dx.doi.org/10.1215/9780822377351.

Joseph, Gilbert, and Daniel Nugent, eds. *Everyday Forms of State-Formation: Revolution and the Negotiation of Rule in Modern Mexico*. Durham: Duke University Press, 1994.

Knight, Alan. "The Mexican Revolution: Bourgeois? Nationalist? Or Just a Great Rebellion?" *Bulletin of Latin American Research* 4, no. 2. (1985): 1–37.

———. "Racism, Revolution, and Indigenismo: Mexico, 1910–1940." In *The Idea of Race in Latin America, 1870–1940*. Edited by Richard Graham. Austin: University of Texas Press, 1990.

Lame Chantre, Manuel Quintín, and Gonzalo Castillo Cárdenas. *En defensa de mi raza*. Bogotá: Rosca de Investigación y Acción Social, 1971.

Larson, Brooke. *Trials of Nation Making: Liberalism, Race, and Ethnicity in the Andes, 1810–1910*. Cambridge: Cambridge University Press, 2004.

Lasso, Marixa. "Revisiting Independence Day: Afro-Colombian Politics and Patriot Narratives, Cartagena, 1809–1815." In *After Spanish Rule: Postcolonial Predicaments of the Americas*, edited by Andrés Guerrero and Mark Thurner, 223–47. Durham: Duke University Press, 2003.

Laurent, Virginia. *Comunidades indígenas, espacios políticos y movilización electoral en Colombia, 1990-1998: Motivaciones, campos de acción e impactos*. Bogotá: Instituto Colombiano de Antropología e Historia, 2005.

Legrand, Catherine. *Frontier Expansion and Peasant Protest in Colombia, 1850–1936*. Albuquerque: University of New Mexico Press, 1986.

———. "Labor Acquisition and Social Conflict on the Colombia Frontier, 1850–1936." *Journal of Latin American Studies* 16, no. 1 (1984): 27–49.

Levine, Daniel H. *Popular Voices in Latin American Catholicism*. New Jersey: Princeton University Press, 1992.

———. *Religion and Political Conflict in Latin America*. Chapel Hill: University of North Carolina Press, 1986.

Lopez, Javier Ocampo. "El Maestro Orlando Fals Borda. Sus ideas educativas y sociales para el cambio en la sociedad colombiana." *Revista Historia de la Educación Colombiana (RHE-LA)* 12 (2009): 13–41.

Medina, Álvaro. *El arte colombiano de los años veinte y treinta*. Santa Fé de Bogotá: Colcultura, 1994.

Melo, Jorge Orlando. *Predecir el pasado: ensayos de historia de Colombia*. Santa Fe de Bogotá: Fundación Simón y Lola Guberek, 1992.

Méndez-Gastelumendi, Cecilia. "The Power of Naming, or the Construction of Ethnic and National Identities in Peru: Myth, History and the Iquichanos." *Past & Present* 171 (May 2001): 127–60.

Meschkat, Klaus. "Helpful Intervention? The Impact of the Comintern on Early Colombian Communism." *Latin American Perspectives* 35, no. 2 (March 2008): 39–56.

Mina, Mateo. *Esclavitud y libertad en el valle del Río Cauca*. Bogotá: Fundación Rosca de Investigación y Acción Social, 1975.

Molano, Alfredo. "50 años de la FARC." http://elsalmonurbano.blogspot.com/2014/06/alfredo-molano-50anos-de-las-farc.html.

Moses, Wilson Jeremiah. *The Golden Age of Black Nationalism, 1850–1925*. New York: Oxford University Press, 1988.

Ng'weno, Bettina. *Turf Wars: Territory and Citizenship in the Contemporary State*. Stanford: Stanford University Press, 2007.

Oquist, Paul. *Violence, Conflict, and Politics in Colombia*. New York: Academic Press, 1980.

Ortiz Sarmiento, Carlos Miguel. *Estado y subversión en Colombia: la violencia en el Quindío, años 50*. Bogotá: CIDER, UNIANDES, 1985.

Ortiz, Sutti Reissig. *Uncertainties in Peasant Farming, A Colombian Case*. New York: Humanities Press, 1973.

Pallares, Amalia. *From Peasant Struggles to Indian Resistance: The Ecuadorian Andes in the Late Twentieth Century*. Norman: University of Oklahoma Press, 2002.

Pava Salazar, Simón de la. *Antonio García Nossa: un pensamiento revolucionario para Colombia y Latinoamérica*. Colombia: S. de la Pava Salazar, 2004.

Pecaut, Daniel. *Ordén y violencia: Colombia 1930–1954*. Bogotá: Siglo XXI Editores, 1987.

Peñaranda, Ricardo. "De rebeldes a ciudadanos: El caso del Movimiento Armado Quintín Lame." In *De las armas a la política*, edited by Ricardo Peñaranda, Javier Guerrero, and Jaime Zuluaga Nieto, 75–131. Santafé de Bogotá: IEPRI, 1999a.

Peñaranda, Ricardo, Javier Guerrero Barón, and Jaime Zuluaga Nieto. *De las armas a la política*. Santafé de Bogotá: IEPRI, 1999b.

Perry, Jimena. "Biografía intelectual de Gregorio Hernández de Alba." Tesis de Grado, Universidad de los Andes, 1994.

Pineda Camacho, Roberto. "Antonio García y el indigenismo en Colombia." *Noticias Antropológicas* 73 (1982): ix–5.

———. "La reivindicación del Indio en el pensamiento social colombiano (1850–1950)." In *Un siglo de investigación social en Colombia,* edited by Jaime Arocha and Nina S. Friedemann. Bogotá: Etno, 1984.

———. "Pueblos indígenas de Colombia: una aproximación a su historia, economía y sociedad." In *Tierra profanada: Grandes proyectos en territorios indígenas de Colombia,* edited by Organización Nacional Indígena de Colombia, Centro de Cooperación al Indígena, and GhK. Santa Fé de Bogotá: Disloque Editores, 1995.

———. *Tierra profanada: grandes proyectos en territorios indígenas de Colombia.* Santafé de Bogotá, D.C., Colombia: Disloque Editores, 1995.

Pinzón Sánchez, Alberto. *Monopolios, misioneros y destrucción de indigenas.* Bogotá: Ediciones Armadillo, 1979.

Pumarada Cruz, Yesenia C. *Othering Modernization: The Nasa Margins of Colombia (1890–1930s).* PhD diss., University of Wisconsin at Madison, 2013.

Rappaport, Joanne. "Between Sovereignty and Culture: Who Is an Indigenous Intellectual in Colombia?" *International Review of Social History* 49 (2004): 1111–32.

———. *Cumbe Reborn: An Andean Ethnography of History.* Chicago: University of Chicago Press, 1994.

———. *Intercultural Utopias: Public Intellectuals, Cultural Experimentation, and Ethnic Pluralism in Colombia.* Durham, NC: Duke University Press, 2005.

———. *The Politics of Memory: Native Historical Interpretation in Colombian Andes.* Cambridge: Cambridge University Press, 1990.

Reissig Ortiz, Sutti. *Uncertainties in Peasant Farming: A Colombian Case.* New York: Humanities Press, 1973.

Rivera Cusicanqui, Silvia. *Política e ideología en el movimiento campesino colombiano: el caso de la ANUĆ (Asociación Nacional de Usuarios Campesinos).* Bogotá: CINEP, 1982.

Rojas, José Maria, and Elías Sevilla Casas. "El campesinado en la formación territorial del Suroccidente Colombiano." In *Territorios, regiones, sociedades,* edited by Renán Silva, 153-79. Bogotá, Colombia: Cerec, 1994.

Roldán, Mary. *Blood and Fire: La Violencia in Antioquia, Colombia, 1946–1953.* Durham, NC: Duke University Press, 2002.

Romero Loaiza, Fernando. *Manuel Quintín Lame Chantre: el indígena ilustrado, el pensador indigenista.* Pereira, Colombia: F. Romero Loaiza, 2005.

Rueda Enciso, José Eduardo. *Ficha bibliográfica de Juan Friede.* http://www.lablaa.org/blaavirtual/biografias/friejuan.htm.

Sabato, Hilda. "On Political Citizenship in Nineteenth-Century Latin America." *The American Historical Review* 106, no. 4 (2001): 1290–1315.

Saether, Steinar A. "Independence and the Redefinition of Indianness around Santa Marta, Colombia, 1750–1850." *Journal of Latin American Studies* 37, 1 (Feb. 2005): 55–80.

Safford, Frank. "Race, integration, and progress: Elite attitudes and the Indian in Colombia, 1750–1870." *Hispanic American Historical Review* 71 (1991): 1–33.

Sánchez, Gonzalo. "Rehabilitación y violencia bajo el frente nacional." *Análisis político* no. 4 (May–August 1988): 21–42.

———. "The Violence: An Interpretative Synthesis." In *Violence in Colombia, the Contemporary Crisis in Historical Perspective,* edited by Charles Bergquist, Ricardo Peñaranda, and Gonzalo Sánchez, 75–124. Wilmington, DE: Scholarly Resources, 1992.

———. "Violencia, guerrillas, y estructuras agrarias." In *Nueva historia de Colombia,* 6 vols., edited by Alvaro Tirado Mejía, 2 I 27–54. Bogotá: Editorial Planeta, 1989.

Sánchez, Gonzalo, and Donny Meertens. *Bandits, Peasants, and Politics: The Case of "La Violencia" in Colombia.* Austin: University of Texas Press, 2001.

Sanders, James E. "Belonging to the Great Granadan Family: Partisan Struggle and the Construction of Indigenous Identity and Politics in Southwestern Colombia, 1849–1890." In *Race and Nation in Modern Latin America*, edited by Appelbaum et al., 56–86. Chapel Hill: University of North Carolina Press, 2003.

———. "Citizens of a Free People: Popular Liberalism and Race in Nineteenth-Century Southwestern Colombia." *Hispanic American Historical Review* 84, no. 2 (2004): 277–313.

———. *Contentious Republicans: Popular Politics, Race, and Class in Nineteenth-Century Colombia.* Durham: Duke University Press, 2004.

Sandt, Joris Jan Van de. "Behind the Mask of Recognition: Defending Autonomy and Communal Resource Management in Indigenous *Resguardos*, Colombia." University of Amsterdam, 2007.

Sendoya M., Mariano. *Caloto ante la historia*, vol. 1. Cali: Imprenta Departamental del Valle del Cauca, 1975.

Sevilla Casas, Elías. *La pobreza de los excluidos: Economía y sobrevivencia en un resguardo indígena del Cauca, Colombia.* Cali, Colombia: Ethnos, 1986.

Sieder, Rachel. *Multiculturalism in Latin America: Indigenous Rights, Diversity, and Democracy.* New York: Palgrave Macmillan, 2002.

Silva, Renán. *República liberal, intelectuales, y cultura popular.* Medellín: La Carreta, 2005.

Stavenhagen, Rodolfo. *Agrarian Problems and Peasant Movements in Latin America.* Garden City, NY: Anchor Books/Doubleday & Co, 1970.

Steward, Julian Haynes. *Handbook of South American Indians.* Washington DC: U.S. Government Printing Office, 1948.

Stoll, David. *Fishers of Men or Founders of Empire?: The Wycliffe Bible Translators in Latin America.* London: Zed P., 1983.

Stoller, Richard. "Alfonso López Pumarejo and Liberal Radicalism in 1930s Colombia." *Journal of Latin American Studies* 27, no. 2 (May 1995): 367–97.

Tate, Winifred. *Counting the Dead: The Culture and Politics of Human Rights Activism in Colombia.* Berkeley: University of California Press, 2007.

Taussig, Michael. *The Devil and Commodity Fetishism in South America.* North Carolina: University of North Carolina Press, 1980.

Tello Lozano, Piedad Lucía. "Vida y lucha de Manuel Quintín Lame." Undergraduate thesis, Universidad de los Andes, 1982.

Theidon, Kimberly Susan. *Intimate Enemies: Violence and Reconciliation in Peru.* Philadelphia: University of Pennsylvania Press, 2013.

Torres Giraldo, Ignacio. *La cuestión indigena en Colombia.* Bogotá: Fundación Rosca de Investigación y Acción Social, 1975.

Troyan, Brett. "Ethnic Identity and State Formation in the Cauca, Colombia from 1930–1991." PhD dissertation, Cornell University, 2002.

———. "Gregorio Hernández de Alba (1904–1973): The Legitimization of Indigenous Ethnic Politics in Colombia." *European Review of Latin American and Caribbean Studies* 82 (2007): 89-106.

———. "Re-Imagining the 'Indian' and the State: *Indigenismo* in Colombia, 1926–1947." *Canadian Journal of Latin American and Caribbean Studies* 33, no. 65 (2008a): 81–106.

———. "Ethnic Citizenship in Colombia: The Experience of the Regional Indigenous Council of the Cauca in Southwestern Colombia from 1970 to 1990." *Latin American Research Review* 43, no. 3 (2008b): 166–91.

Tumiña-Pillimue, Francisco. *Nuestra gente: Namuy Misag: tierras, costumbres y creencias de los indios Guambianos.* Popayán: Instituto Etnológico Nacional, Universidad de Cauca, 1949.

Uribe, María Tila. *Los años escondidos: sueños y rebeldía en la década del veinte.* Bogotá: CEREC, 1994.

Valencia Llano, Alonso. Empresarios y políticos en el estado soberano del Cauca, 1860–1895. Santiago de Cali: Editorial Facultad de Humanidades, Universidad del Valle, 1993.

———. *Estado soberano del Cauca: federalismo y regeneración.* Bogotá, D.E., Colombia: Banco de la República, 1988.

Valencia Tovar, Alvaro. *Testimonio de una época.* Santafé de Bogotá, D.C., Colombia: Planeta, 1992.

Van Cott, Donna Lee. *The Friendly Liquidation of the Past: The Politics of Diversity in Latin America.* Pittsburgh: University of Pittsburgh Press, 2000.

Vanegas, Isidro. "International Links to Early Socialism in Colombia." *Latin American Perspectives* 35, no. 2 (March 2008): 25–38.

Vasco Uribe, Luis Guillermo. "Quintín Lame: resistencia y liberación." Online publication: http://www.luguiva.net/%5C/articulos/detalle.aspx?id=68.

Vasco Uribe, Luis Guillermo, and François Correa. *Encrucijadas de Colombia amerindia*. Santafé de Bogotá, Colombia: Instituto Colombiano de Antropología, Colcultura, 1993.

Vega Cantor, Renán. *Gente muy rebelde, protesta popular y modernización capitalista en Colombia (1909–1929)*. Vol. 2: Indígenas, campesinos y protestas agrarias. Bogotá: Ediciones Pensamiento Crítico, 2002.

Wade, Peter. *Blackness and Race Mixture: The Dynamics of Racial Identity in Colombia*. Baltimore: Johns Hopkins University Press, 1995.

Warren, Kay B., and Jean E. Jackson. *Indigenous Movements, Self-Representation, and the State in Latin America*. Austin: University of Texas Press, 2002.

Weisman, Alan. *Gaviotas: A Village to Reinvent the World*. White River Junction, VT: Chelsea Green Pub, 1998.

Wilches-Chaux, Gustavo. "Breve historia ntural del Cauca." In *Homenaje al Cauca*. Bogotá, Colombia: Villegas Editores, 1991.

Index

About the Author

Brett Troyan holds a PhD in Latin American History from Cornell University and lives in Ithaca, New York. Before she began her graduate studies at the State University of New York at Stonybrook, she lived in Bogotá, Colombia, for four years. She is an associate professor of history at Cortland College, State University of New York. She has published a number of peer reviewed journal articles on the Colombian indigenous movement; one of her articles, published by the European journal *CEDLA*, was republished and translated into German in 2010. The article, which accompanies a Colombian indigenous artist's work and an anthropologist's annotations, is now part of a book, *Unsere Leute Namuy Misag: Land, Bräuche und Glaubensvorstellungen der Guambianos. Nacherzählt von Gregorio von Hernandez de Alba.* Her research was funded by the Fulbright Program, National Endowment for Humanities (summer and year-long fellowships), United States Institute of Peace, and the Woodrow Wilson Foundation for Democracy (junior grant).

CPSIA information can be obtained at www.ICGtesting.com
Printed in the USA
BVOW05*1552020615

402615BV00002B/2/P

9 781498 502283